FOUNDATIONS
OF ACCOUNTING

Edited by
RICHARD P. BRIEF
New York University

A GARLAND SERIES

ACKNOWLEDGMENTS

It has been six and one-half years since I purchased my trusty TRS-80 and started this project. I can no longer remember my original purpose, and my thinking has been influenced by so many discussions, comments, books, and papers that it is very difficult to credit all of the appropriate accounts.

Intellectually, I was born in the economics department at the University of Chicago, during the changing of the guard from Knight and Simons to the younger leadership of Friedman and Stigler. Their influence on my way of thinking about economic problems has been so profound that it is useless to try to isolate it.

My interest in accounting stems from my days at Ohio State University, where I had extensive discussions with Tom Burns, Paul Fertig, Mel Greenball, and Leslie Livingston, among others, about various accounting problems. I also benefitted from discussions and coments by Dick Epaves, Elise Jancura, Erich Obersteiner, and Abba Spero at Cleveland State University, and John Cook at the College of Wooster. The works of Yuji Ijiri and Robert Sterling have also had an important influence on my approach to accounting.

Most of the economists I have worked with recently have agreed, sometimes relucantly, to discuss accounting issues which were of only marginal interest to them. I think of Ed Bell, Jon Harford, Dick Marcus, Vijay Mathur, Sheldon Stein, Doug Stewart, and Allan Taub at Cleveland State, and David Cleeton, Luis

Acknowledgments

Fernandez, and Jim Zinser at Oberlin College. Finally, two old friends, Carl Christ and Jack Hirshleifer were kind enough to make comments on Chapter 2, which is the heart of the economic analysis underlying this work.

I must also apologize for the paucity of references to the literature. This stems from two sources. 1) Professor Knight always told his students that it was impossible to say anything new in economics, and that if we did it was sure to be wrong. I can no longer remember the source of most of my ideas, and simply do not have the interest, or the time, to try to chase the ideas back to their origins. I take it for granted that it has all been said before, and that my contribution, if any, comes in rejecting some old ideas, and in reorganizing some of the remaining ones. 2) It is clear to me that accounting, like economics, has a rich "unwritten" tradition. I cannot believe that anyone really thinks, for example, that cash receipts are sometimes revenue. There is no way that debits "are" credits. The possibility nevertheless remains that Sterling is right in suggesting that sloppy language may well lead to sloppy thinking, and vice versa [40, p. 37]. I do not know when accountants really mean what they say, and when they are using a well understood, but unwritten, shorthand, and decided not to pursue this intellectual history.

Finally, custom requires that I give credit to my long-suffering wife and family, even though my children have long

ii

Acknowledgments

since left home, and I do not have the impression that my work habits have changed noticeably in recent years. My wife's encouragement, long after most of my other friends were too embarrassed to inquire about my progress, kept me going until Tom Burns and Dick Brief finally convinced me that nothing was to be gained by further procrastination, and persuaded me to accept a deadline for completion.

Oberlin, Ohio

January, 1988

Chapter I

Introduction and Summary

Academic accountants have recently been concerned with the foundations of accounting, and the FASB has finally completed a major series on "Financial Accounting Concepts." With the major exception of Ijiri [22], the current trend is to argue that accounting should provide information for business decisions.

This monograph is a throwback to an earlier era when accountants thought that they were to describe economic events, and let other disciplines deal with decision making. It is more in line with Ijiri's emphasis on "performance measurement" [22, Chapter 3], than Sterling's conclusion than accountants "should examine economic decision models in order to discover what attributes are specified by those models." [40, p. 87]

I still think that the primary concern of the accountant should be to measure the variables which economists have identified as the most important in describing the performance of an economy, and the entities in the economy. The two most important are wealth and income. Product (GNP) is also an important economic variable, but there is less agreement among economists about how national product should be attributed to producing entities. I adopt, with some trepidation, the "capitalist" view that identifies productive income with product, both for the economy as a whole (where there is a consensus), and for individual entities.

My approach, however, is that of an economist. Instead of trying to describe the real world, which is the unavoidable job of the practicing accountant, I start by accounting for a simple economic model of a Crusoe economy, and then try to draw some (perhaps unwarranted) inferences about the real world. The procedure is not unlike that of the physicist who starts (at least when I went to college) by studying the laws of motion of an object sliding down a frictionless plane into a vacuum. I look for an economic model which has two characteristics: 1) it is simple enough that I can solve it, and 2) it hopefully has enough content that it has some interest for the real world.

The procedure differs from the traditional accounting approach mainly in that accountants usually start by looking at the world and making simplifying assumptions. This leads to what economists think of as a partial equilibrium model. There is no overall structure into which the pieces fit. An economic model of a Crusoe economy is a total equilibrium model. I must therefore develop interdependent criteria for national income accounting, business accounting, and household accounting.

This point deserves emphasis. Traditional accounting is concerned with accounting for entities which do not have to coordinate their accounts. If Crusoe sets up a firm, traditional accounting has no principles which address the question of whether the firm should carry its shares on its books at $100 when Crusoe carries them at $200. Indeed, Littleton [27, pp. 197-8] argues that firms should ignore "outside" facts in constructing their accounts, which suggests that different entities should use different accounting principles to account

for the same financial instruments. To my knowledge, the more
modern decision-making approach has also not addressed this
question, but would presumably permit different valuations of
the same financial instrument if this were called for by the
appropriate decision models. A general equilibrium model
determines the appropriate valuation ("description") of a share,
and requires all entities to conform to this valuation. There is
an overall structure into which all accounts must fit.

Strangely enough, the use of a model also gives meaning to
the idea that accounting should be "empirical" and "represent"
the real world. Thomas [42 and 43] has criticized accounting
allocations (e. .g, depreciation) on the grounds that they are
arbitrary and do not reflect "reality," a conclusion which has
also been approved by Sterling [40, Chapter 6]. Solomons [36, p.
211] argues that an accounting number which "more faithfully
represents the economic events and conditions relating to the
enterprises" is to be preferred.

While I certainly agree that acounting should try to
reflect real economic events (and cannot understand the meaning
of the idea that depreciation is an "allocation" rather than a
"valuation"), I have never been quite sure what this meant. The
world is a very complicated place, and can be described in many
ways. If I say that I know that some accounting number does not
describe the world, this must mean that I know what the world is
really like, and the accountant does not.

An economic model provides the basis for such a judgement.

If a particular accounting scheme describes the model better than another, it is therefore more realistic and "better" within the context of the model. We do not have to argue about the "facts," because the model determines the facts.

The applicability of a model to the real world is of course a matter of judgement. Different people will try different models, and the profession will select. My view is that simple models can create a strong presumption that some accounting principles are inappropriate, but are much less convincing about appropriateness. That is, if an accounting principle gives a poor description of a simple Crusoe model, I find it very difficult to believe that it will provide a reasonable description of a more complicated model. If you cannot account for Crusoe, you probably cannot account for anyone else.

It also seems likely that procedures which are appropriate for Crusoe will have to be modified in more complicated models. This awaits further research. I hope that some of the research will follow the general equilibrium method, rather than the partial equilibrium which currently prevails in accounting.

The book is divided into three parts. Part I contains this introduction, and a chapter presenting the Crusoe model. Part II presents an accounting model which is appropriate for the Crusoe model. Part III discusses some accounting problems which arise in the real world. Part III should be considered as speculative, since the models for which I am accounting are not rigorously specified.

Part I: The Crusoe Model

My   model is   adapted   from   Hirshleifer [21,   Chapter   6].
Crusoe   is assumed to divide his time between leisure   and work.
When   he works, he produces one of two consumer goods, which   he
must consume   immediately,   or capital, which is carried forward
to the next period.   Using a   certainty model, he maximizes his
welfare over a long time horizon, subject to constraints imposed
by homogeneous production   functions,   which may   change through
time.   All   goods are valued at   shadow   prices   which   measure
opportunity costs.   The economy   is artificially divided into   a
firm   which   maximizes   profit subject   to   a   known   production
function,   and a consumer who maximizes a known welfare function
subject to a wealth   constraint.   I   therefore account for three
entities: a firm, a household, and a society.

From   an   accounting point   of   view,   the   most   important
conclusions are 1) that   the appropriate price   index to   use in
the measurement   of   "real"   variables   is   a general   index   of
consumer   goods   prices, 2)   that   the   appropriate   measure   of
capital maintenance   is   the preservation   of the real   value   of
capital (current value   corrected   for changes   in the   CPI), 3)
that the only way   to   estimate income   is to measure wealth, and
4) that the   firm's balance   sheet will   "balance" if shares are
priced at   the discounted value of   future dividends and   assets
are valued at current market.

The last point   is   of particular interest because   it says
both that firms   have   no   net   wealth, and   that   there   is   no

conflict between measuring the values of individual assets, and measuring the value of the firm. Since many models suggest that there is a difference (for example, Bodenhorn, [5], Sections IV and VI), accountants frequently say that their job is to measure individual assets, not the firm. It also provides an answer to Sterling's criticism that "the 'value of the firm' or 'going concern value' is invariably undefined." [40, p. 173] One of the advantages of a general equilibrium model is that such terms are defined. In addition, it provides a challenge to those who think that there is a difference between asset value and firm value to explain why their models produce this result.

Part II: The Accounting Model

The accounting model, Chapters 3-8, is based on the premise that a balance sheet should measure wealth, and an income statement should measure income. Income is divided into two parts, productive income and financial income, and productive income is used as a measure of product or production. Since financial income aggregates to zero for the society, we have the familiar result that national income equals national product. For smaller accounting entities, financial income need not be zero, and product need not equal income.

The formal accounting utilizes, of course, the standard double-entry bookkeeping. It is based on two familiar concepts: 1) positive numbers are recorded as debits, and negative numbers as credits, and 2) the inventory equation which says that opening inventory (stock) plus inflows and minus outflows equals the closing inventory.

Balance sheets account for the values of the economic instruments which comprise Crusoe's wealth. There are two classes of economic instruments. Productive instruments are the arguments in the production and welfare (utility) functions, but not including welfare (utility) itself. Financial instruments are agreements that A will pay B something in the future. In a Crusoe economy, the only financial instrument is shares. Within classes, instruments may be aggregated or disaggregated arbitrarily.

It is also important to be explicit about how negative balance sheet values arise. We adopt the convention that exchanges which increase inventories (purchases) involve positive quantities, whereas exchanges which decrease inventories (sales) involve negative quantities. The value of any instrument is the price, which is always taken as positive, multiplied by the quantity, which will be negative if we have sold short, i. e., if outflows are larger than inflows.

It is also convenient to assume that there is a "medium of exchange" which is different from cash, and whose quantity is always identically zero. Every exchange then involves the sale of an economic instrument for "medium," and the purchase of another instrument with the "medium" obtained from the sale. Such a convention is virtually necessary in a Crusoe economy, since there exists no cash. It is also a convenient convention if there is cash. We then obtain cash by selling "medium." All assets, including cash, must be purchased. The net flow of "medium" is always identically zero, with no inventory.

A balance sheet records the values of all instruments owned by the entity, at a specified point in time. Positive values are debits, and negative values are credits, with a balancing entry for "Net Wealth," if necessary. This procedure is virtually required by double-entry bookkeeping procedures, but complicates the interpretation by making (positive) net wealth a credit entry, when other credit entries are negative values.

Negative balance sheet values arise if the inventory (stock) of an economic instrument is negative. While this is impossible for productive instruments, it is routine for financial instruments. Consider, for example, a mortgage which I take out at a bank. This is not a financial instrument until I sign it and sell it to the bank for $100,000 of "medium," which I then use to buy a deposit from the bank. Since I started with a zero inventory of mortgages, and sold one, I now have an inventory of -1, and it has a value of -$100,000. (The bank, of course, has an inventory of +1 with a value of +$100,000.) I therefore record a credit of $100,000 for the mortgage on my balance sheet, and call it a "liability."

This differs in important ways from Ijiri's treatment [22, Chapters 4 and 5]. His "axiom" of quantities (pp. 55-60, 68, 74) requires that quantities be nonnegative. In his view, each exchange involves an "initiator" and a "terminator." The mortgage exchange I have described above is "initiated" by my receipt of $100,000 from the bank, and will not be "terminated" until I have repayed the bank.   An "unterminated" exchange is then regarded (defined) as negative control (ownership) by the individual who will be required to decrease his resources (me) when the exchange is "terminated."   The end result is very much the same.   I define the quantity as negative. Ijiri defines the control as negative.

Nevertheless, I do not regard this as a good description of a financial instrument. Consider a retail purchase on "account." In my view, this is a "complete" exchange. The merchant sells me merchandise.   I sell him a financial instrument. At this point, he may decide to sell the instrument in the secondary market (to MasterCard or Visa), or to keep it himself. He can "terminate" the transaction any time his portfolio analysis suggests that he should do so. His portfolio decision has nothing to do with the original sale.

My behavior with respect to the financial instrument is also unconnected with the original purchase. When I get my Visa bill, I can pay whatever fraction I want to pay, and I have no way of knowing which exchanges have been "terminated" and which are still outstanding unless I pay my bill in full. I also do a portfolio analysis and decide how much debt I want to have.

There is of course a difference in risk, depending upon what financial instrument the merchant receives. If he buys cash, the risk is minimal. If he buys a Visa account, the risk increases. If he buys a personal check or an open account, there are different risks, and different transactions costs. The initial exchange, however, should be regarded as "terminated" when the merchant gets a financial instrument, which will be the same time that I get my merchandise. We then make subsequent, and largely independent, decisions about when and how to exchange the financal instrument.

The suggestion that the receipt (purchase) of cash "terminates" a transaction because the risk of default is small, whereas the receipt (purchase) of an account receivable does not "terminate" the transaction because the risk is larger, certainly is inappropriate in a Crusoe economy where there is no risk. I do not think it is an appropriate distinction, even in the real world. Formally, cash is a financial instrument like any other, and experience with hyperinflations demonstrates that it is not riskless. The purchase and sale of financial instruments is governed by economic considerations in much the same way as the purchase and sale of productive instruments. The quantity convention which I advocate makes more sense to me than Ijiri's "control" convention.

The question of how negative balance sheet values arise is not frequently discussed in the literature because of the elegance of the double-entry bookkeeping scheme. Routine book-keeping solves the problem before the question is raised. If we borrow money, we automatically credit a liability account, and debit cash. The balance in the liability account becomes a credit, which is a negative number, with no necessity to provide

an "explanation," other than to say that credit entries increase
liabilities, while debit entries reduce them.

Flow Accounts and the Measurement of Income. We start with
balance sheet accounts, which record market values at a point in
time, and for which credits "balance" debits in the sense that
the sums are equal in absolute value, but are opposite in sign.
These accounts are all "closed" to flow accounts, which cover a
specified time period. The flow accounts therefore start with an
appropriately signed inventory, and have debits which exactly
offset credits. Initially, there is one flow account for each
economic instrument on the balance sheet. Additional accounts
may be required if the entity purchases or sells an instrument
which was not on the opening balance sheet. Additional accounts
are also required to keep track of income.

All purchases and sales of economic instruments are
recorded in flow accounts, as they occur during the period.
Purchases have positive quantities, positive values, and are
debit entries. Sales have negative quantities, negative values,
and are credit entries. In every case, the account which is
entered is the account for the economic instrument bought or
sold. There are no "revenues" or "expenses." If we sell
automobiles for $1,000, we credit the automobile flow account
for $1,000. We receive $1,000 of "medium," which we immediately
spend to buy a financial instrument, and we debit the flow
account for the instrument received. The books must continue to
be in balance, because the exchange involves the purchase of one

economic instrument and the sale of another, for the same amount of "medium."

At the end of the period, a new balance sheet is prepared, in the same way that the initial balance sheet was prepared. We have an inventory of economic instruments, both productive and financial. The balance sheet shows the market value of these inventories, as of the balance sheet date.

At the end of each period, we make two entries to the flow accounts:

1) We record a flow of inventory from the flow account to the ending balance sheet account. This is the counterpart of flowing the inventory from the starting balance sheet to the flow account at the start of the period. However, the signs are reversed. If we consider a typical asset account with a debit balance sheet value, the initial flow from the balance sheet will credit the balance sheet account and debit the flow account. The ending inventory will be a credit to the flow account (to take the value out of the flow account) and a debit to the balance sheet account (to put the value into the balance sheet account).

2) We "close" each flow account. While the closing must eventually be to the "Net Income" account, the value in any productive instrument flow account may be "transferred" to another productive flow account, and so indirectly to an income account. For example, we may credit raw materials and debit goods-in-process, and then credit goods-in-process and debit

finished goods before closing finished goods to an income account. Furthermore, we may set up income "segment" accounts for either productive or financial income, such as "Operating Income," "Interest Income," "Gains or Losses on the Disposal of Assets," etc., and close these accounts to "Net Income."

It cannot be overemphasized that the same procedures are followed for all accounts. We do not have separate rules for asset accounts and liability accounts and shareholders' equity accounts. Debit entries do not "increase" asset accounts and "reduce" liability accounts, as we are told in the textbooks. Debit entries increase the algebraic value of whatever account is entered. Shares are no different from other financial instruments, as far as accounting procedures are concerned, even if they are different from a decision-making perspective.

If the entity is a business firm, it has no net wealth, and the "Net Income" account closes of its own accord, since the debits balance the credits for the accounts which are closed to it. We know in advance that the net income of the firm will be zero. The purpose of the closing procedure is not to measure net income, but to measure its components, which we can do either by grouping the entries within the "Net Income" account, or by opening sub-income accounts to measure different segments of income, and closing these accounts to "Net Income."

Entries which close flow accounts for an economic instrument to "income" accounts are called "Value Added" by the instrument. Each instrument flow account can be interpreted by a value-of-inventory equation: opening inventory + purchases − sales + value added = closing inventory. Purchases are always debits, sales are credits. Opening inventories are debits if they are positive, credits if they are negative. Closing inventories are credits if they are positive, debits if they are negative. Value added may be either positive (a debit entry to close the flow account) or negative (a credit entry to close the account).

If the closing inventory is more valuable than it "should" be on the basis of the opening inventory, purchases, and sales, 1) a debit entry is required to "close" the account, and 2) the firm must have created some positive value by its activities during the period. If the closing inventory is less valuable than it "should" be, 1) a credit entry is required to close the account, and 2) the firm has "destroyed" or "lost" some value on the basis of its activities, and the value added is negative.

Consider a simple numerical example. Crusoe produces and consumes wheat and corn, and also produces equipment. At t_0, he sells his firm $10,000 worth of equipment, and the firm sells him $10,000 worth of shares. Between t_0 and t_1, he sells the firm $2,000 of labor, and buys $2,000 of corn and $1,500 of wheat. The firm must pay him a dividend of $1,500, to keep the "medium" flow at zero. At t_1, the equipment and the shares are worth $9,000. There are no inventories of corn or wheat.

The balance sheets of the firm show market values:

	t_1	t_0		t_1	t_0
Equipment	$9,000	$10,000	Shares	$9,000	$10,000

We need flow accounts for each economic instrument: equipment, shares, labor service, corn, and wheat. The equipment account shows only flows to and from the balance sheet. The share account shows dividends in addition to the balance sheet flows. The dividend is associated with the shares, and must be treated as either a purchase or a sale. Since the medium flows from the firm to Crusoe, the firm is (re)purchasing some of the shares it originally sold Crusoe. The remaining accounts show only the purchases and sales.

Journal entries to record flows from the opening balance sheet:

Equipment Flow from t_0 B. S.	$10,000	
Equipment, t_0 B. S.		$10,000
Shares, t_0 B. S.	10,000	
Share Flow, from t_0 B.S.		10,000

Journal entries to record purchases and sales, ignoring the "medium" account, since it has a zero balance:

Share Flow (Dividend)	$1,500	
Labor Service Flow (Purchase)	2,000	
Wheat Flow (sale)		$1,500
Corn Flow (Sale)		2,000

Journal entries to record flows to closing balance sheet:

Equipment, t_1 B.S. $9,000

    Equipment Flow, to t_1 B.S. $9,000

Share Flow, to t_1 B.S.   9,000

    Shares, t_1 B.S.   9,000

The trial balance for <u>flow</u> accounts is:

Equipment Flow $1,000

Labor Service Flow   2,000

Share Flow   500

    Wheat Flow $1,500

    Corn Flow   2,000

These accounts are now closed to various income accounts. They may also be aggregated, providing that a strict separation between productive and financial instruments must be maintained until the final closing to the "Net Income" account. The intermediate accounts reflect the artistry of the accountant in describing what is going on.

For example, the accountant may think that he has seen Crusoe spending $500 of labor time producing wheat. I cannot overemphasize the fact this this is pure fantasy, in my model. There is absolutely nothing in the model which permits the allocation of the labor cost to the production of wheat, corn, or anything else. My model is entirely consistent with Thomas' [42, 43] conclusion that such allocations are arbitrary and "incorrigible," i. e., cannot be refuted by any possible empirical observation.

A traditional cost accountant might therefore decide to

"capitalize" some labor services, and some depreciation:

Wheat Flow, Labor Cost	$500	
Corn Flow, Labor Cost	600	
Wheat Flow, Depreciation Cost	200	
Corn Flow, Depreciation Cost	300	
Labor Service Flow		$1,100
Equipment Flow		500

These transfers do not change total assets. They reclassify productive instruments to reflect the accountant's interpretation of the production process. He might then decide to measure "Operating Margins," perhaps to improve the quality of pricing decisions. He closes the flow accounts to "Income:"

Wheat Flow, Value Added	$800	
Income, Wheat Operating Margin		$800
Corn Flow, Value Added	1,100	
Income, Corn Operating Margin		1,100
Income, Loss on Labor Overhead	$900	
Labor Flow, Value Lost		$900
Income, Loss on Equipment Depreciation	500	
Equipment Flow, Value Lost		500
Income, Loss on Shares	500	
Share Flow, Value Lost		500

The algebraic signs are reversed when "instrument" flow accounts are closed to "income flow" accounts. The $800 value added by "Wheat Flow" is positive, and is a debit entry to the Wheat Flow account. It must, however, be a credit entry to the income flow account. This is associated with the idea than "Net Wealth," if any, has the wrong sign. If assets exceed equities, net wealth is plugged in where needed to "balance" the accounts, and this is a credit entry.

Net income flow, if any, will be closed to net wealth, in accordance with the economic definition of income as the increase in net wealth plus consumption. Since income adds to wealth, and wealth is a credit, income must also be a credit.

The final result of closing the four productive instrument flow accounts to "Income," no matter how many "explanatory" accounts are created, is:

Productive Instrument Flow, Value Added $500

Income Flow, Productive Instruments $500

The value added in production of $500 can be allocated to corn production, wheat production, equipment production, depreciation expense, and labor expense,   almost at will, in conformity with GAAP.   Depreciation can be pulled out of a hat, and capitalized as cost of wheat, cost of corn, or expensed as "administrative" or "overhead," pretty much at random. Similarly, the labor cost can be capitalized or expensed.

The reason why I permit these allocations while Thomas deplores them is that Thomas knows that GAAP permits the allocations to influence the balance sheet measurements, and the measurement of productive income. My procedures do not permit this.   Allocations "explain" the "sources" of the productive income, but do not influence its measurement.   Productive income is determined by the market values of productive instruments held at the beginning and end of the accounting period, and the observed purchases and sales of productive instruments. There is no "matching." There are no "accruals." There need not be any "allocations," "revenues," or "expenses."

The firm started the year with $10,000 of productive instruments. During the year it purchased $2,000 and sold $3,500. It should therefore have had $8,500 of productive instruments at year-end. In fact, it has $9,000 of productive instruments. We infer that the firm "produced" or added $500 of value to the productive instruments, thereby generating $500 of productive income.

Allocations, while arbitrary, do no influence the measurement of income, or the balance sheets. My scheme satisfies Thomas' definition of "allocation free."

I turn to a consideration of the share flow account. Since there is only one financial instrument in this scheme, aggregation is not possible. The account must be closed to the "Net Income" account:

Income, Financial Loss on Shares $500

Share Flow, Value Lost $500

The firm started with shares valued at -$10,000. During the course of the year, the firm paid Crusoe $1,500 in respect of these shares. The simplest way to think of this transaction is old-fashioned "coupon clipping." We can think of the share as a set of coupons, each of which entitles the owner to dividends "when and if declared." The owner clips the coupons, and sells them to the firm on the coupon date. The share price, at any point in time, is the value of the remaining coupons, which is the present value of the dividends which will be declared.

This means that the firm has bought $1,500 of coupons, and the value of the remaining coupons "should" be -$8,500 to the firm, or +$8,500 to Crusoe. The market, however, says that the value to the firm is -$9,000, which is $500 less than it ought to be. The firm has lost $500 of value on its share operations, and this is negative financial income.

While this may seem strange, since this accounting loss is usually called "profit" or "net income," it is consistent with finance theory. The shareholder's financial income is measured as the increase in the value of his shares (capital gain) plus net cash received. I apply the same definition to the firm. Its income is the increase in the value of its shares plus net cash received. The share value was -$10,000 at t_o, and -$9,000 at t_1, which is a capital gain of $1,000 for the firm (and a capital loss of $1,000 for Crusoe). The net cash received by the firm is -$1,500, which is the amount paid for the dividend coupon. The sum of the capital gain and cash received by the firm is a net financial income of -$500. It is also a positive financial income (+$500) for Crusoe, since the only difference between Crusoe and the firm is that all of the signs are reversed. Positive values for Crusoe are negative for the firm. Crusoe's net cash receipts are net cash payments for the firm.

The problem apparently arises because of the standard economic assumption that firms act in the interests of their shareholders, which is also part of the "stewardship" idea in accounting. In a formal sense, firms generate income from productive activities, and transfer this to other entities by engaging in financial activities. Firms therefore generate product, but not income, for the society. All of the firm's productive income is transferred, in the Crusoe case, to shareholders. In the real world, there will usually also be debtholders and government.

It is in the shareholders' interest for firms to maximize shareholder income (or wealth). As we have seen, the definition of financial income arising from any financial instrument requires that net social financial income be zero, since positive income for one party (owner) is negative income for the other. Shareholder income is firm loss, and shareholders want firms to maximize their (the firms') financial loss on shares.

On another level, the idea that a firm's "profit" is not really "income" is well understood. Nobody measures national income by adding corporate profits to shareholder income, because this is obvious double-counting.

Formally, accounting for bonds is identical to accounting for shares. A financial instrument is sold short. The quantity held by the firm is negative. "Interest" payments are purchases of coupons from debtholders. If the value is unchanged, the financial loss (expense) to the firm is the cash paid. In all cases, the income equals the capital gain, recognizing that the values are negative, less the payment from the firm to the debtholder.

No harm is done if the accountant wants to explain the financial loss by accruing an interest expense. Using our numerical example, but assuming that the financial instrument is a bond rather than a share, the accountant may think that the interest rate was 7% when the bond was issued. He would then record:

> Income, Interest Expense $700
>
> Bond Flow, Value Lost on Interest $700

The bond flow account would then have a credit balance of $200 after the payment of $1,500 and the transfer of $9,000 to the closing balance sheet. A closing entry would be required:

> Bond Flow, Value Added $200
>
> Income, Capital Gain on Bonds $200

The net income from the bond is -$500, as before. If the accountant were to use an interest rate of 4%, the interest expense would only be $400, but the capital gain would be -$100. The interest accrual is not required, and simply has the effect of dividing the $500 loss into two parts, interest and capital gain, for explanatory purposes.

Thomas would object to interest accruals because he knows that the GAAP accountant would first apply an "accrual principle," which says something like: "Interest should be accrued on financial instruments whether it is realized or not, unless the instrument is called a share, an account receivable, deferred taxes, etc., etc." Then he would apply a "realization principle," which says something like: "Capital gains should not be recognized unless they are realized, unless the firm is a mutual fund, the financial instrument is part of a portfolio whose cost basis is above its market value, the management has revealed that the investment is really long-term, etc., etc."

The net result is very likely to be that the interest expense is recognized, and the capital gain is not. The value transferred to the balance sheet will not be $9,000, and the interest accrual will in fact influence both income measurement and balance sheet values.

My accounting requires that the balance sheet value be the market value of $9,000, and that the income be -$500. The accountant can "explain" this any way he wants, but he cannot "explain" why this is wrong.

The fact that the motivation of management is different with respect to shareholders and debtholders does not influence our accounting principles. Both groups have bought financial instruments from the firm, and both expect to get a return, be it interest, dividends, or capital gains, from those instruments. The buyers' gain is the sellers' loss, as far as financial instruments are concerned. The firm expects to generate enough productive income to provide income for both groups of lenders.

Economists want to measure both productive and financial

income, even though these must add to zero for business firms. We do this because we are also interested in accounting for households and societies, and these entities need not have zero income. In almost all economic models, social financial income must be zero. We therefore say that social income and social product are equal, although the double-entry bookkeeping procedures reverse the sign of the income. Social income is associated exclusively with productive income, i. e., income generated by producing instruments which can generate welfare, either immediately as consumer goods, or later as capital goods.

In the Crusoe economy, financial activities transfer income between entities without either increasing or reducing social (national) income. Crusoe's real consumption and income are not influenced by his financial activities. Value added by productive activities increases national product, and is therefore frequently called "production." Value added by the financial activity does not increase national product and is never called "production." Automobiles are "produced." Stocks and bonds are "issued."

This accounting structure is, of course, consistent with GAAP, even if the terminology is somewhat different. The flow accounts must start with the balance sheet entries, and record market transactions. They must also record value added (lost) and closing inventories. The difference between my approach and GAAP is that GAAP frequently measures value added directly (usually by an "allocation"), and "plugs" the inventory which goes to the closing balance sheet. I define this procedure as "matching," since the "allocation" is usually designed to match revenues and expenses.

My procedure never "matches." It <u>always</u> measures balance sheet values at market, and plugs value added. This follows from the definition of wealth as the market value of economic instruments, and the definition of income as the increase in wealth plus consumption. Income is conceptually a residual which is derived from observable wealth.

The total abandonement of "matching" is advocated in other accounting studies. The reasons are frequently an appeal to decision-making, or a search for empirical content or representational faithfulness.

Chambers [8] advocates valuing assets at "market resale prices," since "The only observable financial magnitude of an asset at a given date is its price, and market prices are one of the key elements of choice." [8, p. xiii]. Valuation at market determines the balance sheet value, and prevents matching.

Chambers' model is typical of accounting models. He makes "postulates" which approximate the "real world," and concludes: "Our postulates are a selection from an extensive range, if not an infinite range, of possible statements about the environment of action and of accounting which could have been selected. ... Nevertheless, there is abundant evidence ... to support the belief that our conclusions are not not materially in error, ..." [8, p. 370]. I interpret this to mean that Chambers

believes that he would have arrived at the same conclusions had
he emphasized different aspects of reality.   His conclusions,
however, differ significantly from others who adopt the same
approach, including the FASB.

Sterling [40] also abandons matching, primarily on the
grounds measurements which cannot be verified empirically are
not "scientific."   Wealth is "command over goods" or "value in
exchange" [40, p. 161], while income is the change in wealth
after adjusting for consumption [40, p. 191].   While his major
emphasis is decision-making, rather than description, his
approach resembles mine in its examination of relatively simple
cases. He devotes considerable attention to accounting for a
firm which has only one depreciable asset. The economic model,
however, is an approximation of "reality," and not a theoretical
model of a simple economy.

Thomas' [42, 43] attack on "allocations" is clearly a call
for the abandonment of matching. His primary concern is the lack
of empirical content ("incorrigibility") of balance sheet values
derived from the allocation or matching process.

Ijiri [22] and Mattessich [29] are difficult to analyze
from this point of view. They both try to present simplified
descriptions of the "real world," which Mattessich calls
"assumptions" [29, p. 32] and Ijiri calls "judgments" or
"axioms" [22, p. 74]. My impression is that my model could well
be consistent with Mattessich's assumptions, and might therefore
be thought of as a special case. However, "matching" might well

be another   special case.   Ijiri's model is also consistent with
matching.

Other   studies,   however,   continue   to   advocate matching,
starting   with   Edwards and Bell [12] important work.   They   are
remarkably   "modern" in   their emphasis   on decision-making, but
define "current operating profit" as "the excess of the value of
output sold during a period over the current cost of the related
inputs," and argue that this concept is "relatively unambiguous"
[12, p. 111].   It is, to repeat, undefined (perfectly ambiguous)
in my Crusoe model, and their model is also a loosely   specified
approximation of "reality."

By far the most important endorsement of matching, however,
is the recent study of accounting "concepts" by the FASB.   Their
endorsement   of   "matching,"   "accruals,"   and "allocations"   is
unambiguous [16, paragraphs 134 - 150].   This   endorsement may
well   inhibit   the   evolution   of   accounting into   an empirical
discipline for the rest of this century.

Part III: The "Real World"

The final three chapters, 9 to 11, abandon the Crusoe model
and   follow the accounting   tradition of   picking out   carefully
selected aspects of the "real world" for emphasis. I then try to
apply the lessons learned from Crusoe.

Chapter   9 considers the possibility that   a society   might
set up a government, with power to tax and subsidize. I continue
to assume that   only households have wealth, and that artificial
entities like firms and governments have no wealth.

This requires that future tax receipts (payments) and future subsidy payments (receipts) be capitalized and treated as if they were financial instruments. The government then has one asset, future tax receipts, and two equities, future subsidies and debt. Assets must equal equities to satisfy the zero wealth assumption.

Two problems are created. 1) Firms' balance sheets are thrown out of balance by the liability to pay future taxes, which must be recorded because I continue to assume that financial instruments add to zero. 2) The "value" of economic instruments becomes ambiguous. In a Crusoe economy, all valuations are the same. With taxes, there are "distortions," which means that market prices do not always reflect both value in consumption and opportunity costs.

I make a hopefully successful attempt to solve both problems by using the "productive" value of economic instruments instead of the "market" value for balance sheet purposes. The not surprising result is that the measurements are not useful for private decision making, since market values measure private opportunity costs in most cases.

Chapter 10 is concerned with banks and financial institutions. They differ from Crusoe's firm in two important respects. 1) Their assets are primarily financial, and they perform financial services such as portfolio management, and insurance. 2) They frequently do not charge a fee for services rendered, but instead reduce the interest rate which they pay on borrowed money. This makes it look as though they have negative productive income, since their purchases of productive resources exceed their sales.

My solution is to impute fictitious sales of productive services, and fictitious interest payments of equal magnitude, in much the same way that it is done in National Income accounting. The difference is that my "adjustments" make the productive income equal to a risk-adjusted "normal" rate of return on productive assets, while the National Income accounts "adjustment" makes productive income equal a normal return on shareholders' equity.

Chapter 11 makes some comments about business accounting in the "real world." I start by observing that Crusoe accounting could be based on "costs," or on "service potential," instead of market values.

The service potential approach would value all economic instruments according to the present value of the future cash flows which the instrument will generate. There are two serious drawbacks: 1) the future is difficult to predict, and 2) there is no theoretically correct way to allocate future cash flows (even if they were known) to the various productive instruments which the firm holds.

I suggest a cost-based approach, since it both avoids forecasting, and more closely resembles traditional accounting. Purchases of assets are "costs," sales are "cost recoveries." Purchases and sales of equities are not costs, but an interest

cost is accrued on all equities, including shares, in much the
way that Anthony suggested in his brilliant book, Accounting for
the Cost of Interest [1].   Assets are carried at "unrecovered
cost," and equities are carried at "book value," including the
accrued interest.

While this gives the correct measurements of total assets,
productive and financial income in the Crusoe economy, there are
two major problems even in the Crusoe case, and a third problem
for real-world economies which are not in long-run equilibrium.

1)   It   is   impossible to associate the sales (cost
recoveries) of productive instruments with particular purchases,
If a firm buys materials and labor, and sells wheat, there is no
way of knowing whether the labor cost or the materials cost was
recovered.   We   therefore cannot value individual productive
assets at "unrecovered" cost.   This problem does not arise in
connection with financial instruments.

2)   In much the same way, it is difficult to allocate the
interest cost to specific assets. We can allocate an interest
cost equal to the interest "yield" on financial assets, but are
again in trouble with productive assets.

My suggested solution is to try to define "projects," much
as Ijiri does [23].   The hope is to be able to associate
purchases and sales with projects, rather than individual
assets, and keep track of the unrecovered costs.   Interest cost
would be allocated to projects on the basis of the cost of
capital associated with the projects, which is also the discount

rate used in analyzing the project for profitability in modern
capital budgeting procedures.

3) This procedure generates a "normal," risk-adjusted rate
of return on all financial instruments, and all projects. In
economic terminology, there are no "pure" profits or losses.
While this is correct for a Crusoe economy, it is not correct in
the real world, and we must therefore face the question of
determining the evidence which we require to "recognize" pure
profit or loss.

One possibility is to compare actual costs and recoveries
to "standard" costs and recoveries, which have been projected on
th basis of previous information. Variances would lead to
revaluations of assets and equities if they were deemed to be
permanent.

Market prices should also be used to revalue assets and
equities. These would include 1) outside offers for the entire
firm or any of its parts (projects), 2) the issue of new shares,
or the purchase of treasury shares, and 3) market values of
financial instruments, although a smoothing process might well
be appropriate to reduce the wild swings sometimes observed in
the stock market. The very least that should be done is to
require firms to revalue all shares when new shares are issued.
The firm should not issue new shares unless it has enough assets
to provide a "normal" return to all shareholders, including the
holders of previously issued shares.

Chapter II

The Crusoe Model

I. SUMMARY

The purpose of this chapter is to "account" for a Crusoe economy, in the broadest sense of the term. In particular, at t_1, I "account" for what has happened between t_o and t_1, on the basis of "observed" variables, which I call a "data base."

Section II presents a certainty model in which Crusoe maximizes his welfare over time subject to annual production functions. This solves his behavioral problems, and determines the quantities produced, consumed, and held in inventory until the end of his time horizon. The Section also introduces shadow prices and "own" rates of interest, which I call "synthetic"[1] accounting variables, to distinguish them from the "observed" variables.

Section III introduces nominal prices, a nominal interest rate and money, and sets up two decision centers, a household (consumer) and a firm. The household knows the welfare function, but not the produuction functions. The firm knows the production functions but not the welfare function.

Section IV considers the "synthetic" accounting variables which the household must use in decision-making as a substitute for the production functions, and which the firm must use as a substitute for the welfare function. These "decision" variables lead the household and the firm to the same behavior we observe in Section II.

The required synthetic decision variables include the

nominal prices and interest rates, although these would be
"observed" (rather than synthetic) variables in a competitive
economy. Nominal prices, when discounted at the nominal interest
rate, reflect opportunity costs.

In addition, there are "agregate" decision variables:
nominal wealth, nominal consumption, nominal product, and
nominal marginal products. No variables corrected for changes in
the price level ("real" variables), are decision variables
either for the household or the firm.

Section V introduces a class of "descriptive" synthetic
accounting variables. These are not necessary for decision
making, but are used to describe the behavior of the economy.
These include income, the rate of inflation, and the various
"real" variables: real product, income, wealth, interest rates,
consumption, and marginal products. We have more leeway in
defining these variables, since no decisions are made on the
basis of these variables.

We have three classes of accounting variables:
observations, synthetic decision variables, and synthetic
descriptive variables.

All synthetic variables are generated from observed
variables on the basis of economic theory. Synthetic decision
variables are associated with testable hypotheses: the theory
says that individuals (firms) behave as if they were using these
variables in a maximizing process.

Synthetic descriptive variables have no testable

implications. They describe economic theory, not the real world. There is no such "thing" as "real" income or the "real" marginal product of capital. They are mental constructs which the economist finds useful in describing and understanding the way an economic system works, within the context of an economic theory. The choice between definitions (of income, for example) must be made on the basis of economic theory, not on the basis of economic behavior or "facts."

I present accounting definitions which describe the Crusoe economy better than the traditional measurements if my economic model is correct. The advantage of using a Crusoe model is that it is easy to describe and understand, so that a better judgment about accounting measurements is possible.

Section VI biefly reviews the major differences between my approach and the GNP approach.

The major results of this chatper are:

1. Consumption should include leisure ("full" consumption), if it is to be a proxy for utility.

2. The general price index should include the prices of all consumer goods, including leisure, and exclude the prices of capital goods.

3. "Real" values should be calculated by correcting for changes in the general price index, not for changes in sector prices. In particular, the real t_1 value of t_0 capital is the nominal t_0 value corrected for changes in the general price index

between t_0 and t_1, not corrected for changes in the price of capital goods. The same is true for other sectors such as consumer durables or consumer services. There should be only one price deflator, not a different deflator for each sector.

4. Capital maintenance should be defined in terms of maintaining the real value of the capital, not in terms of maintaining physical quantities. This applies to the measurement of real investment, and the real marginal product of capital.

5. There is a "real" rate of interest, calculated by correcting the nominal interest rate for changes in the general price level. In equilibrium, it is independent of the rate of inflation. It measures the real marginal productivity of all kinds of capital goods, and the real return on financial instruments. The "own" rate of interest is not a good measure of the marginal productivity of a capital good.

II. THE BASIC MODEL

Crusoe gets "utility" each year, and "welfare" over his lifetime. His utility function (U) covers one year at a time, and is the same every year

(1) $U_t = V(x_t, y_t, R_t)$,

where $\underline{x}$ and $\underline{y}$ are consumer goods, and $\underline{R}$ is leisure (rest). There are $\underline{M}$ hours per year, with $\underline{L}$ spent working, and $M = L + R$.

His welfare (H) depends upon his annual utilities:

(2) $H = H(U_0, U_1, \ldots, U_n)$.

He maximizes welfare, not utility in any one year. I do not specify the number of years in his time horizon. He maximizes welfare subject to annual production functions, which may change over time.

(3) $W(x_o, y_o, L_o, K_{-1}, K_o) = 0$

$T(x_1, y_1, L_1, K_o, K_1) = 0,$

where $\underline{W}$ governs the year from t_{-1} to t_o, $\underline{T}$ governs the following year, and $\underline{K}_i$ is the capital at t_i. I assume constant returns to scale.

All of the arguments of the production functions are physical goods. $\underline{x}$, $\underline{y}$, and $\underline{L}$ are flows. $\underline{K}$ is a stock of physical capital. The physical characteristics of $\underline{K}$ do not change through time. I use an implicit production function because it does not require knowing how much $\underline{L}$ is devoted to the production of $\underline{x}$, $\underline{y}$, or $\underline{K}$, and because the results generalize readily for additional kinds of consumer goods, labor, and capital.[2]

I also assume that the welfare function exhibits positive marginal welfare of utility, and positive marginal utility for the "consumer goods," $\underline{x}$ and $\underline{y}$, and leisure, $\underline{R}$.

It is convenient to define the production functions so that the partials will have the same signs as the partials of the utility function with respect to $\underline{x}$ and $\underline{y}$. The partials of opening capital and labor input are therefore negative while the partial of closing capital is positive:

(4) $\qquad H_{Ut}, V_{xt}, V_{yt}, V_{Rt} > 0,$

$\qquad W_{xo}, W_{yo}, W_{Ko}, T_{x1}, T_{y1}, T_{K1} > 0,$

$\qquad W_{Lo}, W_{K-1}, T_{L1}, T_{Ko} < 0,$

where $\underline{H}_{Ut}$ represents the partial derivative of the function, $\underline{H}$, with respect to the subscripted variable, $\underline{U}t$.

At some time in the past, Crusoe has selected all future quantities to maximize welfare, $\underline{H}$, subject to $\underline{n}$ production function constraints like (3), within a framework of perfect knowledge. This implies forming a Lagrangian function and setting the first partials with respect to future $\underline{x}$'s, $\underline{y}$'s, $\underline{R}$'s, and $\underline{K}$'s equal to zero. I assume that the second order conditions are satisfied.

This establishes shadow prices, which measure opportunity costs, as the slopes of the indifference curves or the slopes of the isoquants. Using the shadow price of $\underline{x}$ at t_o, ps_o^x, as the numeraire, yields:

(5) $\qquad ps_o^x = V_{xo}/V_{xo} = W_{xo}/W_{xo} = 1,$

$\qquad ps_o^y = V_{yo}/V_{xo} = W_{yo}/W_{xo},$

$\qquad ps_o^L = ps_o^R = V_{Ro}/V_{xo} = -W_{Lo}/W_{xo}.$

There is also a shadow price for capital, defined in terms of the partials of the production functions, so that the shadow price measures opportunity cost. The price of capital is not directly related to utility, since capital is not an argument in the utility function. Capital does influence welfare, however, because it permits Crusoe to maximize welfare by trading utility between years. Next year's consumption has an opportunity cost in terms of this year's consumption.

The "own" rate of interest on $\underline{x}$ between t_0 and t_1, rx_1, is defined in terms of the shadow price of $\underline{x}$ at t_1 so that $ps_1^x = ps_0^x/(1+rx_1)$. Crusoe can obtain 1 unit of $\underline{x}$ at t_1 by sacrificing $1/(1+rx_1)$ units at t_0, or can obtain $(1+rx_1)$ units at t_1 by sacrificing 1 unit at t_0. He does this by first reducing $\underline{x}_0$ and increasing $\underline{K}_0$, while leaving $\underline{y}_0$ and $\underline{L}_0$ unchanged, and then increasing $\underline{x}_1$ while leaving $\underline{y}_1$, $\underline{L}_1$, and $\underline{K}_1$ unchanged.

The remaining shadow prices and own rates of interest:

$$
\begin{aligned}
(6) \quad ps_0^K &= W_{Ko} / W_{xo}, \\
ps_1^K &= -(T_{K1}/T_{Ko}) * (W_{Ko}/W_{xo}), \\
&= ps_0^K/(1+rK_1), \\
ps_1^x &= -(T_{x1}/T_{Ko}) * (W_{Ko}/W_{xo}), \\
&= (H_{U1}/H_{Uo}) * (V_{x1}/V_{xo}), \\
&= ps_0^x / (1+rx_1), \\
ps_1^y &= -(T_{y1}/T_{Ko}) * (W_{Ko}/W_{yo}) * (W_{yo}/W_{xo}), \\
&= (H_{U1}/H_{Uo}) * (V_{y1}/V_{yo}) * (V_{yo}/V_{xo}), \\
&= ps_0^y / (1+ry_1), \\
ps_1^L &= (T_{L1}/T_{Ko}) * (W_{Ko}/W_{Lo}) * (W_{Lo}/W_{xo}), \\
&= (H_{U1}/H_{Uo}) * (V_{R1}/V_{Ro}) * (V_{Ro}/V_{xo}), \\
&= ps_0^L / (1+rL_1).
\end{aligned}
$$

Each shadow price falls continuously at a rate given by its own rate of interest. The own rates of interest for any commodity are different in different years, and are different for different commodities in the same year.[3] Equation (6) shows that $rx_1 = ry_1$ if and   only if $ps_1^x/ps_0^x = ps_1^y/ps_0^y$, so that the relative prices of $\underline{x}$ and $\underline{y}$ are the same at t_0 and t_1.

Crusoe's "real" or "behavioral" problems have now been resolved. He knows what he should produce and consume for t=0 ... n, without having to determine his income, his product, or any other synthetic accounting variable.

For illustrative purposes, I assume the following behavior at t_0 and t_1.

TABLE   I

t	x	psx	y	psy	L	psL	K	psK
0	100	1.0	200	1.00	250	1.00	312	1.00
1	120	.9	200	.95	260	.85	250	.94

The own rates of interest can be calculated by dividing the t_0 shadow price by the t_1 shadow price, so that $(1+rx_1) =$ 1.111, $(1+ry_1) = 1.052$, $(1+rL_1) = 1.176$, and $(1+rK_1) = 1.064$.

III. PRELIMINARY ACCOUNTING

I modify the model in three ways before starting to "account." The purpose is to make the Crusoe economy resemble a competitive economy.

1) I introduce nominal prices and a nominal interest rate such that the present value of each nominal price is the opportunity cost. 2) I divide the economy into two parts, a firm which maximizes financial "profit" subject to restrictions imposed by production functions, and a consumer who maximizes welfare subject to financial constraints. 3) I introduce money as a unit of account and as a medium of exchange, but not as a

store of value.

1) Nominal prices and interest rates.

Nominal prices make the Crusoe economy resemble the usual competitive model more closely by avoiding the continuous decline in prices, and permitting the arbitrary determination of the price level each year, perhaps by monetary policy.

Nominal prices can be equated to shadow prices at any arbitrarily chosen time, and I select t_o. Nominal prices at t_1 are determined by multiplying each shadow price by the same arbitrary constant $(1+rn_1)$, so that relative nominal prices at t_1 are the same as relative shadow prices at t_1. Nominal prices therefore reflect opportunity costs at any given time. However, the nominal prices do not reflect opportunity costs between years, as the shadow prices do.

This defect can be cured by introducing a nominal interest rate, rn_1, and calculating the present (t_o) value of one unit of $\underline{x}$ at t_1 as $pn_1^x/(1+rn_1) = ps_1^x$. The present value of the nominal price is the shadow price, and measures the opportunity cost.[4]

There is only one nominal interest rate, even though there are four "own" interest rates. The nominal interest rate is determined arbitrarily to specify the price level, and is not related to the "own" rates.[5]

The nominal prices are formally defined:

$$(7) \quad pn_o^x = ps_o^x,$$
$$pn_1^x = ps_1^x * (1+rn_1) = ps_o^x * (1+rn_1) / (1+rx_1),$$
$$pn_1^y = ps_1^y * (1+rn_1) = ps_o^y * (1+rn_1) / (1+ry_1),$$

with the understading that nominal prices for $\underline{L}$ and $\underline{K}$ are similarly defined.

I modify Table I to introduce the nominal prices obtained if Crusoe inflates all t_1 prices by $(1+rn_1) = 1.2$. The nominal interest rate between t_0 and t_1 is therefore 20%. The "own" rates are the same as before.

TABLE II

DATA BASE

t	x	pnx	y	pny	L	pnL	K	pnK	1+rn
0	100	1.00	200	1.00	250	1.00	312	1.000	
1	120	1.08	200	1.14	260	1.02	250	1.128	1.2

I assume as part of my "certainty" model that Crusoe knows all future nominal prices and interest rates.

2) A firm and a household.

I next decentralize Crusoe's decision making by creating two accounting entities, a household (or consumer sometimes called Crusoe) and a firm. The household knows the welfare function, which it maximizes subject to financial constraints without knowledge of the production functions. The firm knows the production functions. It maximizes a financial target subject to restraints imposed by those functions without knowlegde of the welfare function. I return to the determination of the financial constraints and objectives in Section IV.

3) Money and Interest.

I now assume that both Crusoe and his firm use money as a unit of account, and as a medium of exchange for all transactions. Since there is no physical money to use as a store of value, the net flow of "medium" at any point in time must be identically zero, so that neither accounting entity starts with nor accumulates any "cash."

Crusoe starts his firm at t_o by lending it $K_o*pn_o^K$ = \$312, so that it can buy its initial capital from him. The net flow of "medium" at t_o is therefore zero. At t_1, Crusoe pays his firm $x_1*pn_1^X + y_1*pn_1^Y$ = \$357.60 for   (consumer) goods, and the firm pays Crusoe $L_1*pn_1^L$ = \$265.20 in wages.   These are called "productive" cash flows because they pay for goods and services which are arguments of the production function. There must be an additional "financial" flow (FF_1) from the firm to Crusoe equal to the difference between sales and wage costs (\$92.40), or Crusoe would not have the "medium" required to make his purchases, and the firm would acquire a stock of cash.

This financial flow is divided into an interest payment, and a payment (positive or negative) of principal.

The model requires that the interest rate on financial obligations be rn_t. Since I have assumed constant returns to scale,[6] Euler's theorem says:

(8) $x_1*T_{x1} + y_1*T_{y1} + L_1*T_{L1} + K_o*T_{Ko} + K_1*T_{K1}$
        $= T(x_1, y_1, L_1, K_o, K_1) = 0.$

The definitions of shadow and nominal prices imply:

(9.1) $x_1*ps_1^X + y_1*ps_1^Y - L_1*ps_1^L - K_o*ps_o^K + K_1*ps_1^K = 0,$

which I multiply by $(1+rn_1)$, to get

       $x_1*pn_1^X + y_1*pn_1^Y + K_1*pn_1^K = L_1*pn_1^L + K_o*pn_o^K*(1+rn_1),$

(9.2) $\quad x_1*pn_1^X + y_1*pn_1^Y - L_1*pn_1^L$

$\qquad = K_0*pn_0^K*rn_1 - (K_1*pn_1^K - K_0*pn_0^K) = FF_1.$

$\quad K_1*pn_1^K = K_0*pn_0^K * (1 + rn_1) - FF_1.$

(9.3) $\quad K_0*pn_0^K = (K_1*pn_1^K + FF_1) / (1 + rn_1).$

Equation (9.3) is a standard finance equation which says that the present (t_0) value of an asset is the sum of the t_1 value and the t_1 cash flow, discounted to t_0. I define interest in the usual way, as the difference between the t_1 wealth ($K_1*pn_1^K + FF_1$) and the t_0 wealth ($K_0*pn_0^K$) associated with the debt of the firm to Crusoe. This implies that the financial flow ($92.40) consists of an interest payment ($62.40) of 20% on the original loan of $312, and a principal payment ($30) of $K_0*pn_0^K - K_1*pn_1^K$, bringing the debt to $K_1*pn_1^K$ ($282).

Equation (9.2) shows that the present value of the future financial cash flows from the firm to Crusoe is the value of the firm's capital, and of the firm's debt to Crusoe. In general, the financial flow from the firm to Crusoe, FF_i, is the difference between the money paid by Crusoe for consumer goods, and the money received by Crusoe for labor services:

(10) $\quad FF_i = x_i*pn_i^X + y_i*pn_i^Y - L_i*pn_i^L$

$\qquad = K_{i-1}*pn_{i-1}^K *(1+rn_i) - K_i*pn_i^K$

$\quad K_0*pn_0^K = (FF_1 + K_1*pn_1^K)/(1+rn_1)$

$\qquad = [FF_1 + \{FF_2 + K_2*pn_2^K\}/(1+rn_2)]/(1+rn_1)$

$\qquad = FF_1/(1+rn_1) + FF_2/[(1+rn_1)*(1+rn_2)] + \ldots$

This is consistent with finance theory which says that the value of shares should equal the present value of the future cash flows to shareholders, and with capital theory which says that capital assets should reflect the value of future services. This is another interpretation of the statement that Crusoe receives interest at the rate rn on his loan to the firm.

No net assets or liabilities are created by setting up two decision-making accounting entities. Offsetting financial assets and obligations are created. The firm gets all of the productive assets, but issues financial instruments, which in this case are shares, but might also be debt, to obtain them. This makes the firm's assets equal its liabilities, with no net wealth required to "balance" the balance sheet. The household has only financial assets, which equal the value of the firm's obligations, and the value of the firm's real assets. Discounting at the interest rate of rn keeps the firm's balance sheet in balance.[7]

The nominal interest rate was introduced in the model to avoid the steady deflation of prices which is required by using shadow prices, and was used to deflate nominal prices to obtain opportunity costs. With the introduction of a firm, the nominal interest rate is also the interest rate paid on loans.

IV. Decision Variables

In this section I consider the synthetic variables which Crusoe and his firm find useful for decision purposes, which I call decision variables. I consider the household first, and then the firm.

1) The household's decision variables

The household maximizes welfare, $\underline{H}$, subject to a financial

constraint without knowledge of the production functions. I
assume that Crusoe is making decisions at t_o, and that the
decisions are to cover his behavior at t_o and for the future.

There are numerous ways of presenting the financial
constraint, the most common of which is that the present value
of the (current and future) purchases of $\underline{x}$ and $\underline{y}$ (but not $\underline{R}$)
cannot exceed the present value of the (current and future)
labor sales plus the value of the financial instruments at t_o.

$$(11)\quad x_o*pn_o^X + y_o*pn_o^Y + (x_1*pn_1^X + y_1*pn_1^Y)/(1+rn_1) + \ldots$$
$$\leq K_o*pn_o^K + FF_o + L_opn_o^L + L_1*pn_1^L/(1+rn_1) + \ldots$$

Since present values measure opportunity costs, this
constraint generates the same decisions as Section II, when he
maximized subject to physical rather than financial constraints.
The raw data which Crusoe needs to make his decisions are
therefore a) his welfare function, b) present and future values
of pn_X, pn_Y, pn_L, and $\underline{rn}$, and c) the current value of his
financial assets, including the dividend received at t_o.[8] He
does not need to know the value of physical capital, nor the
production functions.

This constraint suggests defining synthetic decision
variables for (personal) consumption ($\underline{C}_i$), financial wealth
($\underline{FW}_i$), human capital or wealth ($\underline{HW}_i$), and total (personal)
wealth ($\underline{W}_i$):

$$(12)\quad C_i = x_i*pn_i^X + y_i*pn_i^Y$$
$$FW_i = K_i * pn_i^K + FF_i$$
$$HW_i = L_i*pn_i^L + (L_{i+1}*pn_{i+1}^L)/(1+rn_{i+1}) + \ldots$$

$$\overline{W}_i = FW_i + HW_i.$$

(9), (10), (11) and (12) also imply the following relationships through time:

(13) $FW_{i+1} = (FW_i - FF_i) * (1+rn_{i+1})$

   $HW_{i+1} = (HW_i - L_i*pn_i^L) * (1+rn_{i+1})$

   $W_{i+1} = (W_i - C_i) * (1+rn_{i+1})$

This defines human capital as the present value of current and future labor sales, and measures wealth after the dividends and wages have been received, but before the consumption has been paid for. The constraint (11) can be rephrased to say that the present value of current and future consumption cannot exceed current wealth. The decision problem is to decide when to consume one's wealth.

While this definition of consumption is consistent with national income accounting, it is more consistent with modern consumption theory[9] to reformulate constraint (11) by adding the present value of current and future leisure ($\underline{R}$) to both sides of the equation, with the understanding that the price of leisure, pn_i^R, equals the price of labor, pn_i^L. Noting that $L_i + R_i = M$, we rewrite (11):

(14) $x_0*pn_0^X + y_0*pn_0^Y + R_0*pn_0^L$

   $+ (x_1*pn_1^X + y_1*pn_1^Y + R_1*pn_1^L)/(1+rn_1) + \ldots$

   $\leq K_0*pn_0^K + FF_0 + M * [pn_0^L + pn_1^L/(1+rn_1) + \ldots]$

This equation suggests that Crusoe works M hours per day at a wage of p_L, and spends some of these "earnings" buying leisure. It requires a redifinition of the synthetic variables,

consumption and human capital, to obtain "full" consumption (FC)
and "full" human capital (FHW):

$$(15) \quad FC_i = x_i * pn_i^X + y_i * pn_i^Y + R_i * pn_i^L$$

$$= C_i + R_i * pn_i^L$$

$$FHW_i = M * [pn_i^L + pn_{i+1}^L/(1+rn_{i+1}) + \ldots]$$

$$= HW_i + R_i * pn_i^L + R_{i+1} * pnL_{i+1}/(1+rn_{i+1}) + \ldots$$

The equations in (12) for financial and total wealth are not
changed, nor are equations (13), except that FC and FHW must be
substituted for C and HW.

This formulation has the advantage of defining consumption
so that it includes all of the variables in the consumption
function, which makes it preferrable for descriptive purposes.
For decision purposes, the information required by Crusoe is
identical to (11).

Equations (5), (6), and (7) were used to define the
(shadow) prices and interest rates. When we divide the economy
into two parts, they become the first-order conditions for the
maximizing behavior of Crusoe and the firm. We assume that
Crusoe knows the prices, and that he controls the values of the
partial derivatives by his consumption decisions. The
first-order conditions for welfare maximization are that he
should select the values for the $\underline{x}$'s, $\underline{y}$'s, and $\underline{R}$'s so that these
equations will hold.

We can also use the first-order conditions to develop
decision variables. If we define the marginal utility of $\underline{x}$ as
v_x, then (5) shows that the marginal utility of a dollar's worth

of each consumer good   equals the marginal utility of a dollar's worth of every other   consumer good,   since nominal   prices are proportional to shadow prices, for   any t. We can then refer to this as the marginal utility of a dollar's worth of consumption.

If we consider a   two-year   period, as in equations (6) and (7), we   must define marginal   welfare (H_v * V_x) rather than marginal utility.   We then obtain from (7) the standard result that welfare maximization requires that the marginal welfare of a dollar's worth of nominal consumption must   rise from   year to year according to the nominal interest rate, rn. If the interest rate between t_0 and t_1 is 20%, as in our example, the marginal welfare of \$1.00 of nominal consumption at t_0 must equal the marginal welfare of \$1.20 of nominal consumption at t_1.

Crusoe's constraint is wealth, divided into financial wealth and (full) human wealth, and the choice variables are (full) consumption in t_0 and beyond. We conclude that his decision   variables   are   financial   and human wealth, and consumption.   We note that Crusoe does not need to measure his income, the rate of inflation, or any "real," as opposed to "nominal," prices or interest rates.   These   are apparently descriptive variables, not decision variables.

2) The firm's decision variables

The firm maximizes a synthetic financial decision variable (frequently called "profit") subject to the physical constrains imposed by the production functions, without knowledge of Crusoe's utility or welfare functions. I assume that the firm, like Crusoe, is making decisions at t_o, and that the decisions cover its behavior at t_1 and the future.[10]

There are different ways of presenting the variable which the firm must maximize if it is to behave the way that Crusoe behaved before he decentralized the decision-making. The simplest statement is that the firm knows the value of its t_o capital $(K_o*pn_o^K)$, and maximizes Crusoe's t_1 nominal financial wealth:

(16) $FF_1 + K_1*pn_1^K$

$= FF_1 + FF_2/(1+rn_2) + FF_3/[(1+rn_2)*(1+rn_3)] + \ldots$

$= x_1*pn_1^X + y_1*pn_1^Y - L_1*pn_1^L + K_1*pn_1^K,$

subject to production function $\underline{T}$, and the initial endowment of $\underline{K}_o$. Since financial wealth is the only constraint on Crusoe controlled by the firm, maximizing is in Crusoe's interest. It also leads to the same decisions as in Section II, because the prices reflect the relative values to Crusoe.

The firm therefore needs to know only the prices at t_1 and the production function, $\underline{T}$. The price of capital at t_1 incorporates all of the necessary knowledge about future prices and interest rates.[11] The firm will behave optimally if it maximizes this synthetic variable.

It is usual, however, to state the objective function of the firm in terms of a flow, usually thought of as "profit," rather than in terms of a stock of wealth. One simple way to convert (16) into a flow, without trying to define "profit," is to subtract the initial capital value, which generates a synthetic variable which can be called the firm's (net) nominal product (NFP):

$$(17) \quad NFP_1 = FF_1 + K_1 {*} pn_1^K - K_0 {*} pn_0^K.$$
$$= x_1 {*} pn_1^X + y_1 {*} pn_1^Y - L_1 {*} pn_1^L + K_1 {*} pn_1^K - K_0 {*} pn_0^K$$

This definition of the firm's product is consistent with the normal "inventory" approach to the definition of product. The firm has a stock of productive resources valued at $K_0 {*} pn_0^K$ at t_0, purchases an additional $L_1 {*} pn_1^L$ of resources and sells $x_1 {*} pn_1^X$ and $y_1 {*} pn_1^Y$. It therefore "ought" to have a stock of $K_0 {*} pn_0^K + L_1 {*} pn_1^L - x_1 {*} pn_1^X - y_1 {*} pn_1^Y$ at t_1. Any difference between this amount and what it actually has, $K_1 {*} pn_1^K$, must be its product, and is given by (17).

Nominal product is the increase in inventory plus sales, less purchases, and plus net transfers (donations made less gifts received). I assume that the stocks of inventories are directly observable, and that the flows of sales, purchases, and transfers are observed by the economic accountant, and recorded as "transactions" between Crusoe and the firm. Product is an (unobserved) event which "explains" the discrepancy between the increase in inventories and the sales, purchases, and transfers.

We can now redefine the objective of the firm is the maximization of a synthetic decision variable called nominal product. Real product, defined to take account of changes in the price level, must therefore be a descriptive variable rather than a decision variable.

We can again think of the first-order maximizing conditions

(5), (6), and (7), as creating more decision variables, in this case, marginal products. The marginal products are defined in terms of the total differential of the production function, $\underline{T}$:

(18) $dx_1 {}^* T_{x1} + dy_1 {}^* T_{y1} + dL_1 {}^* T_{L1} + dK_0 {}^* T_{K0} + dK_1 {}^* T_{K1} = 0,$

Labor $(\underline{L}_1)$ and capital $(\underline{K}_0)$ each have three marginal products, one each producing $\underline{x}_1$, $\underline{y}_1$, and $\underline{K}_1$. We define the marginal product of labor (mp_{L1}) producing $\underline{x}_1$ as dx_1/dL_1, assuming $dy_1 = dK_0 = dK_1 = 0$, with the marginal products of labor producing $\underline{y}_1$ and $\underline{K}_1$ defined similarly. We define the $\underline{gross}$ marginal product of $\underline{K}_0$ capital[12] (gmp_{K0}) producing $\underline{x}_1$ as dx_1/dK_0, assuming $dy_1 = dL_1 = dK_1 = 0$, with the gross marginal product of capital producing $\underline{y}_1$ and $\underline{K}_1$ defined similarly.

(19) $dx_1/dL_1 = mp_{L1}^{x1} = - T_{L1}/T_{x1}$

$dx_1/dK_0 = gmp_{K0}^{x1} = - T_{K0}/T_{x1}$

Equations (5), (6), and (7) imply that the value of the marginal product of labor (vmp_{L1}) must be the same in all its uses, and must equal the wage rate.

(20) $vmp_{L1} = mp_{L1}^{x1} * pn_1^x = mp_{L1}^{y1} * pn_1^y$

$= mp_{L1}^{K1} * pn_1^K = pn_1^L$

Since $\underline{K}_0$ is not a decision variable, the three equations (20) and the production function $\underline{T}$ provide enough information for the firm to determine $\underline{x}_1$, $\underline{y}_1$, $\underline{L}_1$, and $\underline{K}_1$ to maximize (16) or (17).

Equations (5), 6), and (7) imply that the value of the gross marginal product of (t_0) capital must be the same in all (three of) its (t_1) uses. The value of the gross marginal product ($vgmp_{KO}$) is, however, not its t_O price, since the product will not be available until t_1. The t_O price must be accumulated for the year at an interest rate of rn_1.

Finally, there is a marginal rate of substitution between $\underline{K}_O$ and $\underline{L}_1$, assuming $dx_1 = dy_1 = dK_1 = 0$ (T_{KO}/T_{L1}), which can also be looked upon as a marginal product of capital. The value of the labor saved at t_1 by producing additional capital at t_O must also equal the accumulated price of the t_O capital.

$$(21) \quad vgmp_{KO} = gmp_{KO}^{x1} * pn_1^x = gmp_{KO}^{y1} * pn_1^y$$
$$= gmp_{KO}^{K1} * pn_1^K = pn_O^K * (1+rn_1)$$
$$= (T_{KO}/T_{L1}) * pn_1^L.$$

Equations (21), like equations (20), provide enough information for the firm to determine $\underline{x}_1$, $\underline{y}_1$, $\underline{L}_1$, and $\underline{K}_1$, to maximize (16) or (17).

V. Descriptive Variables

I now turn to the definition of descriptive synthetic variables. These variables are not required by either the household or the firm for decision-making. They have no operational significance. They are developed by economists for the purpose of gaining a better understanding of or insight into the operation of the economic system.

They also differ from decision variables in that, by convention, they are based on information about the past and the present, and do not require information about the future or about the production functions or the welfare functions.

I assume a "data base" for the generation of descriptive

variables, consisting of past and present nominal prices, nominal interest rates, inventories, and quantities exchanged, as in Table II. In a market economy, this data would be available from market observations, company records of physical inventories, and transactions.[13] In a Crusoe economy, I simply assume that the data is available.

The descriptive measures with which I shall be primarily concerned distinguish real from nominal values. I shall be concerned with real consumption, which seeks to determine whether Crusoe obtains greater utility in one year than another, real product, which seeks to determine whether Crusoe has produced more in one year than another, and real income, which seeks to determine how much Crusoe's potential real consumption has risen. These variables lead to the measurement of the rate of inflation, the real rate of interest, and the real net marginal product of capital.

1) Consumption and the Rate of Inflation.

The objective is to find a single number, called real consumption, which will serve as a proxy for utility, since utility is not directly measurable. It should rise when utility rises, and fall when utility falls. We are going to consider the measurement of real consumption at t_o and at t_1.

We take the total differential of Crusoe's utility function (1):

(22) $dU = V_x*dx + V_y*dy + V_R*dR,$

   $dU = U_1 - U_o,$

$$dx = x_1 - x_o; \quad dy = y_1 - y_o; \quad dR = R_1 - R_o$$

We define $\underline{D}_o$, $\underline{D}_1$, and $d\underline{D}$:

$$D_o = V_x*x_o + V_y*y_o + V_R*R_o,$$

$$D_1 = V_x*x_1 + V_y*y_1 + V_R*R_1,$$

$$dD = D_1 - D_o = dU.$$

Since $D_o > 0$ and $D_1 > 0$, the ratio $D_1/D_o > 1$ if and only if $dU > 0$.

To obtain the ratio D_1/D_o, we divide numerator and denominator by V_x, and substitute the shadow prices[14] for the ratio of the partials:

$$(23) \quad D_1/D_o = (x_1*ps^X + y_1*ps^Y + R_1*ps^L)/$$

$$(x_o*ps^X + y_o*ps^Y + R_o*ps^L).$$

We define nominal (full) consumption, $\underline{NC}$, as in (15):

$$(24) \quad NC_1 = x_1*pn_1^X + y_1*pn_1^Y + R_1*pn_1^L > 0$$

$$= 129.6 + 228 + 754.8 = \$1112.4$$

$$(24a) \quad NC_1 = M*pn_1^L + K_o*pn_o^K*(1+rn_1) - K_1*pn_1^K,$$

$$= 1000*1.02 + 312*1.2 - 282 = \$1112.4,$$

where (24a) follows from the assumption of constant returns to scale (9).[15]

We now distinguish two measures of consumption at any time, $\underline{t}$: 1) nominal consumption, $\underline{NC}_t$ (24), in which no correction is made for changes in the price level, and 2) real consumption of year $\underline{t}$ in base-year $\underline{B}$ dollars, $\underline{RC}_{t,B}$, in which all prices are restated in dollars of year $\underline{B}$. Since all prices in (24) are associated with the same year, real and nominal consumption are the same in the base year, i.e., $\underline{NC}_i = \underline{RC}_{i,i}$.

Difficulties arise in measuring real consumption of one

year in dollars of another base year, i. e., in measuring real
consumption at t_0 in t_1 dollars, $\underline{RC}_{0,1}$, and real consumption at
t_1 in t_0 dollars, $\underline{RC}_{1,0}$. The objective is to measure $\underline{RC}_{1,0}$ so
that $RC_{1,0} - RC_{0,0} = RC_{1,0} - NC_0 > 0$ if and only if $dU = U_1 - U_0$
> 0, and to measure $RC_{0,1}$ so that $RC_{1,1} - RC_{0,1} = NC_1 - RC_{0,1} >$
0 if and only if $dU > 0$. Changes in real consumption in
base-year dollars should have the same sign as changes in
utility.[16]

Equation (23) suggests that the use of the same prices to
measure $RC_{1,1}$ and $RC_{0,1}$, and the same prices to measure $RC_{1,0}$
and $RC_{0,0}$ should produce the desired result. That is, if we
define $RC_{1,0}$

(25) $RC_{1,0} = x_1 * pn_0^X + y_1 * pn_0^Y + R_1 * pn_0^L = \$1060,$

and $RC_{0,0} = x_0 * pn_0^X + y_0 * pn_0^Y + R_0 * pn_0^L = \$1050,$

then $RC_{1,0} - RC_{0,0} > 0$ if and only if $dU > 0$.

If we define $RC_{0,1}'$

(26) $RC_{1,1} = x_1 * pn_1^X + y_1 * pn_1^Y + R_1 * pn_1^L = \$1112.40,$

and $RC_{0,1}' = x_0 * pn_1^X + y_0 * pn_1^Y + R_0 * pn_1^L = \$1101,$

then $RC_{1,1} - RC_{0,1}' > 0$ if and only if $dU > 0$.

There are two problems with these measurements. First, they
do not always give the same results, which is the usual index
number problem. In calculating the total differential, dU (22),
dx, dy, and dR are assumed to be so small that the partials, e.
g., V_X, are the same whether they are evaluated at t_1 or t_0. For
finite changes, prices (the ratios of the partials) are not the
same at t_1 and t_0. The mathematics says that $D_1 - D_0 > 0$ implies

dU > 0 only in the limit as the quantity changes approach xero, so that the price changes also approach zero.

In the finite case, the two sets of prices yield different measures of the changes in real consumption. If $RC_{1,1} - RC'_{0,1}$ and $RC_{1,0} - RC_{0,0}$ have the same sign, then this must be the sign of dU. If real consumption rises on one measurement and falls on the other, it is not possible to determine which sign is correct (has the same sign as dU) without knowing the utility function. There is no theoretical preference between (25) and (26).

Second, the two formulations, (25) and (26), give different measurements of the rate of inflation $(1+rf_1)$ between t_0 and t_1. The rate of inflation is defined as real consumption in t_1 dollars divided by real consumption in t_0 dollars. (25) implies

$$(27) \quad (1+rf_1) = RC_{1,1} / RC_{1,0},$$
$$= (x_1*pn_1^X + y_1*pn_1^y + R_1*pn_1^L) / (x_1*pn_0^X + y_1*pn_0^y + R_1*pn_0^L)$$
$$= 1112.4/1060 = 1.0494,$$

which is the Paasche price index showing the increase in price of the t_1 market basket.

Equation (26) implies

$$(28) \quad (1+rf'_1) = RC'_{0,1} / RC_{0,0},$$
$$= (x_0*pn_1^X + y_0*pn_1^y + R_0*pn_1^L) / (x_0*pn_0^X + y_0*pn_0^y + R_0*pn_0^L)$$
$$= 1101/1050 = 1.0486,$$

which is the Laspeyres price index showing the increase in price of the t_0 market basket.

In general, rf_1 (27) will not equal rf'_1 (28), and there is no criterion for selecting one rather than the other. The only virtue is consistency. If $RC_{1,o}$ is defined from (25), then $(1+rf_1)$ should be defined from (27), and $RC_{o,1}$ defined so that $RC_{o,1}/RC_{o,o} = (1+rf_1)$:

(29) $RC_{o,1} = RC_{o,o} * (1+rf_1) = 1050 * 1.0494 = \$1101.91$.

If $RC'_{o,1}$ is defined from (26), then $(1+rf'_1)$ should be defined from (28), and $RC'_{1,o}$ defined so that $RC_{1,1}/RC'_{1,o} = (1+rf'_1)$:

(30) $RC'_{1,o} = RC_{1,1} / (1+rf'_1) = 1112.4/1.0486 = \$1060.87$.

I shall use (25), (27), and (29), which are Laspeyres quantity indices and Paasche price indices, in my examples.

No matter how we define the rate of inflation, our results agree with modern consumption theory: we must use <u>full</u> consumption if consumption is to be a proxy for utility.

2) Income, Wealth, and the Real Rate of Interest.

Real (full) consumption is a proxy for current utility, and does not take into account the fact that Crusoe may have changed his future prospects by saving or dissaving. The idea of income is to measure not only current consumption, but activities which enhance future consumption.

The most common definition of income is the maximum consumption which an individual can sustain during a year without being worse off at the end of the year than he was at the beginning.[17] This is often interpreted to mean that income is potential consumption, rather than actual consumption.[18]

This is not true in our model. If we define potential consumption as the maximum amount Crusoe could consume during

the year, this is his wealth, not his income. Furthermore, since
Crusoe maximizes welfare, rather than utility, he would be
"worse off" (get less welfare) if he consumed either more or
less than we "observe." If "income" is the maximum Crusoe can
consume without being worse off, then income is consumption.[19]
In our model, Crusoe's welfare is the same at t_1 and t_0, since
he selects his utility through time to maximize welfare.

We can still ask, however, whether his activities during
the year changed his wealth (potential consumption), and
interpret an increase in wealth as making provision for the
future, which is a standard interpretation of the idea of
saving. If his wealth has risen, he is not "better off" in the
sense that his welfare is higher, but in the sense that he has
saved and increased his maximum possible consumption for the
following year.

We define "income" between t_0 and t_1 as actual consumption
at t_1 plus the increase in wealth between t_0 and t_1, measuring
wealth after consumption on both dates.[20] Income is therefore
the maximum amount he can consume at t_1, less the amount he
decided not to consume at t_0. Actual consumption at t_1 reduces
wealth at t_1, but not income.

There are two major difficulties with using wealth as
defined in (13) and (15) as the basis for measurement of income:
a) it overstates potential consumption, and b) it requires
information not available to the accountant.

a) Crusoe could not consume all of his wealth and continue

to provide the labor services whose present value is part of this wealth. In making his consumption decision, Crusoe acts as though he could sell his human capital and his financial resources and turn them into present consumption. This suggests that Crusoe could either sell himself into slavery to his firm, or could borrow an equivalent sum (his human capital) from the firm. Neither action would change his wealth. If he sold himself into slavery, he would use the proceeds to buy a financial asset from the firm (and provide the firm with the "medium" required for the purchase), thereby substituting financial wealth for human capital. Similarly, if he borrowed against his future earnings, he would buy a financial asset which would offset the financial liability, and leave his net financial wealth unchanged.

In either event (sale or borrowing), he incurs an obligation to perform labor services in the future, either to "justify" the sale price (interpreting the sale as a promise to deliver labor services in the future), or to repay the loan. This means that he cannot consume his entire wealth since this would reduce his future consumption below the starvation level and he would be unable to meet his obligations.

We should therefore correct the constraint (14) by subtracting the consumption required to maintain the productivity of human capital from both sides of the equation. The constraint would then say that the present value of future "discretionary" consumption (full consumption less maintenance) should equal the present value of "net" labor earnings (full earnings less maintenance) plus financial assets. The present value of "net" labor earnings is the market value of the human capital (slave), or the maximum amount which Crusoe could borrow against his future labor earnings, if the lender could be certain of future repayment.

Our preferred definition of wealth is therefore the (full) value of (net) human capital plus the value of financial assets. This represents the maximum amount that Crusoe could consume at any point in time if he could convert his wealth into consumer goods at going prices, and still maintain his human capital to the extent required to fulfill the obligations which he has made for the future.

The model implies that Crusoe thinks that he can convert all of this wealth into immediate consumption. In fact, Crusoe could not do this, since it would take time to convert the physical capital into consumer goods, and he could not consume today the goods he will not produce until next year. He will nevertheless make the correct decisions if he acts as though he were constrained by prices, rather than production functions. In a more realistic model, any single individual can make the conversions if he is a small enough element in the system, although all individuals can not do so simultaneously.

b) The present value of human capital, gross or net of maintenance, is not part of the data base available to the economic accountant for the development of synthetic variables.

The information is not available in a market economy since slavery is illegal, and the amount that an individual can borrow against future labor earnings is very difficult to estimate.

Therefore, we do not usually include human capital as part of wealth in the definition of income. This means that 1) wealth underestimates potential consumption to the extent that individuals can borrow against future earnings even when slavery is illegal, and 2) income is underestimated (overestimated) by the amount of the increase (reduction) in human capital during the accounting period.

If Crusoe holds no real assets, his nominal income ($\underline{NY}_1$) is 1) the increase in (financal) wealth after he consumes at t_0 and before he consumes at t_1, or 2) nominal consumption at t_1 plus the increase in financial assets between t_0 and t_1, after consumption on both dates, or 3) labor earnings plus (normal) interest on the financial holdings at t_0:

(31.1) $NY_1 = K_1*pn_1^K + FF_1 + M*pn_1^L - K_0*pn_0^K$,

$\qquad = 282 + 92.4 + 1020 - 312 = \$1082.40$,

(31.2) $\qquad = NC_1 + K_1*pn_1^K - K_0*pn_0^K$,

$\qquad = 1112.4 + 282 - 312 = \$1082.40$,

(31.3) $\qquad = M*pn_1^L + K_0*pn_0^K*rn_1$,

$\qquad = 1020 + 62.4 = \$1082.40$.

These nominal measures of wealth and income, however, do not take into account changes in the purchasing power of the dollar between t_0 and t_1. We can define Crusoe's real wealth at t_0 in t_1 dollars ($\underline{W}_{0,1}$) as $K_0*pn_0^K*(1+rf_1)$ ($\$327.42$), since this

measures the amount he would need at t_1 to have the same
purchasing power over consumer goods that he had at t_o. We then
define __real__ income ($\underline{RY}_{1,1}$) as   the amount he could consume at t_1
and still maintain his real t_o wealth.   His real   income, $\underline{RY}_{1,1}$,
measured in t_1 dollars, is therefore

(32.1) $RY_{1,1}$ = $K_1 * pn_1^K + FF_1 + M * pn_1^L - K_o * pn_o^K * (1 + rf_1)$

= 282 + 92.4 + 1020 - 312*1.0494 = \$1066.98

(32.2)   = $RC_{1,1} + K_1 * pn_1^K - K_o * pn_o^K * (1 + rf_1)$,

= 1112.4 + 282 - 327.42 = \$1066.98,

(32.3)   = $M * pn_1^L + K_o * pn_o^K * (rn_1 - rf_1)$,

= 1020 + 312*(.20 -.0494) = \$1066.98.

Equation (32.3) suggests that some of Crusoe's __nominal__
interest is not __real__ interest. Crusoe starts the year with real
wealth of $K_o * pn_o^K * (1 + rf_1)$ = \$327.42, and receives a financial
payment of FF_1 = $K_o * pn_o^K * (1 + rn_1)$ - $K_1 * pn_1^K$ = \$92.40, divided
into $K_1 * pn_1^K - K_o * pn_o^K * (1 + rf_1)$ = \$45.42 of __real__ principal and
$K_o * pn_o^K * (rn_1 - rf_1)$ = \$46.98 of __real__ interest. The __real__ interest
rate, rr_1, is therefore $(rn_1 - rf_1)/(1 + rf_1)$ = \$46.98/\$327.42 =
14.3%.

Real income therefore equals (real) wages plus a real
return of rr_1 on the initial wealth, $W_{o,1}$:

(33) RY_1 = $M * pn_1^L + K_o * pn_o^K * (1 + rf_1) * rr_1$,

An equivalent, and more familiar, equation for the __real__
interest rate, __rr__, is

(34) $(1 + rr_1)$ = $(1 + rn_1)/(1 + rf_1)$ = 1.2/1.0494= 1.143.

In equilibrium, the real rate is independent of the nominal

rate, and the rate of inflation. If Crusoe had decided to inflate shadow prices (Table I) by 50% instead of 20%, the nominal rate of interest would become 50%, but all prices would be 25% higher so that the new rate of inflation would be 31.175%, and the real rate would be unchanged at 14.3%. The real rate does depend, however, on whether we use a Paasche price index (27) or a Laspeyres index (28).[21]

The model now has six rates of interest, plus a rate of inflation. The four own rates are the ratios of the shadow prices from Table I. The nominal rate is arbitrarily determined by Crusoe to prevent continuous deflation. The real rate depends upon which price index is used to measure the rate of inflation, but not upon the actual rate of inflation. The nominal interest payment is the nominal rate multiplied by the nominal debt. The real interest payment is the real rate multiplied by the real debt.

We can also measure real t_1 income in t_0 dollars, $\underline{RY}_{1,0}$. From (27), (32), and (34), we get:

(35) $RY_{1,0} = RY_{1,1}/(1+rf_1) = 1066.98/1.0494 = \$1016.72,$

(35.1) $\quad = RC_{1,0} + K_1*pn_1^K/(1+rf_1) - K_0*pn_0^K,$

$\quad = 1060 + 268.72 - 312 = \$1016.72,$

(35.2) $\quad = M*pn_1^L/(1+rf_1) + K_0*pn_0^K*rr_1,$

$\quad = 971.95 + 44.76 = \$1016.72.$

(35.1) simply restates Crusoe's consumption and wealth in t_0 dollars by deflating all t_1 values by $(1+rf_1)$. (35.2) deflates his wage earnings by $(1+rf_1)$, and says that his real interest, in t_o dollars, is at the rate $\underline{rr}_1$.

Finally, we note that the firm has neither consumption nor income, on these definitions.   The firm cannot consume since consumption is a proxy for utility and the firm has no utility. Its income would therefore simply be the increase in its wealth between t_o and t_1. However, the firm has no wealth, since the value of its physical assets always equals the value of its debt to Crusoe.   The increase in wealth is therefore zero, as is the income.

This means that our first two descriptive variables, consumption and income, really apply only to the household (and the society), and not to the firm. Our third variable, product, will, however, apply to both entities.

3) Product.

We introduced the decision variable, product, as a variable which the firm might maximize in Crusoe's interests.   We now introduce product as a descriptive variable, with a definition which is very close to our definition of income.

One of the basic conceptions of income is the increase in maximum potential consumption after consumption at t_o and before consumption at t_1. Income, however, can arise either from labor earnings (production), or from financial activities. Product can arise only from productive activities, not from financial activities.

We look at the society as a whole, and define social or national product as the increase in the quantity of economic goods and services which would be observed if there were no consumption during the accounting period. This means that social product a) is the increase in the stock of goods (and services) plus consumption, b) is independent of financial activities, and c) equals social income, even though income and product may differ for any entity within the society.

We note again that we have, by convention, excluded human capital from wealth in the measurement of income. We must also exclude the production of human capital from the measurement of product, if we equate social income and product.

We start by considering nominal product ($\underline{NP}_1$), which means that we do not take account of price changes between t_o and t_1, and therefore measure the increase in the stock of goods (excluding human capital) to be $K_1 * pn_1^K - K_o * pn_o^K$:

$$(36) \quad NP_1 = x_1 * pn_1^X + y_1 * pn_1^Y + R_1 * pn_1^L + K_1 * pn_1^K - K_o pn_o^K,$$

$$= NC_1 + K_1 * pn_1^K - K_o * pn_o^K,$$

$$= M * pn_1^L + K_o * pn_o^K * rn_1,$$

$$= NY_1,$$

so that nominal product is the same as nominal income, since there is no social financial income.

The measurement of real product at t_1 in t_1 dollars ($\underline{RP}_{1,1}$) requires that we measure the increase in the real quantity of economic goods, rather than the increase in the nominal value of the stock. This raises the problem of defining economic quantities. In general, we argue that economic quantity should measure the ability of the goods to generate utility.

We are therefore interested in the productivity of the capital goods, not in their physical quantity. If Crusoe does not change the physical quantity of capital goods, but manages to increase their productivity, the real quantity of economic resources available to him has increased, and he has produced economic resources. The price of capital goods equals the present value of the future cash flows which Crusoe will get from these goods, and Crusoe behaves as though he could turn these flows into consumption. If the price of capital rises more than the price level of consumer goods, the productivity of a physical unit of capital has increased. The _real_ value of capital, i.e., the nominal value corrected for changes in the price level of consumer goods, measures capital quantity[22] and productivity.

This means that $NP_1 = RP_{1,1}$ if $rf_1 = 0$, and the proper way to measure the increase in the real quantity of capital in t_1 dollars is to measure the initial real quantity as $K_0 * pn_0^K * (1+rf_1)$, not as $K_0 * pn_1^K$.

Real product is therefore:

$$(37) \quad \begin{aligned} RP_{1,1} &= RC_{1,1} + K_1 * pn_1^K - K_0 * pn_0^K * (1+rf_1) \\ &= M * pn_1^L + K_0 * pn_0^K * (1+rf_1) * rr_1 \\ &= M * pn_1^L + K_0 * pn_0^K * (rn_1 - rf_1) \\ &= 1066.88 = RY_{1,1}. \end{aligned}$$

Real product is the same as real income, since there is still no financial income.

4) Net Marginal Product.

We have already discussed the marginal product of labor and the gross marginal product of capital, in connection with the firm's decision variables. We now introduce a descriptive variable, the net marginal product of capital. The idea is to attribute the total (nominal or real) product to the two factors of production, labor and capital. Since we are not keeping track of the production or the quantity (stock) of labor, we need not be concerned with the net marginal product of labor. However, we count increases in the quantity of capital as production, which means that we must also keep track of capital destruction (depreciation), or we will double-count the product.

In the measurement of nominal product, we do this by subtracting the value of the initial capital, $K_0*pn_0^K$, from the closing capital, $K_1*pn_1^K$, to measure the net increase in capital, or net nominal investment. In the measurement of real product, we subtract the real (t_1 base) value of the initial capital, $K_0*pn_0^K*(1+rf_1)$ to measure net real investment.

I discuss three definitions of net marginal product of capital: the marginal products of physical capital, nominal capital, and real capital. Each starts from the total differential of T, (18). The gross marginal product (19) is based on the assumption $dK_1 = 0$, so that the increment of capital, dK_0, is not preserved. The net marginal product assumes that dK_0 is "preserved," in one of three ways:[23]

1) The marginal physical product (mpp_K) assumes $dK_1 = dK_0$ (and $dy_1 = dL_1 = 0$), so that physical capital is maintained,

and dx_1/dK_0, from (18), is

(38.1) $mpp_{KO}^{x1} = (pn_1^K/pn_1^X)*rK_1$.

The _value_ of the marginal physical product ($vmpp_K$) is

(38.2) $vmpp_{KO} = pn_1^K*rK_1$.

The rate of return on _physical_ capital (rpc) is the own rate of interest on capital:

(38.3) $rpc_{KO} = rK_1$.

    2) The marginal _nominal_ product (mnp_K) assumes $pn_1^K*dK_1$ = $pn_0^K*dK_0$ (and $dy_1 = dL_1 = 0$), so that _nominal_ product is maintained, and dx_1/dK_0, from (18), is

(39.1) $mnp_{KO}^{x1} = (pn_0^K/pn_1^X)*rn_1$.

The value of the _nominal_ marginal product ($vmnp_K$) is

(39.2) $vnmp_{KO} = pn_0^K*rn_1$.

The rate of return on _nominal_ capital (rnc) is the nominal interest rate:

(39.3) $rnc_{KO} = rn_1$.

    3) The marginal _real_ product (mrp_K) assumes $pn_1^K*dK_1$ = $pn_0^K*(1+rf_1)*dK_0$ (and $dy_1 = dL_1 = 0$), so that _real_ capital is maintained, and dx_1/dK_0, from (18) is

(40.1) $mrp_{KO}^{x1} = (pn_0^K/pn_1^X)*(1+rf_1)*rr_1$.

The value of the _real_ marginal product ($vmrp_K$) is

(40.2) $vrmp_{KO} = pn_0^K*(1+rf_1)*rr_1$.

The rate of return on _real_ capital (rrc) is the _real_ interest rate:

(40.3) $rrc_{KO} = rr_1$.

    In all cases, the value of the marginal product, and the

rate of return are independent of pn_1^X. This means that vmp and the rate of return are the same no matter which commodity the capital is used to produce.

There is a measurement of (net) social product which corresponds with each of these measurements of the net marginal product of capital, in the sense that the social product can be attributed to the factors of production:

$$\text{Social product} = K_o * vmp_{Ko} + L_1 * vmp_{L1}.$$

These measurements of social product can all be formulated so that product equals consumption plus net investment. They all measure consumption in the same way, but measure net investment differently.

The marginal <u>real</u> product of capital (40) measures net real investment, $\underline{RI}_{1,1}$, as:

(40.4) $RI_{1,1} = K_1 * pn_1^K - K_o * pn_o^K * (1+rf_1) = -\$45.42.$

The definition of net real investment is identical to the definition of net real investment in (37). Since (37) is our definition of real social product, the marginal real product, as defined in (40), is the economically appropriate definition of marginal (real) product.

Marginal <u>nominal</u> product (39) measures net nominal investment (NI_1) as:

(39.4) $NI_1 = K_1 * pn_1^K - K_o * pn_o^K = -\$30.$

This definition of net nominal investment is identical to the one in (36), and is therefore the appropriate definition of marginal nominal product of capital.

Marginal _physical_ product measures   net physical investment ($\underline{PI}_1$) and net social product ($\underline{NNP}_1$) as:

(38.4) $PI_1 = (K_1 - K_o)*pn_1^K = -\$69.94,$

(38.5) $NNP_1 = x_1*pn_1^x + y_1*pn_1^y + (K_1-K_o)*pn_1^K = \$287.66.$

These definitions are consistent with the GNP accounts.   My accounting   scheme,   however,   has   no   definition   of   product, nominal or   real, which is consistent   with   this concept of the marginal (physical) product of capital.

VI Comparison with GNP accounts.

There are   five major differences   between this   accounting scheme and the GNP accounts:

1)   GNP   accounts   measure   only   consumption   of market goods, rather than full consumption, including leisure.

2) GNP accounts correct   components (e. g., consumption or investment) of product for changes   in prices by constructing separate   price indices for each component. We use the   general consumer   price   index   to   corect   all   components,   including investment.

3)   GNP   accounts   measure   physical   investment   (38.4) rather than real investment (40.4).

4)   In   the   GNP   accounts, nominal product   equals   real product   in   the base year. In our   accounts, nominal   and   real product are equal in the base year only if there is no inflation during that year.

5)   GNP accounts   measure   both gross and   net   product, while we measure only net product.

The first differences has already been adequately covered. We discuss the remaining four, in order.

2) Corrections for price changes. The fundamental issue is the use of separate price indices for separate components.[24] If there were no changes in the consumer price index, all price changes would represent changes in relative prices. Our scheme would not correct any component of nominal income or product in measuring real values, i. e., all real values would equal nominal values.

The GNP accounts, however, measure real (t_1 base) consumption of $\underline{x}$ as $x_0 * pn_1^X$ at t_0, and as $x_1 * pn_1^X$ at t_1. The increase in real consumption is $(x_1 - x_0) * pn_1^X$ in t_1 dollars, and the percentage increase is $x_1/x_0 - 1$, whether or not there has been a change in the general level of prices.

Our model measures the real (t_1 base) consumption of $\underline{x}$ at t_0 as $x_0 * pn_0^X * (1+rf_1)$, and the percentage increase in real consumption as

$$[x_1 * pn_1^X] / [x_0 * pn_0^X * (1+rf_1)] - 1.$$

The GNP measurement of real t_0 consumption of $\underline{x}$ depends only upon the change in the price of $\underline{x}$, and not on changes in the price level. Our measurement takes into account the change in the price of $\underline{x}$ relative to other price changes.   It is preferable for two important reasons.

First, the GNP model does not correctly measure the fraction of real resources devoted to the production of $\underline{x}$ at t_0. Opportunity costs at t_0 are measured by t_0 prices, so that the ratio $x_o * pn_o^X / NC_o$ measures correctly the fraction of total real consumption devoted to x at t_o. The GNP model uses t_1 prices to determine the relative importance of the commodities at t_o, even if relative prices have changed, and says that the ratio $x_o * pn_1^X / RC_{o,1}$ measures the fraction of total real consumption devoted to x at t_o.

The use of t_1 prices to measure real total consumption, $RC_{o,1}$, does not require that they be used to measure components of that consumption. Once $RC_{o,1}$ has been defined from (25), with the associated price index, $(1+rf_1)$ from (27), the price index can and should be used to correct all subtotals (x, y, and R) for changes in prices between t_o and t_1.

The second reason is equally important. The purpose of measuring real consumption is to provide a proxy for utility. If the marginal utility of x has risen, then a physical unit of x represents a larger contribution to utility, and should be counted as a larger quantity of real consumption. The marginal utility of a real dollar's worth of x is greater at t_1 than at t_o if x has risen in price relative to other prices, i.e., if $pn_1^X / pn_o^X > (1+rf_1)$. If pn_1^X reflects the marginal utility of x at t_1, then $pn_o^X * (1+rf_1)$ reflects the marginal utility of x at t_o, and $x_o * pn_o^X * (1+rf_1)$ is the best available measure of the real consumption of x at t_o in t_1 dollars.

The GNP model does not take account of this change in the marginal utility of individual commodities, and says that a physical unit of x represents as much real consumption (utility) at t_0 as at t_1, no matter what has happened to relative prices. Our model takes account of the changes in marginal utility of x. For example, if the price of oil rises dramatically during the year, its marginal utility also rises, and consumption of a gallon represents more real consumption at the end of the year than at the beginning.

These arguments are equally strong when we measure capital goods and investment. In the absence of inflation, our measure of investment is $K_1 * pn_1^K - K_0 * pn_0^K$, since we do not make any corrections for relative price changes. The GNP accounts correct the t_0 inventory of capital goods for the change in the price of capital goods, pn_1^K/pn_0^K. This is equivalent to measuring the quantity of capital goods produced as $K_1 - K_0$, and valuing this quantity in t_1 prices, i. e., as $(K_1 - K_0) * pn_1^K$.

Our model counts this product, but also counts the increase in the (relative) value of the t_0 capital, $K_0 * (pn_1^K - pn_0^K)$, because changes in relative prices reflect changes in productivity and economic quantity. The GNP accounts do not count changes in the prices of existing inventories as product[25], on the grounds that there have been no changes in the physical characteristics of the commodity.

Finally, I argue that the best price index to use is the consumer price index, not a GNP deflator which includes the prices of capital goods.[26] There is no reason why Crusoe should consider the price of capital goods in measuring his real financial wealth. He is interested only in the consumption made

possible by the wealth. The same is true of the measurement of
capital and investment. We are not interested in the ability of
capital goods to produce capital goods, but in their ability to
produce consumer goods and utility. We must use the same price
index to correct both nominal savings and investment if we want
real savings to equal real investment. Since Crusoe must use the
consumer price index to deflate nominal savings, it should also
be used for capital goods.

3) The use of physical measures of capital (38) in the GNP
accounts leads to two undesirable inconsistencies, which are
avoided by using the real value approach (40).

First, it implies a real return to physical capital of $\underline{rK}_1$,
which does not equal Crusoe's real return on financial loans of
$\underline{rr}_1$.   When he measures his nominal t_0 wealth of $K_0 * pn_0^K$ in real
t_1 dollars, he corrects for changes in the general purchasing
power of the dollar, and gets real wealth of $K_0 * pn_0^K * (1+rf_1)$. He
therefore gets a real return of $\underline{rr}_1$, defined in (34).

If we use the marginal physical product (38.3), we get a
rate of return on capital of $\underline{rK}_1$, which does not equal $\underline{rr}_1$
unless we define the rate of inflation exclusively in terms of
capital goods, i. e., $(1+rf_1) = pn_1^K/pn_0^K$.[27] It is difficult to
make sense of the idea that Crusoe's real return on loans to the
firm differs from the firm's real return on the money borrowed.
Our formulation measures both real returns as $\underline{rr}_1$.

Second, additional inconsistencies arise if there is
another kind of capital, $\underline{J}$, which would be expected even in a

Crusoe economy. If we use the marginal physical product, the real rate of return on $\underline{J}$ capital is its own rate of interest, $\underline{rJ_1}$. This would equal the real rate of return on $\underline{K}$ capital, $\underline{rK_1}$, only if relative prices of $\underline{K}$ and $\underline{J}$ do not change, which suggests a steady state equilibrium. A difference in the productivity of the two kinds of capital suggests that Crusoe could have increased his t_1 product by shifting resources from the less productive capital to the more productive capital at t_0.[28]

There is no useful purpose in measuring capital productivity so that it implies that Crusoe should change his behavior when he is maximizing welfare. Economists are trained to think that equilibrium exists only if the rate of return on a dollar's worth of capital is the same for both $\underline{K}$ and $\underline{J}$. Our model produces this result by measuring the real rate of return as $\underline{rr_1}$ for all kinds of capital goods and on all loans, while the nominal rate of return is $\underline{rn_1}$. The use of physical capital (38) instead of real capital (40) generates misleading differences between the real return to physical capital and the real return to financial capital, and between the real rates of return on different kinds of capital goods.

4) This concerns the equality of nominal and real product in the base year. The GNP accounts make an "inventory valuation adjustment" to remove inventory gains from product in measuring both nominal product and real product. Nominal investment in t_1 prices is $(K_1 - K_0) * pn_1^K$. There are no t_0 prices in the GNP measurement of nominal t_1 product, and nominal and real t_1

product are identical no matter what happens to prices during the year. Since we measure nominal investment as $K_1*pn_1^K - K_0*pn_0^K$, and real investment as $K_1*pn_1^K - (1+rf_1)*K_0*pn_0^K$, nominal product equals real product only if $\underline{rf_1} = 0$.

This difference follows from the use of specific price indices, rather than a general price index, as noted above.[29]

5) GNP accounting measures both net and gross product, by distinguishing empirically between capital created during the year, and capital on hand at the start of the year. There is no way to measure gross product within the context of our model, since the production function does not specify how much of the capital in existence at t_1 also existed at t_0. Furthermore, there is no description of the economic system which suggests the measurement of gross product.

In our example, GNP could be estimated on the assumption a) that all 250 units of t_1 capital also existed at t_0, b) that all of the t_0 capital had been replaced, so that none of the capital in existence at t_1 also existed at t_0, or c) anything in between. In case a), there would be no "gross" investment at t_1, 62 units of physical depreciation, valued at pn_1^K ($1.128), for depreciation of $69.94 and net investment of -$69.94. In case b), there would be "gross" investment of 250 physical units @ $1.128, or $282. Depreciation would be 312 units @ $1.128, equal to $351.94, leaving net investment at -$69.94. Case c) would have gross investment between 0 and $282, with net investment still -$69.94. If we include leisure in consumption, this leads to a GNP between $1112.40 and $1394.40, and a NNP of $1042.46.

The NNP is always the same. The GNP has no economic meaning.

Chapter III

Double-entry Bookkeeping and Economic Accounting

The purpose of this chapter is to develop the basic ideas of a double-entry bookkeeping system. This system will be applied to different kinds of entities, the society, households, and firms, in later chapters.

1. Overview of Double-entry Bookkeeping.

Double-entry bookkeeping starts from a data base which records all of the information available to the accountant. Ideally, this information includes the market prices of relevant economic instruments at balance sheet dates, and transactions with other entities between balance sheet dates. Balance sheets are prepared for t_0 and t_1, on the basis of the price information. Accounts with positive values are recorded as debits, and usually treated as assets, although they may sometimes be treated as contra-liabilities. Accounts with negative values are recorded as credits and are usually treated as equities, although they may sometimes be treated as contra-assets.

Since the sum of the credits must equal the sum of the debits, for each balance sheet, a balancing entry called "Net Wealth" is created, if necessary. Equities are further divided into three categories: liabilities which represent legal claims against the firm, owners' equity which represents the owners' interest in a firm, and net wealth which represents the net assets of a household.

Flows between the accounting entity and other entities

between t_0 and t_1 are recorded in flow accounts, again so that the sum of credits equals the sum of debits.

The flow accounts are opened by "transferring" the balances from the initial (t_0) balance sheet to the flow accounts, to record the opening inventories in the accounts. This amounts to "closing" the balance sheet stock account to the flow account which is concerned with the next accounting period. If the balance sheet account has a positive (debit) balance, it is closed with a credit entry, and the flow account is opened with a debit entry. If the balance sheet account has a negative (credit) balance, it is closed with a debit entry, and the flow account is opened with a credit entry. The flow accounts therefore start with balances which are identical to the balance sheet accounts, with positive inventories as debits and negative inventories as credits. By convention, positive net wealth is a credit balance, to make the balance sheet balance.

The ending inventories are similarly transferred from the flow accounts to the ending (t_1) balance sheet, to record the closing inventory. If the balance sheet account is positive (debit balance), the flow account must be reduced with a credit entry, and the balance sheet account opened with a debit entry. If the balance sheet account is negative (credit balance), the flow account must be increased with a debit entry, and the balance sheet account opened with a credit entry.

The transactions are recorded in the flow accounts, with additions to inventory recorded as debits, and subtractions from

inventory recorded as credits.   Each transaction is required to
"balance" debit and credit entries.   Inventory increases must
equal inventory reductions for each transaction.

The flow accounts are "closed" to the income flow account,
to measure value added and income. If the flow account "closes"
with a debit entry, this is positive value added, and the
corresponding credit to the income flow account is positive
income (gain).   If the closing entry to the flow account is a
credit, this is value lost, and the corresponding debit entry to
the income flow account is negative income (loss).

The income flow is "closed" to the wealth flow account, to
measure net value added and net income. The wealth flows account
is automatically "closed" when net income is closed from the
income flow account.

The most critical difference between economic accounting
and traditional (GAAP) accounting is that economic accounting
bases the balance sheet entirely on current market prices.
Economic accounting requires no knowledge of flows to prepare a
balance sheet, unless some prices are unavailable and flows
provide information which may be used to estimate prices.[1]
Traditional accounting is based on the assumption that analysis
of observed flows can be used to measure income, and balance
sheets can be prepared without knowledge of current prices.

2. Balance Sheets

In economic accounting, the balance sheet records the
values of stocks (inventories) of economic instruments owned by

the entity, with positive values recorded as debits, and negative values recorded as credits. Any difference between the sum of debits and the sum of credits is recorded as "Net Wealth," to make the balance sheet balance. No balancing entry is required for firms, since any residual becomes a part of owners' equity.

Both the quantities and the market prices of all economic instruments should be part of the "data base." If the prices are not available, it is the job of the economic accountant to estimate them.

Economic instruments are classified as either "productive," or "financial." Productive instruments are real goods or services which are arguments in production or utility functions, except that utility itself is not a productive instrument, and is not accounted for. Financial instruments are pieces of paper which record financial obligations of one entity to another, and are not arguments in either production or utility functions.

The value of an economic instrument is, on our definitions, always a quantity multiplied by a market price and is never a price alone. The price is always taken as positive, but the quantity may be either positive or negative.

The inventory quantity (stock) of any instrument is calculated by counting purchases as positive quantities (additions to the quantity already held), and sales as negative quantities (subtractions from the quantity already held). Quantities owned can be negative if the entity has sold "short," i.e., has sold instruments which are not on its books at the time of sale. In addition, quantities can be changed by "producing" or "adding" value, which will be discussed in the next section.

All quantities of productive instruments owned by an entity are positive, since we treat all short sales as financial activities rather than productive activities. However, it is very common for entities to "own" negative quantities of particular financial instruments, since the "issue" of shares, bonds, accounts payable, debt, and other equities, is in effect a short sale. These instruments are not on a firm's books (are not part of "physical" inventory) prior to sale. When a firm sells shares or bonds, the quantity recorded by the seller is negative, and the quantity recorded by the buyer is positive, as with any other sale. The quantity (inventory, stock) held by the seller is therefore negative, and the quantity held by the buyer is positive. The value recorded on the balance sheet of the seller is therefore negative (a credit) while the value recorded by the buyer is positive (a debit).

We can illustrate these ideas with simple examples. If A sells B 10 lbs of productive instruments @ $2/lb, the quantity for A is -10 lbs, and for B is +10 lbs. Each entity can keep track of its physical inventories by adding the quantity involved in the transaction to previous inventories. Accountants keep track of value inventories rather then physical inventories, so that entity A adds -$20 to the value of

productive   instruments owned with a credit   entry, while B adds
+$20 with a debit entry.

Similarly, if A sells B 10 shares of GM common stock @ $50,
A adds -10 shares to his physical inventory and -$500 to his
value inventory with a credit entry, while B adds +10 to his
physical inventory and +$500 to his value inventory with a debit
entry. It makes no difference whether either A or B is GM, or
whether they are trading in the shares of a third firm.

If A is GM, the quantity of GM shares which it owns has
declined by 10, and the value of shares owned has declined by
$500. The previous inventory may be   zero in both   quantity and
value, in which case the new inventory is -10 valued at -$500.
If GM's inventory was negative to start with, GM adds -10 shares
to the quantity and -$500 to the value. Shares issued have
negative quantities and negative values.

We record the sale by GM:

Cash (Flow Account) $500

    Shares (Flow Account) $500

If this is the original and only issue, and is the value on
the balance sheet date, we transfer $500 to the ending balance
sheet:

Shares (Flow Account) $500

    Shares (Balance Sheet Account) $500

The balance sheet account shows a credit (negative) balance,
since shares were sold short, and the quantity "held" by GM is
negative.

A reversing entry will transfer the balance sheet account to a new flow account, which will record flows for the following accounting period.

However, our basic definitions in Chapter 2 require that all entities use the market price in recording the value of all economic instruments which they "hold," or "own." Each financial instrument is recorded on the balance sheets of two entities, once as a debit (by the buying entity, or lender), and once as a credit (by the selling entity, or borrower). In the aggregate, in a closed society, these financial entries add to zero.

This means that the entry transferring the balance to the balance sheet depends on the market value as of the balance sheet date. If this value were $600, the journal entry would be:

        Shares (Flow Account) $600

            Shares (balance Sheet Account) $600

The flow account would have a $100 debit balance, which we will account for when we measure income.

Productive instruments are "held" or "owned" by one and only one entity, and appear on only one balance sheet, as a debit entry.

It is important to understand that this represents a sharp departure from traditional business accounting, in four important respects:

    1. The balance sheet can be constructed from a data base which does not include any flows, or any information about past (or future) prices. All instruments are valued at current market

price.   Generally accepted accounting principles (GAAP) usually
require   that   current balance   sheet   values   be   calculated by
"adjusting" previous balance sheet values.

2. GAAP do not say that economic instruments should be
valued at market. This is not a question of the availability of
data.   It   is a question   of accounting principle. GAAP permits,
for example,   the   use of FIFO or LIFO to determine the value of
finished   goods   inventories.   Both of   these procedures   permit
different physical units of identical instruments be carried at
different prices   at the same   time. The traditional   procedures
for valuing   financial instruments (either   purchased or issued)
frequently   also result in the recording of different prices for
identical instruments at the same time, by the same entity. GAAP
is not designed to estimate market prices. If it were, all units
of the same instrument would be carried at the same price.

3. GAAP does not say formally that credits   are negative
values, although   this is   a common interpretation. Ijiri,   for
example, says "Negative numbers   are   avoided   by   setting   up a
different column or a separate account in which negative numbers
are grouped and recorded as positive." [24, p. 5] The important
conceptual point is that credits can never "equal" debits.   They
are of opposite sign.   The balance   sheet balances if the sum of
aggregate debits plus   the   sum of   aggregate credits   is   zero,
i.e.,   if   credits   equal debits in   absolute value,   but are of
opposite   sign. We   shall   therefore   say   that   debits "offset"
credits, rather than saying that debits equal credits.

4. Net wealth is not the same as "net worth" or "owners' equity." For a corporation, owners' equity is represented by a financial instrument called a share. Our procedure says that this instrument should be listed on the balance sheet at market, just like any other economic instrument owned by the firm. Net wealth is the net wealth of the entity for which we are accounting, not the wealth of some other entity. Shareholders are "other" entities, from the point of view of the firm. In a Crusoe economy, firms have no net wealth, and the balance sheet balances on the basis of the values of the economic instruments owned by the firm.

Only households or societies have net wealth. For the society, net wealth is the value of productive assets. Households also have financial wealth, which represents the value of productive assets owned by firms.

As we saw in Chapter 2, economic accounting treats sole proprietors as if they were firms, and accounts for owners' equity just as if shares had been issued. For partnerships, we have trouble, since the partners are individually liable for the debts of the firm. There is "joint" ownership of the debts, and each partner is liable for 100% of each debt. This reduces the risk to the debtor, but violates the idea that financial instruments add to zero in a closed economy. Our principles do not permit separate accounting for entities which have joint assets or liabilities. We cannot account separately for husband and wife, or for other partners.

3. Flows

In economic accounting, we keep track of flows to explain or understand, but not to measure, changes in stocks, since stocks are measured at current market price. In traditional accounting, flows are frequently recorded to help measure the ending stock.

In either case, we are guided by the fundamental inventory equation:

Opening stock + additions = subtractions + ending stock.

Since we are accounting for values rather than quantities, additions are purchases and value added, while subtractions are sales, consumption, and value lost, where the value lost is not due to consumption.

Consumption is the only flow that affects only one entity. Consumption reduces the stock of a productive instrument to create utility for the entity, which must therefore be a household rather than a firm. Destruction of one economic resource to produce another, according to rules governed by a production function, is not consumption. It is part of the "value lost." We assume that information about consumption is part of the data base, although in practice we usually have to estimate consumption from other observed stocks or flows.

The effect of consumption is to reduce the value of productive instruments held, and to reduce net wealth. We do not "account" for the utility obtained from consumption. It is not part of the data base, has no market price, has no physical units of measurement, and has no economic value.

Consumption is the only flow required to measure the income of an entity, since income is the increase in net wealth plus consumption, and net wealth depends only on the prices of economic instruments. Firms have no consumption, income or net wealth.

All other flows in the data base are "transactions" or "exchanges" between two entities. They are categorized as either "fair" or "unfair." A "fair" exchange is one in which the items exchanged have equal value, and is the only possible exchange in the perfectly competitive model we have been discussing. In the real world, governments frequently require tax payments which are not "fair," and entities sometimes make or receive gifts.

The critically important implication of "fair" exchanges is that they do not change the wealth of either entity. Since income is defined as the change in wealth plus consumption, income can never be generated by a fair exchange. All income is generated by what accountants call holding gains or losses, which we call "value added" or "value lost." This is a common characteristic of economic models, as in Bodenhorn [5], and differentiates economic accounting from GAAP. Under GAAP, purchases are usually assumed to be fair exchanges. Sales, however, are frequently unfair: income is "realized" when a transaction takes place if the (book) value of the item sold is different from the sales price. Under economic accounting, income is never realized when a transaction occurs. The book value (balance sheet value) equals the current price whether or not a transaction occurs.

Conceptually, it is convenient to break all exchanges into two parts: a sale and a purchase. For this purpose, we conceive of an imaginary "medium of exchange," as we did in the last chapter. Since this "medium" is imaginary, it is impossible to hold any stock, so that purchases and sales must mirror each other, in what we call an "exchange" or a "transaction."

Every exchange involves the sale of an economic instrument for "medium," and the purchase of another instrument with the medium acquired. If a "sale" is made for cash, we say that the "medium" of exchange acquired in the sale was itself used to purchase an asset (store of value) called "cash." Similarly, a purchase with cash is the sale of a financial asset (cash) for "medium," and a subsequent purchase using the "medium."

If we follow this procedure, we can use our basic inventory equation for every economic instrument for which we account, including "cash." If we do not follow this procedure, we can increase our cash balance as an asset without a purchase, and we need special procedures for handling cash as an asset.

This procedure requires that all transactions with outside entities be defined as purchases and sales of economic instruments. There can be no "borrowing," no "issuing" of debt or equity, no "payment" of interest or dividends. Every transaction must be a purchase and a sale. "Borrowing" money is the sale of a financial instrument for "medium," and the

purchase of cash with the medium. "Issue" of shares is the sale
of a financial instrument and the purchase of cash.

Interest presents interesting problems. A 10-year bond
calling for semi-annual interest payments is really a "compound"
financial instrument which consists of 21 "primitive"
instruments. Each of the primitive instruments calls for a
specified payment on a specified date: 20 interest payments, and
one repayment of principal. The payment of interest is then the
sale of one of these primitive instruments by the lender to the
borrower. A coupon is "clipped" or "stripped" from the bond and
sold to the issuer. The sale is recorded by the lender:

        Cash   XX

              Bonds   XX

No "revenue" or "expense" is recorded when a transaction
takes place. In principle, we can keep an inventory flow account
for every economic instrument which we either buy or sell,
although in practice we usually consolidate or aggregate the
flow accounts for several instruments. Every transaction results
in a debit (addition) to one flow account pertaining to the
inventory of an economic instrument, and a credit (subtraction)
to another flow account. Every transaction exchanges one
economic instrument for another, and every transaction is fair.
Debits are always offset by credits. The books always balance.

The "value added" by each economic instrument (or group of
instruments) is simply the "closing" entry to the flow account,
after 1) the opening inventory has been transferred ("flowed")

in, 2) ending inventory has been transferred out, and 3) all transactions - purchases, sales, and consumption - involving the instrument(s) have been recorded.

In economic accounting, value added is always a residual or a plug. Stocks are measured at market. Transactions are recorded as they take place. Any discrepancy is called "value added," with the understanding that this may be positive (increasing inventory with a debit entry) or negative (decreasing inventory with a credit entry). In GAAP, value added is frequently not a plug, but is estimated (arbitrarily) by the accountant, and the ending inventory becomes the plug.

It should also be noted that this is not the usual economic definition of "value added." The more common definition does not increase stocks of productive resources when labor services are purchased. Our definitions require that all purchases be capitalized, i. e., recorded as "assets." If the market does not confirm this by increasing the market value of assets held, we record value lost. If the market increases asset values by more than the value of the resources purchased, we record value added. The usual definition used in national income accounts does not anticipate that the purchase of labor services will increase asset values, so that value is recorded if market value exceeds the value of non-labor resources bought. On our definitions labor services are "value added" by the household producing the services. In GNP accounting, labor services are "value added" by the purchaser of the services.

Economic instruments are also classified as "productive" or "financial." A "productive" instrument is an argument in a production function or a utility function. A "financial" instrument is a (negotiable) piece of paper defining future financial obligations. As we have seen, a "primitive" financial instrument obligates a single payment on a specified date. In practice, financial instruments can be quite complicated, and involve considerable risk and uncertainty.

Value added by productive instruments is frequently called "product" or "production." In a Crusoe (perfectly competitive) economy, this definition attributes (assigns) the total national product to the entities which comprise the nation, and is sometimes interpreted to mean that each factor of production "produces" its marginal product.

Various economists and accountants, from Marx to Thomas [42, 43] have, however, objected to this attribution on various grounds. We employ it because it is accepted in national income accounting: world product is attributed to nations using this procedure.

The fundamental problem is that there is no agreement as to what is meant by the statement that "A produces X and B produces Y," when A and B cooperate in the production of X+Y. Marx, for example, insists that only labor can produce anything. To him, the fact that capital has a marginal product does not demonstrate that capital "produces" anything, but only that additional capital makes labor more productive. Thomas [43, p.

38] objects to the idea that all units of a given resource "produce" their marginal product because the marginal product depends upon how many units are employed, which suggests interaction between the productivity of the different units.

At another level, the problem is that there is no empirical content to the statement that "A produces X." The only observable fact is what A receives as income. We can agree that the owner of a resource gets, as income, the value of its marginal product, in perfect competition. Any additional statement that the income resulting from productive activities is also the "product" of the resource a) adds no additional information, and b) has no generally accepted interpretation.

I nevertheless follow the common practice of identifying "product" with "productive income," even though this definition of "product" is not universally accepted, and may well add nothing to our understanding of the underlying economic events.

Value added in financial activities results in income, as does value added in productive activities, but is never characterized as "production" or "product." No social income or product is generated by financial activities, since our definitions result in offsetting positive and negative incomes arising from each financial instrument.

All flows between entities must aggregate to zero when the entities are added together. This is the result of the convention which says that the quantities involved in the flow are positive for one entity and negative for the other. The

total value of the flow to the two entities involved is
therefore always zero. This permits us to aggregate
(consolidate) or disaggregate without changing income totals,
which is an important characteristic of economic accounting.

4. Measurement of product and income.

If we wish to measure both productive income (product), and
total income, we need four major flow accounts. We need one to
keep track of flows of productive instruments, and a second for
financial instruments. We also open up accounts for income
flows, and wealth flows. We may also create sub-accounts to the
productive flow and the financial flow accounts. Sub-accounts
keep track of individual instruments or groups of instruments,
instead of lumping all productive instruments into one account
and all financial instruments into another account. Sub-accounts
provide additional detail into the sources of income.

The productive, financial, and wealth flow accounts record:

    1)   Opening stocks

    2)   Closing stocks

    3)   Transactions - purchases, sales, and consumption.

The productive account is closed to income flow. Hopefully,
the closing entry will involve positive value added, i. e., the
ending inventory plus sales and consumption will exceed the
opening inventory plus purchases. In this case, the closing
entry will be:

    Productive Flows (value added)   XX

        Income flow (Productive income)   XX

On some occasions, the value added will be negative, i. e.,
the closing inventory will be smaller than it ought to be on the
basis of the opening inventory and the observed flows:

Income flow (Loss in production)   XX

    Productive flows (value lost)   XX

Similarly, the financial flow account is closed to the
income flow account. In this case, a firm would expect its value
added to be negative, i. e., it expects to have negative income
(loss) associated with its (aggregate) financial activities. If
its only financial activity were the sale of shares and the
payment of dividends (repurchase of some of the compound and
complex financial instrument), we would expect the debt to
shareholders, as evidenced by the market price, to be larger
than we can explain on the basis of the opening (negative)
inventory and the transactions.

Income flow (Loss on Shares)   XX

    Financial flows (value lost)   XX

The entries are the same as the entries for productive
accounts, except that the income or loss is identified as
financial instead of as productive.

If we are accounting for a business firm, there is no net
wealth. This means that the wealth flow account shows zero
stocks and flows, and that the income flow account will show a
zero balance after the productive and financial flow accounts
have been closed to it. Business firm have neither wealth nor
income. If they generate value added and income in their

productive activities, this income is transferred to other
entities (debtholders and shareholders) by financial activities.
The purpose of accounting is not to measure the firm's income,
which is known to be zero, but to measure the components of the
income. How much income did the generate by its productive
activities? How much income did the firm generate for its
shareholders? These are not known in advance.

It should also be emphasized that the GAAP practice of
recording internal flows, by depreciation, accrual of interest,
transfers of assets from raw materials inventory to work-in-
process inventory, etc., has no effect the measurement of
productive or financial income. Economic accounting carries
inventories of all economic instruments at market. This means
that value added by productive activities and by financial
activities are market determined.

Since GAAP does not use market prices to generate balance
sheet values, GAAP permits the internal (non-market,
non-transaction) flows to influence the measurement of income.
Elaborate rules must therefore be promulgated regarding
permissible internal flows, to prevent firms from reporting
"misleading" income figures.

If the entity is a household, it must close the income
flow account to the wealth flow account, which will then show a
zero balance, since the balance sheet values have already been
transferred to the account. The closing entry to the income flow
account is net value added, which is positive if the entry is a

debit, and negative if the entry is a credit, as with the productive and finanial flow accounts. The entry to the wealth flow account is net income, which is positive if net value added is positive, and negative if net value added is negative. Positive net income is therefore a credit to net wealth, negative net income is a debit.

Positive income requires a closing entry:

Income flow (net value added)   XX

    Wealth flow (net income)   XX

Double-entry bookkeeping treats household wealth as if it were a financial obligation. This is necessary to keep the books in balance. Assets exceed liabilities. If net wealth were also an asset, we would be double-counting, and the books would not balance. Net wealth is recorded as a credit to balance the books, which means that it is treated as if it were a debt.

5. Real Values.

These measurements are concerned with nominal wealth, income, and product. We have already seen in Chapter 2 how to measure real values in t_1 dollars. Each of the values on the t_0 balance sheet would be adjusted for the changes in the general price level by multiplying by $(1+rf_1)$. If any of the flows were observed before t_1, they should similarly be adjusted for changes in the general price level between the date of the flow and t_1. The measurements in Section 4 would then be followed as before.

Since these statements apply to the estimation of real

values for any entity, we shall have no more to say about accounting for real values. We shall assume that the price level is stable, or that the appropriate corrections are made if real values are desired.

Chapter IV

Social Balance Sheets and Flows.

In this and the following two chapters, we illustrate the
basic ideas of the last chapter by applying them to the problems
of social accounting, household accounting, and firm accounting.

There are two ways to approach the problem of social
accounting. We can either consider each of the "entities" in a
closed society, generate measurements of wealth, income, and
product, and then aggregate to obtain "social" accounts. The
alternative is to treat the society as an entity, and apply the
principles which we have enunciated to measure the wealth,
product, and income of the entity.

It is one of the important precepts of economic accounting,
as distinguished from business accounting, that these two
approaches should lead to the same end result. GAAP are designed
to measure the "income" of an entity, but are not designed so
that the income of two entities should add to the income of the
conglomerate which would be formed if the entities were to
combine, as witness the difference between the "purchase" and
the "pooling-of-interest" methods when one firm acquires
another. The idea that social income should equal the sum
(aggregate) of the incomes of the "entities" which "comprise"
the society has no counterpart in GAAP. It is an important part
of economic accounting.

This chapter considers the social accounts as the accounts
of a single entity. The aggregation of the accounts of different
entities is discussed in Chapter 7, after we have presented the

accounts of the household and the firm.

The society we shall consider is similar to the Crusoe economy of the second chapter. There are only two entities, a household and a firm. We start from a data base which contains the values of the relevant inventories, flows, and consumption.

At t_o, the household owns $5,000 of inventories of consumer goods, while the firm owns $7,000 of capital goods and has an inventory of $1,500 of finished consumer goods. The firm has sold bonds and shares to the household, and they are valued at $3,000 and $6,000, respectively. In addition, the household has an "account payable" to the firm which it uses to make purchases. The value of this account is $500.

The flows which are recorded are $10,000 of consumption by the household, $9,000 of consumer goods purchased on account by the household from the firm, and $9,500 of labor services sold by the household to the firm. The household makes a payment of $9,000 on the account. In addition, the firm makes a payment of $1,300 on the outstanding bonds and pays a dividend of $200. Last, the firm sells $2,000 of new shares to the household.

At t_1, the household has consumer goods inventories of $4,000, the firm has $8,000 of capital goods and $2,400 of finished goods inventories. The bonds are valued at $2,000, the shares are valued at $9,000, and the account is valued at $600. Neither the household nor the firm holds any cash at any time, as in the Crusoe case. We will introduce the idea of cash balances in chapter 9.

The basic definitions of social product and income are:

Social income = Increase in net wealth + Consumption

Social product = Net investment + Consumption

Since the increase in net wealth equals net investment, this leads to the usual statement that social income equals social product.

This statement, however, does not take into account the basic idea of double-entry bookkeeping, which is to enter positive values as debits, negative values as credits, and to have the aggregate debits offset the aggregate credits. To the accountant, income is a negative number, while production is a positive number. Income and product are equal in absolute value, but opposite in sign.

We shall also ignore human capital in this and the next two chapters, since national income accounting does not usually take human capital into account. There are, as we have seen, conceptual advantages to introducing human capital, but the data problems are formidable.

1. The Social Balance Sheet.

Much of the information in the data base is not used in measuring social accounts. We assume in effect that the two entities merge into one, so that the bonds, shares, purchases and sales, and financial dealings between the two entities are ignored. An entity cannot lend itself money or buy or sell things to itself.

In constructing the balance sheet, this means that the

financial instruments are ignored, and only the productive
instruments remain. The social balance sheet is:

SOCIAL BALANCE SHEET (0)

Assets		Equities	
Capital goods	$7,000.	Net wealth	$13,500.
Consumer goods	6,500.		
TOTALS	$13,500.		$13,500.

In this balance sheet, we add the consumer goods
inventories of the two entities, since we are making no
distinction between them.

Net wealth must be a credit entry, to make the books
balance. This means that we are treating Net Wealth as if were a
debt to "Nature." The society, in effect, issues shares to
Nature, and obtains resources. These shares are accounted for
exactly like any financial instrument issued by an entity. Their
quantity is negative, since they have been sold short. They are
part of the entity's "equities."

Another way to think about this is to say that double-entry
bookkeeping treats (positive) wealth as a negative number. It is
a synthetic variable which is created to "balance" the books. It
can be thought of as an economic instrument not "explained" by
the information in the data base.

This is a concept which we shall use repeatedly in our
development of synthetic accounting variables. Our accounting
system is developed from a data base. The information in this
data base "explains" some of the economic events of interest,

but leaves other events "unexplained." The synthetic variables "account for" the events ("facts") which are not "explained" by the data base.

The ownership of economic instruments which have positive value can be "explained" from the data base by the ownership of economic instruments which have negative value. If an entity borrows money, this creates a financial instrument of negative value to the entity, and "explains" how the entity could afford to gain ownership of instruments with the same positive value. If the entity owns more instruments of positive value (assets) than it owns of negative value (liabilities), the entity has "unexplained" assets. We then infer that this entity must have "net wealth," which must be entered as a credit (negative value, or equity) to "balance" the books. We also find it convenient to "explain" net wealth as if it were a debt to Nature.

In some cases, an entity may have fewer assets than can be explained by its liabilities, so that its net wealth is negative. This requires a debit entry for net wealth (which can then be listed on either side of the balance sheet). The economist usually interprets this to mean that the entity is bankrupt, since the entity has insufficient assets to meet its liabilities. Households, however, usually do not list human capital as an economic instrument on their balance sheets and therefore may have undisclosed assets which keep them from bankruptcy.

On the basis of the data base, the final balance sheet is

SOCIAL BALANCE SHEET (1)

Assets		Equities	
Capital goods	$8,000.	Net wealth	$14,400.
Consumer goods	6,400.		
TOTALS	$14,400.		$14,400.

2. Social Flows.

The procedure for measuring income requires that we transfer the balance sheet values to flow accounts. We divide productive flows into capital goods and consumer goods, and also account for income flows and wealth flows. Financial flow accounts are unnecessary for a society, since there are no financial flows.

The flows "transferred" from the t_o balance sheet close the balance sheet accounts:

Capital goods flow (from t_o B.S.)	$7,000.	
Capital Goods stock at t_o		$7,000.
Consumer goods flow (from t_o B.S.)	$6,500.	
Consumer goods stock at t_o		$6,500.
Wealth stock at t_o	$13,500.	
Wealth flow (from t_o B.S.)		$13,500.

The flows "transferred" to the t_1 balance sheet open the new balance sheet accounts:

Capital goods stock at t_1	$8,000.	
Capital goods flow (to t_1 B.S.)		$8,000.
Consumer goods stock at t_1	$6,400.	
Consumer goods flow (to t_1 B.S.)		$6,400.

Wealth flow (to t_1 B.S.) $14,400.

Wealth stock at t_1 $14,400.

The algebraic signs on the flows from the t_0 balance sheet
are the opposite of the signs of the flows to the t_1 balance
sheet. We close the opening balance sheet to the flow account.
If the balance sheet has a debit balance, the entry to the flow
account is also a debit, since the stock flows from the balance
sheet to the flow account. The flows to the closing balance
sheet are opposite in sign because we are taking the inventory
out of the flow account, and putting it into the balance sheet
account.

This procedure generates flow accounts which have total
credits exactly offsetting total debits, since the both of the
balance sheets were in balance.

We next enter the flows from the data base. These flows
must generate offsetting debits and credits, to keep the books
in balance.

The only observed flow in the social case is consumption.
This flow reduces the quantity of consumer goods owned, and
therefore is a credit entry to the consumer gooods flow account.
It also "explains" a reduction in net wealth, since the society
does not get any economic instrument in return for the
consumption. It is therefore a debit to the wealth flow account.
This confirms our earlier result that positive wealth is a
credit entry. We must debit wealth flow when we record
consumption, and consumption reduces wealth.

Wealth flow $10,000

Consumer Goods flow $10,000

This means that consumption is not a "fair" exchange from the point of view of the accounting system. The "return" that we get from using productive economic instruments for consumption is utility, and we do not account for utility. It has no price, no physical unit of measurement, and no value. From the accounting standpoint, consumption is no different from giving resources away with no return. We make one entry to record the effect on the value of productive resources, and another entry to record the effect on wealth. We make no entry in the income flow account, since consumption does not change income.

3. Measurement of Product and Income.

We measure value added in production (product) as the increase in the value of productive resources not explained by the stocks and flows (observations) in the data base. The society has accumulated $13,500 of productive instruments prior to t_o, and these have been put into (debited to) the flow accounts. The society has consumed $10,000 during the period, and carried forward $14,400 for future use, and these flows have been taken out of (credited to) the flow account. This means that the economy started with $13,500 of productive instruments and used $24,400 of productive instruments. We infer that the $10,900 not explained by the data base were produced by the society.

We account for this by aggregating the two "goods" accounts

into a single "Productive instruments" account:

       Capital Goods flow $1,000

            Productive Instruments flow $1,000

       Consumer Goods flow   9,900

            Productive Instruments flow   9,900

We then close the Productive Instruments account with a debit of $10,900. Since this closing would "unbalance" the books, and since our economic theory says that production generates income, we close the productive flow account to the income flow account with a credit entry of $10,900, which we call "productive" income, since the income is generated by productive activities.

       Productive Flow (value added) $10,900

            Income flow from production $10,900

Our accounting system is based on the idea that product or production is not part of the accounting data base, and is what we call a "synthetic" variable. There may be engineers who "saw" some swords being bent into ploughshares, but this "observation" is not part of the accounting data base. Furthermore, it may not be "production" on our definitions. If the data base records $10 of swords at t_o and none at t_1, records no ploughshares at t_o and $10 at t_1, with no consumption, then the fabrication of poughshares from swords was not "production." There was no "unexplained" change in the value of productive instruments.

Production is an (algebraic) increase in the value of productive instruments which is not "explained" by the data base, and which we therefore sometimes refer to as an "unexplained" increase in value. The "processing" of one physical economic instrument into another may or may not be production, and will be negative production if the aggregate value of productive instruments is reduced by the activity.

This is a "value added" approach to the measurement of product. We look at the value of opening inventories, and the flows during the interval. On this basis, we determine what the value of the closing inventory "ought" to be. If the closing inventory differs from this, the entity has added (algebraically) value to the instruments. We frequently refer to this as the "product" of the entity for the period, although we have seen that this terminology is not universally accepted.

If the sum of credits (outflows) to the productive flow account is larger in absolute value than the sum of debits (inflows), 1) inventories are larger than they "should" be, 2) value added is positive, and 3) the closing entry is a debit. If debits (inflows) exceed credits (outflows) in absolute value, 1) inventories are smaller than they "should" be, 2) value added is negative, and 3) the closing entry is a credit.

We can therefore say that a debit entry to close a productive flow account means that the entity had positive product. It created a greater value of productive instruments than it destroyed or used up. A closing credit entry implies negative product. The entity has destroyed or used up a greater value of productive instruments than it has created.

The productive income generated by production is positive
if the value added in production is positive, negative if the
value added is negative. If production is positive, the closing
entry to the productive flow account is a debit, and the entry
closed to the income flow account is a credit. Since a credit
entry increases wealth, this credit entry is positive income.

If production is negative, the closing entry to productive
flow is a credit, and the entry closed to income flow is a debit
which reduces income and wealth.

Double-entry bookkeeping therefore reverses the algebraic
signs of both income and wealth. Positive wealth and positive
income are credits. Negative wealth and income are debits. We no
longer have income equal to product in a closed economy, we have
income equal to the negative of product: income plus product
equals zero.

For other entities, we measure the creation of financial
value added and financial income, using exactly the same
principles that are used in measuring productive value added and
productive income. In social accounting, there are no financial
instruments or financial income. We shall return to these ideas
when we consider accounting for firms and households.

This implies that there is only one entry into the income
flow account, from the productive instrument flow account. Total
income is productive income, since there is no financial income.

We measure net income by closing the income flow account.
The closing entry is called net value added, and is a debit

(credit) entry if the value added is positive (negative), as is the case with the productive flow account (and the financial flow account).

The income account is closed to the wealth flow account. The entry to the wealth flow account is net income, and income is positive (negative) if the entry is a credit (debit), following the same principles that are used when the productive flow account is closed to the income flow account.

Income Flow (value added) $10,900

Wealth Flow (net income) $10,900.

This entry must also close the Wealth Flow account. The arithmetic of double-entry bookkeeping keeps total debits equal to total credits. Our flow accounts have this property at all times. We have now closed all but one of the accounts, which logically must also close the remaining account. The entries in the Wealth Flow account are now:

Wealth Flow

Transfer to t_1 B.S. $14,400
Consumption   10,000
Transfer from t_o B.S. $13,500
Net Income   10,900

This confirms the basic definition of income as the increase in net wealth plus consumption. The wealth flow account records all of these values, with appropriate signs. Opening net wealth is a credit. Final net wealth and consumption are debits. Income is the entry required to close the wealth flow account.

Furthermore, a closing credit entry implies positive income, since final net wealth is larger than it "should" be, and must have been acquired through positive income. Similarly, a closing debit entry implies negative income (loss) since final net wealth is smaller than it "should" have been on the basis of opening net wealth and consumption.

Our scheme achieves this result by closing the income flow account to the wealth flow account, rather than by closing the wealth flow account to the income flow account. The arithmetic requires that these two procedures be equivalent. The flow accounts are opened with flows transferred from the balance sheets, so that aggregate debits offset aggregate credits. We record all of the flows from the data base, again offsetting debits and credits. We then close the productive and financial flow accounts to the income flow account, and the income account to the wealth flow account. Since aggregate debits offset aggregate credits, the wealth account must close when the other flow accounts close.

The economist defines net wealth as the value of productive instruments. Since net investment is the increase in the value of productive instruments, net investment equals the increase in net wealth, and income equals product according to our basic definitions.

4. Productive Sub-accounts.

This procedure aggregated the productive sub-accounts into a "master" productive instrument account, before measuring value

added and income. This is not necessary. We can close the
sub-accounts directly to the income flow account, and achieve
the same results.

    Capital Goods Flow, from t_o B.S. $7,000.
    Capital Goods Flow, Value Added   1,000
        Capital Goods Flow, to t_1 B.S. $8,000.
    Consumer Goods Flow, from t_o B.S. $6,500.
    Consumer Goods Flow, Value Added $9,900
        Consumer Goods Flow, to t_1 B.S. $6,400.
        Consumer Goods Flow, Consumption $10,000.
    Income Flow, Net Value Added (to Wealth)$10,900
        Income Flow, from capital goods $1,000.
        Income Flow, from consumer goods $9,900.

The wealth flow account will be as before.

The income flow account measures aggregate income, but in
more detail. The flow accounts for capital and consumer goods
measure the production of these types of goods, which add to
social product. We can now break the product into $1,000 of
capital goods and $9,900 of consumer goods, for a total product
of $10,900.

We have not taken into account the use of labor in our
attribution of product to different industries. The sale of
labor is an internal transaction which need not be considered in
social accounting. The breakdown of production is in terms of
what was produced, in terms of capital goods and consumer goods.
We shall see in the next chapter that we are sometimes also

interested in who produced the product, and not just in what was produced. In national income accounting, all product is produced by the only entity in the economy, which we call the society.

Chapter V

Household Accounting

In this chapter, we use the definitions and concepts of Chapters 2 and 3, and the data base of Chapter 4 to account for the household, considered as a separate entity.

The principle difference between a closed society and a household is that households have exchanges with other entities. They are (proper) subsets of a (closed) society. They therefore engage in financial, as well as productive activities, and also may make and receive transfer payments (gifts). This makes the definition of product more complicated, creates financial income. We postpone consideration of transfers until we consider taxes in Chapter 10.

Product is defined as an increase in the value of productive instruments not "explained" by the flows in the data base, using the value added approach outlined in the last chapter. Product generates productive income. We can account for all productive instruments as a group in one "major" account, or account for particular productive instruments in sub-accounts.

Financial value added is defined as an increase in the value of financial instruments not "explained" by the flows in the data base, using the same value added approach that is used in measuring productive value added (production). Financial value added generates financial income. We can account for all financial instruments as a group in one "major" account, or account for particular financial instruments in sub-accounts.

Total income is measured in the Income Flow account, and

equals the sum of productive and financial incomes. The Wealth
Flow account confirms that income also equals the increase in
net wealth plus consumption.

1. Balance Sheets.

The first step is the preparation of balance sheets. We
observe that the account payable has negative value. The
household "owns" a financial instrument called an account
payable, and uses a quantity of -1 since the household sold the
financial instrument to the firm at a time when its inventory
was not positive.   The value to the households is therefore
negative, and the account is recorded as a credit.

The data base from Chapter 4 generates balance sheets:

HOUSEHOLD BALANCE SHEET (0)

Assets		Equities	
Productive	$5,000.		
Financial		Account payable	$500.
Bonds	$3,000.	Net Wealth	$13,500.
Shares	$6,000.		
TOTAL	$14,000.	TOTAL	$14,000.

HOUSEHOLD BALANCE SHEET (1)

Assets		Equities	
Productive	$4,000.		
Financial		Account payable	$600.
Bonds	$2,000.	Net Wealth	$14,400.
Shares	$9,000.		
TOTAL	$15,000.	TOTAL	$15,000.

Human capital is notable for its absence from this balance sheet, nor was it listed on the social balance sheet of Chapter 4. Economic theory says that both human capital and physical capital are productive instruments, which suggests both ought to be listed on the balance sheet.

Furthermore, our discussion in Chapter 2 suggests that net wealth should include human capital, if it is to serve as a decision variable in helping the household determine the appropriate level of consumption.

The most important reason for not carrying human capital on the balance sheet is that we never have a market price, so that the price is never part of the data base, and would have to be estimated by the economic accountant. Problems in estimating the price would arise even in a Crusoe economy where we assume perfect knowledge of shadow prices. In principle, the appropriate price would be the present (discounted) value of the future labor services which the human capital will render, less the expenses incurred in creating these services.

The value of human capital is the value of a slave, with three important caveats, which arise because the slavery is "voluntary" rather than "forced." 1) Crusoe specifies the amount of labor service he wishes to perform in the future as part of the slavery "contract." 2) The expenses incurred in creating the labor services are also specified in the contract, and are provided by the slave owner. 3) Crusoe sells himself into slavery. He gets the money from the sale, and uses it like any

other wealth, providing only that performs the specified labor
services.

There is no accepted theory, however, which would permit us
to   divide consumption into "expenses of   producing labor
services" and "true" or "discretionary" consumption, i. e.,
consumption which creates utility. This means that we could not
determine the value of human capital even if we had all of the
information which we have assumed in chapter 2.

In addition, human capital is fundamentally different from
physical capital, in three respects. First, there is no reason
to expect the market for human capital to be in equilibrium, in
a cost-price sense. Decisions concerning the production of
capital goods are made on the basis of profitability, and
equilibrium requires that the discounted value of future returns
equal the opportunity cost. While economic theory recognizes the
importance of cost-profit considerations in the   production of
human capital, the theory also recognizes that non-pecuniary
considerations are sufficiently important that the opportunity
cost may well not equal the present value of the returns. We did
not attempt in Chapter 2 to present a theory for the optimal
quantity of human capital.

Second, the household cannot in practice convert human
capital into consumption at a given point in time.   This is
important because because net wealth is supposed to measure
maximum potential consumption at a point in time, according to
the ideas in Chapter 2.   It also brings up an important

difference between a Crusoe economy and a market economy. The assumption that Crusoe could convert his physical capital into consumer goods on a dollar for dollar basis at t_o is clearly false, since it would take him time to make the conversion, and the marginal opportunity cost (shadow price) would not prevail if he decided to convert all of his capital. Even so, it would be easier for him to convert his physical capital into current consumption than to convert his human capital into current consumption.

In a market economy, however, any given household can convert its physical capital into consumption at any time, even though the entire society cannot do so because it faces the same restrictions that Crusoe faces. The statement that the value of physical capital represents potential consumption therefore makes more sense in a market economy than in a Crusoe economy.

Human capital, however, cannot be converted into immediate consumption by a household even in a market economy, because there is no market for human capital. Some conversion, however, is possible. Even though human capital cannot be sold outright, it can be used as a basis for borrowing which permits the individual to consume in the present instead of the future. The amount which can be borrowed, however, is usually less than the value of the human capital, and the market is in practice usually far from perfect, so that it is difficult to estimate the amount that could be borrowed.

Third, the usual assumption in economics is that the

purpose of economic activity is to generate utility for human beings. Human happiness is the objective. Economic resources are the means whereby the objective is reached. It does not seem appropriate to regard people purely as economic resources. People are a special category who have some of the characteristics of resources, but they also have other characteristics which distinguish them from purely economic resources.

These differences, in additional to the difficulty of estimating "market" value, lead us to omit human capital from the balance sheet. We also recognize, however, that the possibility of borrowing against the capital means that the net wealth of households (and of the society) is understated. This means that individuals (unlike firms) are not necessarily bankrupt if they have negative net wealth, because they have human capital which may permit them to cover liabilities even though the capital is not listed on the balance sheet.

We shall also find that we must consider human capital when we try to account for taxes in Chapter 10.

2. Flow Accounts

2.1 Measurement of Income and Consumption.

The only flow information that we need to measure income is consumption, since we use the same definition for household income that we use for social income, or the income of any other entity. Income is not influenced by exchanges with other entities. It is always the increase in net wealth plus

consumption.   Net   wealth is measured   from the balance   sheets
without considering any flows, and the increase is t_1 net wealth
less t_0 net wealth, which may be negative. Consumption is a flow
involving only one entity.

Since the   increase in net wealth is $900, and consumption
is $10,000, income must be $10,900.

We   can   also   determine the   wealth flow   account, without
determining the value to be closed from the income account.   We
can   transfer opening and   final net   wealth   from   the   balance
sheets, enter   consumption as a debit, and determine   income   as
the "closing" entry.

Wealth Flows

To t_1 B.S,	$14,400.
Consumption	10,000.
From t_0 B. S.	$13,500
Net income (to close account)	10,900.

The assumption that consumption is part of the data base is
not usual   in economic accounting. The problem   is   that it is a
flow   which   involves only one   entity,   and the   data   base   is
usually confined to exchanges between entities, and inventories.
Consumption must then be inferred from the data base.

The GNP   accounts simplify the   problem   by   assuming   that
households   neither   own   nor   produce   nor   sell   nor   transfer
consumer   goods.   The   observed purchases   of consumer goods are
then identified as   consumption. There are   in   general only six
possible   explanations   for   changes   in   inventory: purchases,

transfers in, sales, transfers out, production (which may be positive or negative), and consumption. If the household has no opening or closing inventories, no production, no sales, and no transfers, then purchases must equal consumption in absolute value, and be of opposite sign: purchases are debits to the productive flow account, consumption is a credit.

Economists do, however, sometimes estimate consumption on the assumption that households hold inventories. The problem is to collect the data, since household inventory information is difficult to obtain. There are no conceptual difficulties. They also assume that households do not produce, sell, or transfer consumer goods, and measure consumption as purchases plus the decrease in the value of consumer goods' inventories held. We have conformed to this convention in our numerical example. The opening inventory of $5,000 plus the purchases of $9,000 equal the consumption of $10,000 plus the final inventory of $4,000.

The assumptions of no sales or transfers of consumer goods are not required to permit the measurement of consumption, but are imposed because of data problems. The assumption that no consumer goods are produced by households is the only crucial assumption if consumption is not part of the data base. If the data base includes neither consumption nor production, it is not possible to infer both. The usual assumption is that production is zero.

Interestingly enough, the suggestion in Chapter 2 that households produce and consume "leisure" also provides a

solution to this problem. In this case, the assumption is that
the household produces leisure during each hour it does not
produce and sell labor (work). The value of the leisure produced
and consumed is the number of leisure hours multiplied by the
wage rate.   This   permits   an   estimate   of the production of
consumer goods if the hours of work are part of the data base.

No serious error is made if the household uses "leisure"
time to produce other consumer goods such as gourmet cooking or
gardening services. The consumption of leisure is overestimated
and the consumption of other goods is underestimated. Total consumption is correctly estimated.   We follow the usual practice,
and do not include leisure as consumption in our example.

2.2 Measurement of productive, financial, and net income.

We transfer the balance sheet entries to the   appropriate
flow accounts, and record the observed flows in these accounts.
We need both productive and financial flow accounts to reflect
the different sources of income, and we close them to the "net"
income account. The income flow account is closed to the wealth
flow account, which reflects the fundamental definition that
income equals the increase in net wealth plus consumption.

We have already discussed the procedures for transferring
the balance sheet accounts, and recording the consumption. We
need not account for exchanges which increase one financial
instrument and reduce another, unless we want to distinguish
different sources of financial income, which we consider in
Section 2.4. We must, however, consider exchanges of productive

for financial instruments, and vice-versa. These exchanges are
the purchase of consumer goods and the sale of labor. Consumer
goods are productive instruments, and the purchase increases
(debits) productive instruments, and reduces (debits) financial
instruments (accounts payable). Since labor is also a productive
instrument, its sale reduces productive instruments with a
credit entry, and increases financial instruments with a debit
entry. We shall elaborate on the meaning of these entries below.

The four major flow accounts are:

Productive Flows

From t_o B.S.	$5,000.	
Purchases of consumer goods	9,000.	
Productive Value Added (Close to Income)	9,500.	
Sales of labor		$9,500.
Consumption		10,000.
To t_1 B. S.		4,000.

Financial Flows

Bonds from t_o B.S.	$3,000.	
Shares from t_o B.S.	$6,000.	
Accounts payable to t_1 B.S.	$600.	
Cash (wages received)	$9,500.	
Financial value added (close to Income)	$1,400.	
Bonds to t_1 B. S.		$2,000.
Shares to t_1 B. S.		9,000.
Accounts Payable from t_o B. S.		500.
Accounts Payable (for Consumer Goods)		9,000.

Income Flow

Net Value Added (Close to Wealth Flow) $10,900

      Productive income $9,500.

      Financial income   1,400.

Wealth Flow

To t_1 B.S. $14,400.

Consumption   10,000.

      Net Income (from income flow) $10,900.

      From t_o B. S.   13,500.

The productive flow account measures productive value added (product) and productive income as $9,500.

The financial flow account measures financial value added and financial income as $1,400. We can ignore the dividend, bond, and share transactions at this time, since they increase one financial instrument and reduce another.

The income flow account records the income generated by productive and financial activities, for a net income of $10,900, which is the increase in net wealth plus consumption.

The wealth flow account is as before, and confirms the fundamental definition of income: opening net wealth plus income exactly offset final net wealth and consumption.

The four flow accounts permit us to isolate two sources of income, which aggregate to net income measured from the change in net wealth and consumption alone. We shall discuss the meaning of these accounts more fully in connection with the sub-accounts.

2.3 Productive sub-accounts.

We gain additional descriptive detail by creating sub-accounts to the productive and financial flow accounts to keep track of individual economic instruments. We can then associate the income and product with individual economic instruments.

If there were any exchanges of one productive instrument for another, we would need to introduce them at this point, as flows between the productive sub-accounts. This, however, is the barter of two productive instruments, and such transactions are relatively rare. We have none in our data base.

We break the productive instruments into two categories: consumer goods and labor services, and need no additional information to generate the sub-accounts. Each of these accounts is closed to the productive flow account.

Flow of Consumer Goods

From t_0 B.S. $5,000.

Purchases   9,000.

     Consumption $10,000.

    To t_1 B. S.   4,000.

This definition of product is more complicated than our definition of social product as net investment plus consumption. If we use an inventory approach to the definition of product, the social definition is based on the idea that there are only two possible sources of goods - opening inventory and production - and only two uses of goods - final inventory and consumption. The flow account therefore listed opening inventory and production as debits, final inventory and consumption as credits, and was in balance.

Entities which are not "closed" can have exchanges with other entities. This opens up the possibility other sources of goods - purchases and gifts - and other uses of goods - sales and gifts. These sources and uses will aggregate to zero in a closed society, but are important to individual entities.

The basic equality is therefore that opening inventory plus production plus purchases plus transfers in must equal final inventory plus consumption plus sales plus transfers out. We have no transfers in our example, but gifts received (donated) would be recorded as debits (credits) to a productive flow account and credits (debits) to the income flow account.

The value added approach introduced in the last chapter modifies this in an important way. Instead of thinking of inventory in a physical sense, we think of inventory in a value sense. Chapter 2 shows that this is the correct approach to the measurement of product. It does little good to know that the entity produced 10 lbs of some good, since some of the economic product may be reflected in the change in the (relative) price of physically unchanged inventory.

We therefore apply our concepts to the value measurements. The values of opening inventories, purchases, gifts received, and product are entered as debits. The values of final inventory, sales, consumption, and gifts given are entered as credits, and the account is in balance.

All of the information for the productive account is part of the data base except the value of production. Production must be calculated as a residual, to "close" the account, and is the increase in value not accounted for (explained) by the data base. All the relevant information from the data base is entered into the account. The closing entry is required because some of the relevant information - production - is not in the data base.

According to our definitions from Chapter 2, adding value to productive resources is production.   If quantities do not change during the accounting period, so that the only entries in the account are opening and final inventory values, the differ-ence is economic product, since it reflects a difference in the ability of the productive instruments to provide utility to consumers (if there are no changes in the general price level).

The household in our example has produced no consumer goods, since there is no unexplained change in inventory value. As we said before, this is the usual assumption in economic accounting. If the consumption is not part of the data base, it is estimated as a residual to make the production of consumer goods by the household equal zero.

We turn to the labor sub-account:

Flow of Labor

From t_o B.S.		0.
Value Added (Close to Productive Flows)	$9,500.	
Sales		$9,500.
To t_1 B. S.		0.

We treat labor like any other economic instrument. There is no starting inventory, since it is a service. The household sold $9,500 which should reduce the inventory value to -$9,500. Since the inventory is still zero, the household must have produced $9,500 of labor services, or it could not have sold them. Product is an increase in the value of inventories which is not "explained" by the data base.

If households do not produce consumer goods, all of their product is labor service, and all of their labor service is product.

We now look at the major productive flow account:

Productive Flows

Value Added (Close to Income Flow)	$9,500.
From consumer goods	0.
From labor	$9,500.

Since the balance sheet values have been transferred to the sub-accounts, they are not transferred to the major account. The productive flow account now shows the particular productive instruments produced by the entity. The aggregate product is the same as when all entries are made directly to the "consolidated" productive instrument account.

2.4 Financial sub-accounts.

There are potentially four financial instruments held by the household in our example: cash, shares, bonds, and accounts payable. We have, however, constructed the example so that cash balances are zero. In Chapter 2, we introduced money as a medium of exchange, but not as a store of value. We shall introduce money as a store of value in Chapter 9.

We create a sub-account for each of the four instruments, and must now account for the four transactions between these accounts. The firm pays $200 to the consumer on behalf of the shares (a dividend), and $1,300 on behalf of the bonds. The household buys $2,000 of new shares from the firm, and pays $9,000 on its account with the firm.

From the point of view of the household, the receipt of the dividend reduces (credits) the value of shares and increases (debits) cash. The share purchase increases (debits) the value of shares and reduces (credits) cash. The receipt of the payment on the bond reduces (credits) the value of the bond and increases (debits) cash. The payment on the account increases (debits) the value of the account and reduces (credits) cash. These entries will be explained more fully later.

The cash flow account balances with no value added:

Flow of Cash   (Medium of Exchange)

From t_o B.S.	0.	
Dividends received	$ 200.	
Payment on Bonds	1,300.	
Wages received	9,500.	
Payment on the Account		$9,000.
Purchase of Shares		2,000.
To t_1 B. S.		0.

The sub-account for share value shows $1,200 value added:

Flow of Share Value

From t_0 B.S. $6,000.

Purchase   2,000.

Value Added (close to Financial Flow)   1,200.

    Dividend Received $ 200.

    To t_1 B. S.   9,000.

We use the same value added approach to financial flows
that we used with productive flows. The value added, which we
called product in connection with productive activities, is an
increase in the value of financial instruments not "explained"
by the data base. Financial value added is not called product,
since productive instruments can create utility, while financial
instruments can not. Nevertheless, financial value added
generates financial income in exactly the same way that
productive value added generates productive income.

We start by observing that the household has financial
instruments (shares) valued at $6,000 at t_0. This means that
there is an outside entity (firm) which owes the household
$6,000. During the year, the household bought additional shares
for $2,000. This "ought" to ("explains" an) increase the value
of shares held to $8,000.

The firm paid a dividend of $200. This "explains" a decline
in the value of shares by $200, to $7,800. While this may look
strange at first, it makes good sense. The firm(s) owed the
household $8,000, and paid $200 in respect of this debt, which
ought to reduce the debt to $7,800.

The conceptual difficulty arises because we tend to think of dividends as increasing the value of a share rather than reducing it. This is, however, really a semantic problem. The value of a share is the present value of the future dividends to be paid on the share. An increase in expected future dividends increases the value of the share.

The payment of the dividend, however, reduces the value of the share. If expected dividends do not change, the present value of future dividends rises as the next dividend payment approaches, and then falls the moment the dividend is paid. The share price falls when the share goes ex-dividend.

This explains why the dividend payment does not create income or wealth for the household. If the dividend were not paid, the value would not fall, and the net financial wealth of the household would not be changed, although the mix would be changed. The transaction reduces the value of the share (one financial instrument) and increases the value of the cash (another financial instrument). We credit shares and debit cash.

The share value should therefore be $7,800 on the basis of the flows in the data base, but in fact is $9,000. There has been $1,200 of value added, and this is a debit entry, so that the household's financial activities in the stock market have generated a positive value added, and the closing procedures will eventually record this as positive financial income (a debit entry to the wealth flow account).

We record the bond flows:

Flow of Bond Value

From t_0 B.S. $3,000.

Value Added (close to Financial Flow)   300.

    To t_1 B.S. $2,000.

    Payment received on loan   1,300.

At the start of the year, the firm had a financial obligation to the household. There was a financial instrument (bond) which recorded this obligation, and the market value of the instrument was $3,000. We assume that the bond called for a payment of $1,300 at t_1, which the firm made. This should have reduced the value of the firm's debt to the household to $1,700. In fact, the market value of the bond was $2,000 at t_1, which is an unexplained increase of $300 in price. The household has gained $300 of value added, which we might think of as interest of 10% on the loan of $3,000.

It would make no difference if there were a formal statement that the firm was to pay $300 interest. There has been a cash payment of $1,300, and finance theory tells us that it makes no difference whether it is called principal or interest. The accrual of interest explains why the market price of the bond rises from $3,000 to $3,300 just before the payment of $1,300 is made, and explains why the payment created no income or wealth for the household. Prior to the payment, it has a bond worth $3,300. After the payment, it has a bond worth $2,000 and cash of $1,300. Net financial wealth is unchanged.

Our calculation of value added is not an attempt to explain

the market price. The market price is part of the data base used for our accounting scheme. We are not interested in explaining this price. That is a matter for economic theory, not accounting measurement. The statement that the firm is paying interest on the loan is not part of the data base, and is not useful information to the accountant who wants to measure value added and income.

This is critically important in understanding our accounting scheme. Traditional accounting starts from an opening balance sheet, uses GAAP to measure income, and then creates a final balance sheet. These balance sheet (book) values usually bear no resemblance to the balance sheet values obtained by our procedures, because the book values are not an attempt to estimate market values.

The traditional accountant needs to know how much interest the firm payed because he needs this information to determine income and the new book value. He will record the t_1 book value as the t_0 value plus accrued interest and less the payment made, and will record the interest as income. We have no need to know the interest, because we use the t_1 market value as the balance sheet value. If there is no active market so that market price is not in the data base, the responsibility of the economic accountant is to make the best estimate of the market value that he can.

This is not a matter of data availability but of accounting principle, as we have observed before. The author borrowed money

from a bank and created a financial instrument known as a
mortage, which has negative value to him and positive value to
the bank. The bank informs him periodically of its book value.
At the time that the book value was about $20,000, the bank
offered to sell the mortgage back to him for about $15,000. The
bank knows the market value, but does not use it on the balance
sheet even when it is known.

Our procedure does not identify income with interest on a
financial instrument, whether the instrument is a share or a
bond. Value added is the increase in the value of the instrument
not explained by the payments made, which means that the lender
(for whom the values of the instrument are positive) measures
value added as the increase in value plus the net cash flow he
receives.

We do not need to know, nor are we interested in, the face
value of the bond or the stipulated interest rate. The $1,300
payment may have been originally planned as $300 of interest and
$1,000 of principal, $200 interest and $1,100 principal, or $400
interest and $900 principal. Our procedure takes into account
only the market values and the cash flows.

This is the usual definition of return on financial
instruments in the finance literature. It is the procedure we
use to measure the household's value added from both shares and
bonds. We do not care whether the payments are "voluntary" as in
the case of dividends, or contractual as in the case of payments
on the bonds.

The principles involving the account payable are exactly the same. The household started with a debt of $500, and made $9,000 of purchases, which should increase the debt to $9,500. It then made a payment of $9,000 which should reduce the debt to $500. The data base tells us, however, that the debt is $600, which means that the household has lost $100 on the deal, presumably finance charges of some sort, possibly interest.

We express this in terms of value, with the appropriate signs. The household started with an financial instrument with a value of -$500. It sold an additional $9,000 with a value of -$9,000 to the household. This reduces the value of the instrument to -$9,500. It then bought back $9,000 of the instrument, increasing its value to -$500. In fact, its value is -$600, which is an unexplained reduction of $100, or -$100 of financial value added and -$100 of financial income.

Flow of Account Payable

To t_1 B.S.	$ 600.	
Payments on account	9,000.	
From t_0 B. S.		$ 500.
Purchases on Account		9,000.
Value Lost (close of Financial Flow)		100.

As in the case of the shares and the bonds, we do not need to know the cause of the $100 loss. This could be interest or penalties for late payments. All we need to know is that the household and the firm agree on the market values at t_0 and t_1, and on the flows during the year.

Since the firm uses the same accounting principles as the household, they will account for their share, bond, and account receivable activities exactly the same way that the household does, and will record financial value added and financial income of -$1,200 from shares, -$300 from bonds, and +$100 from the receivables. The only difference between the borrower and the lender is the sign. Positive values for the lender are negative values for the borrower. Financial income for the lender and the borrower are equal in absolute value but opposite in sign.

The financial flow account becomes:

Financial Flows

Income (Loss) from accounts payable	$ 100.	
Financial value added (close to Income)	1,400.	
Income from Shares		$1,200.
Income from Bonds		300.

This account now records only values closed from the sub-accounts, and the aggregate financial value added which is closed to Income Flow. All of the flows which were in the major account when we had no sub-accounts are assigned to the sub-accounts.

This account now shows the particular financial instruments which were responsible for the financial income of $1,400. Shares generated a gain of $1,200, the bonds generated a gain of $300, and the payables generated a loss of $100.

The Income Flow and the Wealth Flow accounts remain the same as before the sub-accounts were created. The Income Flow account records the income generated by productive and financial activities, and closed from the productive and financial flow accounts. The Income Flow account reflects the fact that net income is the sum of productive and financial incomes, each of which can be positive or negative. Positive income is a credit to the Income Flow account, negative income is a debit.

This definition of income has an important peculiarity. Negative financial income, such as interest paid, is added in before net income in measured. This means that interest paid is subtracted from other income to get net income. Traditionally, interest received is considered to be positive income, but interest paid is not negative income. The GNP accounts now treat interest paid as a separate "use" of income, in addition to consumption, saving, and transfers to foreigners. Our treatment does not differentiate between interest paid and interest received. The sign of the income takes care of itself. The accrual of interest to be received increases net wealth without changing consumption, and is positive income. The accrual of interest to be paid reduces wealth without changing consumption, and is negative income.

As we shall continually emphasize, financial activities transfer income from one entity to another without generating net income. Positive income for one entity is always exactly offset by negative income for another entity. Only productive activities generate net income. For a closed society, productive income equals net income, since financial activities cancel out.

The Wealth Flow account always has only four entries, no matter how many sub-accounts are created. Initial and final wealth are transferred from the balance sheets. Consumption is debited directly to the wealth account. The last entry is the net income closed from Income Flow.

The account always reflects the definition of income as the increase in net wealth plus consumption, suitably rearranged so that there are no negative signs:

Net Wealth at t_1 + Consumption (debits)

= Net Wealth at t_o + Income (credits).

We can therefore measure net income without recording any flow except consumption. If we wish to attribute net income to productive, financial, and transfer activities, we must also account for exchanges (flows) which involve both productive and financial instruments. If we wish to attribute the productive income to individual productive instruments, we must also record exchanges of one productive instrument for another, but we did not consider such barter exchanges. If we wish to attribute the financial income to individual financial instruments, we must also record exchanges of one financial instrument for another.

Chapter VI

Firm Accounting

In this chapter, we apply the definitions and concepts of Chapters 2 and 3 to accounting for the economic activities of a firm. This chapter is concerned with the general principles. We shall discuss some special problems in later chapters.

The principle difference between firms and households is that firms have no net income. One of the fundamental ideas of both economic and business accounting is that the balance sheet balances without requiring an entry for "net wealth." The social net wealth of Chapter 4 is the same as the household net wealth in Chapter 5. There is no net wealth left over for the firm. Consumption is confined to households, since it is related to utility. Since net income equals the increase in net wealth plus consumption, firm income must always be zero.

The firm, therefore, does not need a major flow account for wealth flows, since there would be no entries to the account, just as the society did not need an account for financial flows. There are still flow accounts to measure productive value added and income, and financial value added and income. When these accounts are closed to income flow, they generate offsetting debits and credits so that the net income is zero. The expected result for most firms is that they will have positive productive value added and income, and that this will be offset by negative financial value added and income.

Income generated by productive activities is transferred to other entities - shareholders, bondholders, and the government -

by financial activities (losses) and transfers. The income generated for the firm by its shares equals the income generated for its shareholders in absolute value, but is opposite in sign. The firm earns income for its shareholders by generating positive productive income for itself, and offsetting this with negative financial income from its shares and other financial activities.

If we use only the major accounts, we identify only net productive income and net financial income, as in the case of households. If we use sub-accounts, we attribute the value added to particular productive and financial instruments.

1. Balance Sheets.

On the basis of the data base presented in Chapter 4, the firm's balance sheets are:

BALANCE SHEET (0)

Assets		Equities	
Capital goods	$7,000.	Bonds	$3,000.
Finished goods	$1,500.	Shares	$6,000.
Receivables	$500.		
TOTAL	$9,000.		$9,000.

BALANCE SHEET (1)

Assets		Equities	
Capital goods	$8,000.	Bonds	$2,000.
Finished goods	$2,400.	Shares	$9,000.
Receivables	$600.		
TOTAL	$11,000.		$11,000.

The most important features of these balance sheets are the listing of shares at market, and the fact that they balance with no net wealth.

Both of these ideas are based on the analysis in Chapter 2. One of the important results of that chapter is that the market value of the physical capital will equal the discounted value of the future cash flows from the firm to shareholders. Finance theory shows that the market price of the shares is also the discounted value of the shareholders' receipts. The balance sheet will balance if both productive and financial instruments are carried at market, and the prices are determined in a Crusoe economy.

The valuation of financial instruments at market is also required if the firm uses the descriptive variables as decision variables in its maximizing procedures. The most serious weakness of business accounting is that no variable is generated which the firm can use for decision-making. This is the result of the generation of values which are different from market values. In a Crusoe economy, the firm acts in the social interest if it maximizes productive value added, and it acts in the shareholders' interest if it minimizes its financial income from shares.

We treat the firm in the same way that we treat the society or the household. The problem is to account for the values of all economic instruments held. The firm may have special relationships with various creditors, particularly shareholders.

These relationships, however, are not accounted for on balance sheets or income measurements. The only relevant question is whether we want to account separately for the firm and its shareholders, or whether the relationship is so close that it makes no sense to account separately. Even in the Crusoe economy, the application of our principles leads to sensible measurements. There are apparently no economic reasons for not accounting separately for shareholders and firms.

The other relevant consideration is whether the exchanges between the entity and other accounting entities are (fair) transactions or are transfers. The general accounting problem is whether the exchanges were "arm's length" deals. If they are, they should be accounted for as transactions, i.e., there is a presumption that wealth was not transferred.

This is related to the question of whether we can account separately for the two entities involved in the exchange only to the extent that there as a data problem. There is no accounting reason not to account separately for the different members of a household, and treat husband, wife, children, and dogs as separate accounting entities. The difficulty is that the exchanges between the entities are numerous, difficult to document and value, and there is reason to believe that there are many transfers of wealth and income. The result is that we usually do not attempt separate accounting (except, perhaps, in divorce procedings or wrongful injury or death cases).

Similar problems arise in the case of owner-operated firms,

where it is frequently difficult to determine the extent of the services rendered for the firm by the owner. There is usually no market for the shares, and they are difficult to value. There are, however, no problems of accounting principle.

The basic problem of entity accounting is to account for the entity involved. Exchanges with other entities must be examined to determine whether they involve transfers of wealth or are (fair) transactions. The other relationships between the entities are irrelevant.

We discussed the problem of undervalued assets in connection with the society and households, and observed that human capital is not listed on these balance sheets, and this results in an underestimation of assets. While the firm does not own any human capital, there may still be problems with undervalued assets.

The difficulty is that the concept of economic instrument is ambiguous. Consider a firm which purchases lumber, bricks, and labor and processes these resources into a building. The normal procedure would be for the firm to drop the lumber, bricks, and labor from the balance sheet. The firm would list only the building on its balance sheet.

It also true, however, that the firm still owns the lumber and the bricks. They are not listed on the balance sheet because they are more valuable if they are sold as part of the building than if they are sold separately. It is conceivable, if unlikely, that prices could change in the future and make the lumber and the bricks more valuable if sold separately than they would be if sold as part of a package (building). In this case, the appropriate procedure would be to remove the building from the balance sheet, and restore the lumber and bricks.

This suggests that the firm lists economic instruments on its balance sheet in their most valuable "form," and that this may change from time to time. The various ways to "package" the productive instruments should be valued, and the most valuable "package" should then be thought of as a productive instrument and listed on the balance sheet.

The important point is that the "package" is determined by value considerations, not by technical considerations, and that it may be very difficult to value packages with unique characteristics for which the market is thin if not non-existent.

This problem arises continuously in the real world. There are good reasons to suspect that the most valuable way to package the firm's productive instruments is as a going concern. If this be so, then the firm should list only one productive instrument on its balance sheet, the going concern. The capital goods, finished goods inventories, and so on, usually listed on balance sheets should not be listed separately because they are more valuable as a package. The single productive instrument, going-concern, is a unique package which is difficult to value.

One possible solution is to value the financial instruments at market if the market is active, and then value the going-concern as a residual to make the balance sheet balance, since we know that there is no net wealth.

An alternative is to measure arbitrarily defined productive instruments at market, and use good will as the balancing entry. In an accounting sense, good will exists if the accountant packages the productive instruments incorrectly for listing on the balance sheet. Our assumptions in Chapter 2 ruled out this possibility, but it can arise in practice.

In this chapter, we account for a Crusoe-like economy with no good will. The package consisting of the capital goods and the inventory would sell for $8,500 at t_o and $10,400 at t_1.

2. Flow Accounts

2.1 Measurement of Income and Consumption.

As always, the only information needed to measure net income is net wealth from the balance sheets and consumption. Consumption to the use of productive instruments by households to create utility. Business firms cannot consume, by definition.

The net income of every firm is therefore always exactly zero. No firm ever has net wealth, or an increase in net wealth. No firm consumes. No firm has net income.

2.2 Measurement of productive, financial, and net income.

We set up three flow accounts, one each for productive, financial, and income flows, to measure the major components of income. We do not need a wealth flow account, since it contains only four entries, according to our accounting principles. Opening net wealth and and net income are credits, closing net wealth and consumption are debits. Since all of these entries are known to be zero for all firms, the account can be omitted.

We transfer the opening and closing balance sheet values to the flow accounts, record the necessary flows, and close the productive and financial flow accounts to the income flow account.

As in the last chapter, the information we need to measure productive value added and income, financial value added and income, and net income, consists of the transactions which exchange productive and financial instruments.

These transactions for the firm are the same as the ones we used for the household in the last chapter. The firm buys $9,500 of labor and sells $9,000 of finished goods.

The labor transaction increases productive instruments (a debit) and reduces financial instruments (a credit). The sale of finished goods reduces productive instruments (a credit) and increases financial instruments (a debit).

The three major flow accounts are:

Productive Flows

Capital goods from t_o B.S.	$7,000.
Inventory from t_o B.S.	1,500.
Purchase of labor	9,500.
Productive value added (close to Income)	1,400.
Capital Goods to t_1 B. S.	$8,000.
Inventory to t_1 B. S.	2,400.
Sale of Finished Goods	9,000.

Financial Flows

Receivables from t_0 B.S.	$ 500.	
Shares to t_1 B.S.	9,000.	
Bonds to t_1 B.S.	2,000.	
Receivables from sales of goods	9,000.	
Receivables to t_1 B. S.		$ 600.
Shares from t_0 B. S.		6,000.
Bonds from t_0 B. S.		3,000.
Cash to Purchase Labor		9,500.
Financial value added (close to Income)		1,400.

Income Flows

Financial Income	$1,400.	
Productive Income		$1,400.

Our firm produces $1,400 of productive value added, which in turn generates $1,400 of productive income. This income is used to cover a loss of $1,400 on financial operations.

The financial value added is a credit entry, which means that it is negative value added. On the basis of the information on the opening balance sheet and the flows between productive and financial instruments, the financial instruments on the final balance sheet should have been (algebraically) $1,400 higher than they were. At t_0, the aggregate financial instruments were valued at -$8,500. The value should have declined by $9,500 because of purchase of labor, and increased by $9,000 because of the sales of finished goods. The value therefore should have been -$9,000 at t_1. It was in fact

-$10,400, which is a vlaue added of -$1,400. This negative value added is negative financial income, which is a debit entry to the income flow account.

2.3 Productive sub-accounts.

We provide additional descriptive detail if we create sub-accounts for the productive and financial flow accounts. We can attribute the value added to specific economic instruments.

The additional information which we need to create productive sub-accounts is the barter transactions, and we have assumed that there are none.

The balance sheet and the productive flow account suggest that there are three productive instruments with which the firm is concerned: capital goods, finished goods, and labor. We construct sub-accounts for each.

Capital Goods Flows

From t_o B.S.	$7,000.	
Value added (close to Productive Flow)	1,000.	
To t_1 B. S.		$8,000.

Finished Goods Flows

From t_o B.S.	$1,500.	
Value Added (Close to Productive Flow)	9,900.	
To t_1 B.S.		$2,400.
Sales		9,000.

Labor Flows

Purchase	$9,500.	
Value Lost (close to Productive Flow)		$9,500.

Productive Flows

Income from Labor Product $9,500.

Net Productive Value Added (Close to Income)   1,400.

     Income from capital goods production $1,000.

     Income from finished goods production   9,900.

    This suggests that the firm added $1,000 to the value of capital goods and $9,900 to the value of finished goods, but subtracted $9,500 from the value of labor, for a net value added of $1,400.

    If we think in terms of product, the firm has produced $1,000 of capital goods and $9,900 of finished goods, but produced -$9,500 of labor. The negative production of labor is a destruction of the value of a productive instrument. It can be thought of as a cost of production. The firm "processed" the labor services into other productive instruments, thereby "explaining" a reduction in the value of the labor and an increase in the value of the other instruments.

    It is also common for firms to try to allocate the costs, in our example labor, to particualr productive instruments. We shall not try to determine the principles upon which such an allocation would be based, but shall simply demonstrate the accounting procedures which would be used.

    Suppose, for example, that the accountant decides that $3,000 of the labor should be allocated to the processing of capital goods, $5,000 to the processing of finished goods, and that $1,500 was "expenses." The accountant could then "transfer" labor from the labor flow account to the other accounts:

Labor Flows

Purchases	$9,500.	
Allocated to Capital Goods Flow		$3,000.
Allocated to Finished Goods Flow		5,000.
Value Lost (close to Productive Flow)		1,500.

Capital Goods Flows

From t_o B.S.	$7,000.	
Labor used	3,000.	
To t_1 B. S.		$8,000.
Value Lost (close to Productive Flow)		2,000.

Finished Goods Flows

From t_o B.S.	$1,500.	
Labor Used	5,000.	
Value Added (Close to Productive Flow)	4,900.	
To t_1 B.S.		$2,400.
Sales		9,000.

Productive Flows

Income from production of capital goods	$2,000.	
Income from production of labor	1,500.	
Net value added in production	1,400.	
Income from Production of Finished Goods		$4,900.

Our procedures always measure net value added in production at $1,400, but we have quite different allocations of this value added. This allocation of labor suggests that the firm lost $2,000 on their capital goods production, which the accountant might interpret as depreciation, and made $4,900 on the production of finished goods. The labor "expense" of $1,500 shows up as negative income in the productive flows account.

We could treat the capital goods as being used in the production of finished goods, and "transfer" the "depreciation" from the capital goods account to the finished goods account in the same way that labor is transferred to the other accounts. This would leave no value added in capital goods, and reduce value added in production of finished goods to $2,900.

The allocation of the value added to the different productive activities is a matter of judgment even in simple examples. It becomes even more difficult and judgmental if there is good will, i.e., if the market value of the going concern is not the sum of the market values of the individual productive instruments listed on the balance sheet.

It should be emphasized that complete knowledge of the production function specified in Chapter 2 would not help in allocating the value added to productive instruments. The production function would permit the determination of the marginal products and marginal costs of the various productive instruments. It does not permit the assigning of "costs" or "expenses" to particular products, as required by modern cost accounting.

The GNP accounts do not measure value added in production on the same principles which we use. We treat the purchase of all productive instruments in the same way in our calculations.

This means that we would get the same results if the firm had purchased $9,500 of productive instruments from other firms rather than purchasing them from households.

The GNP accounts ignore purchases of labor services by firms in determining value added in production, but treat purchases from other firms in the same was that we treat all purchases. The difference, as we shall see when we aggregate to obtain social accounts, is that our procedures count labor services as value added by households which sell the services, whereas the GNP procedures count labor services as value added by the firm which purchases the services.

2.4 Financial sub-accounts.

If we want to allocate the financial value added and income to individual financial instruments, we must record the exchanges of one financial instrument for another. We create sub-accounts for cash, receivables, bonds, and shares.

Cash Flows

From t_0 B.S.	$ 0.	
Payment on Receivables	9,000.	
Share Issue	2,000.	
Value Added (Close to Financial Flows)	0.	
To t_1 B.S.		$ 0.
Purchase of labor		9,500.
Dividend Payment		200.
Payment on Bonds		1,300.

Receivables Flows

From t_o B.S.	$ 500.	
Credit extended on sales	9,000.	
Value added (close to Financial Flows)	100.	
To t_1 B. S.		$ 600.
Payments Received		9,000.

Bond Flows

To t_1 B.S.	$2,000.	
Payment made	1,300.	
From t_o B. S.		$3,000.
Value Lost (close to Financial Flows)		300.

Share Flows

To t_1 B. S.	$9,000.	
Dividend payment	200.	
From t_o B. S.		$6,000.
New Issue		2,000.
Value Lost (close to Financial Flows)		1,200.

Financial Flows

Income from bond activities	$ 300.	
Income from share activities	1,200.	
Income from Receivables		$ 100.
Income from Cash		0.
Financial Value Lost (close to Income)		1,400.

The firm broke even on its cash activities. It made positive value added (and income) on its receivables. It held instruments (notes) valued at $500 at the start, and purchased

an additional $9,000 during the year. It   also sold back $9,000
to customers who made payments.   It should have had notes valued
at $500, but the final market value of the notes was $600.   This
is positive value added of $100, presumably interest charged by
the firm.

The bond activities cost the firm $300 of (negative) value
added and income, presumably interest paid on the bonds.   These
numbers are exactly the same as they were for the household   in
the last chapter.

The share activities cost the firm $1,200 of (negative)
value added and income. These values are all exactly the same as
the values for the household in the last chapter, except that
all of the signs are changed.   The firm started the year with
instruments (shares) valued at -$6,000. It bought (back) some of
these instruments with a (dividend) payment of $200, which
should have increased the value of the instruments to -$5,800,
and sold $2,000 which should have reduced the value to -$7,800.
The market value was in fact -$9,000, for a value added of
-$1,200, and a financial income of -$1,200.

The value added for the firm and its shareholders by their
activities with the firm's shares aggregate to zero. Financial
flows can be ignored in a closed society because they cancel
each other out.   The more important point, however, is that the
firm generates positive financial for its shareholders by
generating negative financial income for itself.   It should
therefore be the objective of the firm to minimize the financial

income it generates for itself from shares.

We usually think, however, in terms of maximizing something rather than minimizing. In a world of certainty with no taxes or transfers, there would be only one interest rate, and the firm would act in the shareholders' interests if it maximized its productive value added. Firms are organized to facilitate production, and behave optimally if they maximize product.

In more complicated economic systems, the objective of the firm becomes more complicated. Nevertheless, the firm never retains any income. Whatever income is generated by productive activities must be transmitted to other entities by financial activities or transfers. The society always benefits if the firm produces more productive income, but the shareholders may not benefit from this if debtholders or governments get the income.

The income flow account is not changed by the introduction of productive or financial sub-accounts. Net productive and financial value added are the same as before.

We could emphasize the special relationship between the firm and its shareholders by isolating the share flow sub-account, and consolidating other income earning activities. We could do this by changing the "Financial Flows" account to the "Non-Equity Financial Flows" account, and introducing a new account for "Non-Equity Income Flows." We would close all non-equity financial flow sub-accounts to the "Non-Equity Financial Flows" account, close this account and the "Productive Flows" account to "Non-Equity Income Flows," and close this

account and "Equity Share Flows" to "Income Flows."   The   income
flow account would then   show income   generated by   the firm for
shareholders,   transfer   income,   and   income   generated   by
shareholders for the firm, adding (algebraically) to zero.

Non-Equity Financial Flows

Income from Bonds	$300.
Income from cash activities	$0.
Income from receivable activities	$100.
Value Lost (to Non-equity income flows)	$200.

Non-Equity Income Flows

Non-equity financial income	$ 200.
Non-equity value added (close to Income)	1,200.
Productive Income	$1,400.

Income Flows

Income from equity	$1,200.
Non-equity Income	$1,200.

The income flow account now suggests that the firm "earned"
$1,200, and transmitted it to shareholders.

These accounts also   resemble traditional   business   income
accounts   more   closely than the first set of sub-accounts.   The
major   difference is that   our accounts   always stress the   idea
that   equity activities   generate negative income for the   firm.
There   are   many different   ways   in which sub-accounts   can   be
created and closed, to bring out whatever "facts" the accountant
thinks important.

No matter which sub-accounts are   created, the share   flows are treated in the same way that the bond flows are treated. In both cases, the firm has sold financial instruments short, i.e., sold instruments when it did not have a positive inventory value listed on its balance sheet. The value of financial instruments held is therefore negative, and the instrument is listed on the balance sheet, and in the flow account, as a credit.

Any payment which the firm makes in respect of these instruments is treated as a purchase, and should increase (algebraically) the value of instruments held. It is a debit entry to the flow account, in the same way that the purchase of any other economic instrument is a debit entry to the flow account for the instrument bought (not the cash flow account).

Any payment which the firm receives in respect of these instruments is (treated as) a sale, and reduces (algebraically) the value of instruments held. It is a credit entry to the flow account, in exactly the same way that the sale of any other economic instrument causes a credit entry to the flow account of the instrument sold (not the cash flow account).

Conceptual difficulties arise for two reasons.

1) The terminology with respect to financial instruments is not uniform. We sometimes say that we

a) borrow money from a bank

b) sell bonds or shares issued by a third party

c) issue new bonds or shares

d) withdraw money from a bank

e) buy goods or services on credit

   f) receive dividends or interest.

From our point of view each of these six activities is the sale
of a financial instrument. We receive money for a financial
instrument, which we must therefore be selling.

   2) The idea of value as price times quantity is confusing
for financial instruments, because the quantity is not easy to
define. Most people do not think that the payment or receipt of
interest changes the quantity of financial instruments held. One
way around this is to define the unit of measurement for all
financial instruments as a dollar's worth, so that the price of
financial instruments can never change. If the value changes, it
is because the quantity held changes.

   It is probably easier, however, to forget the quantity
inventory and think exclusively in terms of value inventory. The
accrual of interest on bonds increases its value to the lender.
The receipt of interest reduces their value to the lender, and
is the equivalent of the sale of some of the bonds. It is one of
the fundamental principles of finance theory that the
shareholder does not care whether he receives a dividend or the
increased price which would be associated with retained
earnings. If he wants cash and does not get a dividend, he can
sell shares. The receipt of dividends is the equivalent of
selling shares. The value of the shares has gone down, and we
make a credit entry to the share flow account to record either
the dividend received or the sale.

   This treatment of interest is directly tied to our

statement that interest is a (fair) transaction, and not a transfer payment. Business accounting treats interest received the way we treat a transfer: debit cash flow, credit income flow. We argue that interest is not a gift, since it reduces the (absolute) value of the debt.

In our scheme, no (fair) transaction ever creates or reduces income or wealth for either entity. This is the basic concept of a transaction: the economic instruments exchanged have equal value so that neither party gains nor looses wealth or income during the exchange. Traditional business accounting is ambivalent in its attitude toward transactions. The buyer records a fair exchange. The seller, however, rarely sells anything for its book value, and so usually gains or loses on the exchange. Since we require the seller to carry each instrument at market, our procedures record no gain or loss for either the buyer or the seller.

Production is the change in value of productive instruments held. It never results from a transaction, which does not change values. It can result from processing one productive instrument into another productive instrument of greater value, but also results from price changes with no change in the physical characteristics of the instrument. An increase in the price of a productive instrument is positive product for the owner, and a decline in price is negative product. We call this approach a "value added" approach, since product is the value added to productive instruments when they are owned by the producer.

Production generates productive income. The change in price of a productive instrument is productive income for the owner.

Essentially the same statements can be made about financial instruments, except that adding value by a financial instrument is not called "production." Value added by financial activities results from changes in the values of financial instruments held, and generates offsetting financial income and net wealth for the debtor and the creditor. Transactions never generate value added, nor do they change the net wealth or the income of either entity, whether the transactions involve productive instruments, financial instruments, or both.

The price of a financial instrument equals the present value of the future cash flows. It rises through time because the future flows become less distant and are discounted for shorter periods. This is frequently called the "accrual" of interest. The increase in value is financial value added, and generates income.

The price also changes when flows occur, for example, when interest is paid. This, however, is neither financial value added nor income, because the change in the value of the debt instrument is exactly offset by the change in the value of another financial instrument, cash. The transaction is fair. In our accounting scheme, these flows are part of the data base. They "explain" changes in values, and do not generate value added or income.

If a firm pays interest on a bond, this reduces the value

of the bond and increases cash balances, without generating value added for the bondholder. Value added and income are generated by the accrual of interest, i.e., by the change in the market value of the bond as the interest is "earned." They are not generated by the payment of interest, which simply changes the composition of the lender's financial portfolio without changing its value.

Price changes caused by changes in the rates used to discount future payments, or caused by changes in the expected magnitudes of these payments, are financial value added and income. They change the value of the financial portfolio of the household, and its net wealth. The causes of the change in value are not part of the data base, and the change in value is not explained by the data base.

These statements must be modified slightly for firms, because firms never have net wealth. If firm A owns shares in firm B, and the price of B's shares increases, this generates financial value added and financial income for firm A. If there were no changes in A's other balance sheet values, however, A's balance sheet would no longer balance, and we would need an entry for net wealth. What happens is that the market revalues A's shares upward to keep the balance sheet in balance. Thus the total value of A's financial portfolio is unchanged, although its composition is changed. The financial value added and income generated by the increase in B's shares is offset by the (negative) financial value added and income generated by the increase in A's shares.

When we break the financial flows into sub-accounts, however, we treat the income generated by B's shares separately from the negative income (loss) generated by A's shares. We treat them as two unrelated events, even though our economic theory tells us that they are related.

The same kind of statement applies to productive income. If the value of A's productive instruments rises, this again must be accompanied by an increase in the value of A's shares, or the books will not balance. In this sense the productive value added "causes" offsetting financial value added. Our procedures treat the two events as if they were unrelated.

3. Financial Activities and Transfers

We conclude from this chapter that firms generate product and productive income, and then transfer all of the productive income to other entities either by financial activities (or by transfer payments), leaving the firm with zero net income.

We can now explain why we treat financial activities and transfer payments differently, even though the effect of each is to transfer income from one entity to another without creating any net income, net wealth, or product.

The point is that financial activities transfer income when the price of a financial instrument changes for some reason other than a cash payment. Cash payments are part of the data base, and value added is calculated as a residual - changes in value not explained by the data base. The cash payment is a fair transaction because it generates offsetting changes in the values of two financial instruments: "cash" and "bonds." Tax payments are not fair transactions because there is no financial instrument other than "cash" whose value is changed by the payment.

Suppose that we thought of a tax law as a financial instrument. It would be an asset (have positive value) for the government, and be a liability (have negative value) for firms and households. Its value, like that of any other financial instrument, would be the present value of the future flows, which in this case are tax payments.

We would now handle tax payments in the same way we handle financial payments. The increase in the absolute value of the financial tax instrument (tax law) as the payment date approached would create negative financial income for the taxpayer and positive income for the government. The actual payment would be a fair transaction, since it would generate offsetting changes in the value of the tax instrument and cash.

This treatment would then reduce the "transfer payment" category to voluntary gifts, for which we could not reasonably infer a financial instrument. There is a growing economic literature which argues, however, that gifts should be thought of as part of the utility maximizing process of households. In this case, they should be treated as consumption, since they create utility.

This would eliminate the transfer payment category except

for the voluntary contributions of business firms.

The problem of valuing tax laws as economic instruments
would be at least as formidable as the valuation of human
capital. We can, nevertheless, get insights into tax accounting
by using this approach. We shall return to the consideration of
tax accounting by firms in Chapter 10.

Chapter VII

Aggregation and Consolidation

In this chapter, we show that we can measure correctly the aggregate product and income of different entities either by adding the income and product of the entities, or by consolidating the entities and measuring the income and product of the single consolidated entity.

It is important to economic accounting that we measure income and its components so that the incomes of different entities can be added together (aggregated) to get the income of the economic "sector" to which the entities belong, or of the entire society.

The correct way to measure the income of a sector or an entire society is to "consolidate" the entities. We consolidate entities by constructing accounts which eliminate any (financial) economic instruments held by both entities and any exchanges between the entities, and then apply our general accounting procedures to the remaining instruments and flows. This is what we did in measuring social income in Chapter 4.

We want our accounting procedures to allocate or attribute the income of the consolidated entity to the original entities, in much the same way that we allocate or attribute the income of an entity to individual economic instruments or activities. This means that we should get the same result by aggregating entities which we get by consolidation.

In particular, if we add the productive, financial, and transfer incomes of any two entities, we should get the same result that we would get if we consolidate the entities, and then measure the productive, financial, and transfer incomes of the consolidated entity using our standard procedures.

We do not want to create or destroy income by consolidation, or by breaking the economy into smaller entities. This is important because of the arbitrary nature of the definition of "entity." We do not want our measurements to be influenced by the merger of two entities, or the forced break up of AT&T. We want our measurements to be the same no matter how economic activities are associated with "entities."

In general, any accounting procedure which requires that both the debtor and the creditor value financial instruments at the same (absolute) value will permit correct aggregation, since no net financial income would be generated by financial activities between debtors and creditors. Our procedures require both entities to carry financial instruments at market, and so permit aggregation. Business accounting frequently results in different valuations of the same instrument by different entities, and aggregation is meaningless.

The attribution of income to individual economic instruments may change when we aggregate. The household of Chapter 5 produced $9,500 of labor services, while the firm of Chapter 6 produced $1,400 of consumer goods, capital goods, and (negative) labor services. The allocation by the consolidated firm will depend upon the sub-accounts which are created. It may create sub-accounts to preserve these sub-totals, or may attribute all of its value added to consumer and capital goods, as we did with the social income of $10,900 in Chapter 4.

1. Aggretating Entities

In this section, we consider what happens if we aggregate the balance sheets and the product and income measurements of existing entities. We illustrate this by adding together the various accounts for the household of Chapter 5 and the firm of Chapter 6.

1.1 Aggregating Balance Sheets.

We can illustrate the aggregation of balance sheets by looking at the t_o balance sheets for the two entities. It also simplifies matters if we reduce the number of entries on the balance sheets, and consider only 1) productive assets, 2) net financial assets, and 3) net wealth.

The household of Chapter 5 has $5,000 of productive assets, $8,500 of net financial assets (adding bonds and shares, and subtracting the account payable), and $13,500 net wealth.

The firm of Chapter 6 has $8,500 of productive assets, -$8,500 of net financial assets, and no net wealth.

The sums are $13,500 of productive assets, no net financial assets, and $13,500 of net wealth. The productive assets add without any netting out, since productive assets are always positive in value. The zero net financial assets combines both negative and positive values. Net wealth usually does not involve netting out, since we rarely find negative net wealth for an entity.

Addition of the balance sheet items therefore produces a balance sheet which balances, whether the shares held by the household are shares of the firm, or are shares of other firms, and whether the household and the firm carry shares of the firm at the same (absolute) value.

Similarly, the final balance sheet shows $14,400 of productive assets, no net financial instruments, and $14,400 of net wealth.

AGGREGATE BALANCE SHEET (0)

Assets		Equities	
Productive	$13,500.	Net Wealth	$13,500.

AGGREGATE BALANCE SHEET (1)

Assets		Equities	
Productive	$14,400.	Net Wealth	$14,400.

The process of aggregation therefore yields exactly the social balance sheets which we obtained in Chapter 4. This is because we listed only net financial instruments. If we simply added without netting financial instruments, we would show $9,500 of financial assets and equities at t_o, and $11,600 of financial assets and equities at t_1.

1.2 Aggregating Product and Income.

The household of Chapter 5 had productive income of $9,500, and financial income of $1,400, for a net income of $10,900. The firm of Chapter 6 had a productive income of $1,400, and financial income of -$1,400, for a net income of zero. If we add the values for the entities, we get productive income of

$10,900, and financial income of zero, for a net income of $10,900.

We can also get these results by examining the balance sheets and flow accounts.

Income is the increase in net wealth of $900 plus consumption, which we get by adding the consumption of the household, $10,000, to the consumption of the firm, zero. The income of the two entities is therefore $10,900. This is, of course the same calculation as for the household, since the firm has neither net wealth nor consumption nor net income.

We can break this income into productive, financial, and transfer income by combining the flow accounts of the two entities:

Productive Flows

From t_0 Household B.S.	$ 5,000.
Household Purchases	9,000.
From t_0 Firm B.S.	8,500
Firm Purchases (labor)	9,500.
Value Added (close to Income)	10,900.

To t_1 Household B. S.	$ 4,000.
Household Sales (Labor)	9,500.
Household Consumption	10,000.
To t_1 Firm B. S.	10,400.
Firm Sales	9,000.

Financial Flows

From t_o Household B.S. $ 8,500.

Household Cash Receipts   11,000.

To t_1 Firm B.S.   10,400.

Firm Cash Receipts   11,000.

Financial Value Added (close to Income)   0.

    To t_1 Household B. S. $10,000.

    Household Cash Payments   11,400.

    From t_o Firm B. S.   8,500.

    Firm Cash Payments   11,000.

Income Flows

Net Value Added (Close to Wealth Flow) $10,900.

    Productive Income $10,900

    Financial Income   0.

Wealth Flows

To t_1 Household B.S. $14,400.

Consumption (Household)   10,000.

    From t_o Household B. S. $13,500.

    Net Income   10,900.

We again get the same results we obtained for the society
in Chapter 4. The aggregate income and product of the two
entities coincide, since the two entities form a closed society.
The financial flow account balances without value added. The
transfers from the household's balance sheet exactly offset the
transfers from the firm's balance sheet. The flows between the
household and the firm also offset each other, since each flow

is positive for one entity and negative for the other.

This is a general property of our accounting scheme. For any entity, the difference between productive income and net income is the net financial income, including transfers, which the entity generates for other entities.

This is just another way of interpreting the "Income Flows" account. This account has entries for two kinds of income, productive and financial. When we introduce the idea of transfer payments, there will also be an entry for transfer income. Positive income is entered as a credit, negative income as a debit. There is also a closing entry for net value added, which is the negative of net income. The account therefore says that that net income equals productive income plus financial income plus transfer income. We can rearrange this to say that net income less productive income equals financial income plus transfer income.

If we add two entities together, the difference between net income and productive income will still be financial income plus transfer income. For a closed society, net income must equal productive income, which means that aggregate financial and transfer incomes should both be zero. This will happen only if both entities involved in debtor-creditor relationships keep the financial instruments on their books at the same absolute value. In our example, the financial income of the firm plus the financial income of the household add to zero, since they both value the shares at market. If there were different valuation procedures for the two entities (as in business accounting), financial income would not aggregate to zero, and aggregate income would not equal aggregate productive income.

The significance of the valuation procedure is that income is measured as the increase in inventory value plus the observed cash flows. Both entities normally use the same procedures to measure the flows, but the valuation of inventories causes significant problems in business accounting. Business accountants do not use market values, nor estimates of market values. Furthermore, their procedures are unlikely to result in the same (absolute) valuation by both entities who have a debtor-creditor relationship. If firm A owns shares in firm B, there is no reason for book values to be equal in absolute value. A's financial income from the shares will not offset B's, and aggregate financial income will not be zero.

This problem also extends to the valuation of productive instruments, since the balance sheet must always balance. If shares are not valued at market, then productive instruments are also not valued at market. Business accountants usually value productive instruments according to arbitrarily selected depreciation rules without regard to market prices. The consolidated accounts will not be the same as the aggregate accounts if the consolidated entity uses market values and the "original" entities use different valuation rules.

Aggregation is important to the economic accountant, but has no influence on business accounting. Economists want to get sensible results when they add two entities together.   Business

accountants have no principles related to aggregation.   They

consider only the entity for which they are accounting.

Economists insist, as a matter of accounting principle,

that debtors and creditors carry the financial instrument

involved at the same absolute value.   Aggregation will eliminate

financial income no matter what common absolute value is used.

It does not have to be market value.   One general principle in

economics, however, is that information is transmitted between

entities through the market, so it is appropriate for our

procedures to use market values.

2. Consolidation

2.1 Consolidated Balance Sheets.

The alternative is to consolidate or merge the entities,

and then measure balance sheets, product, and income for the

consolidated entity, as we did in Chapter 4.   In general, if we

consolidate a household and a firm, we must think of the new

entity as a household, since it has net wealth, although it

forms a closed society in our example.   The entity could be the

proprietor of an unincorporated business.

For consolidation, we must know whether the shares owned by

the household were issued by the firm, and whether the flows are

between the two entities or involve third parties.   For

aggregation, we need not know whether third parties are involved

or not.

The balance sheets of the consolidated entity would be determined by first eliminating from the books all financial instruments which appear as assets for one entity and equities for the other. The consolidated entity would not list the same shares, bonds or receivables (payables) as both an asset and a liability. The financial instruments, in effect, would be retired and no longer exist.

This means that consolidation and aggregation of the original entities will result in the same financial entries on the balance sheets only if both of the original entities carry the financial instruments on their books at the same absolute value. In the case of aggregation, the aggregate value will be the algebraic sum of the two values listed on the balance sheets. In consolidation, the financial instruments listed by both entities will not appear no matter what the previous book values had been.

The consolidated entity will then value the remaining instruments, productive and financial, and enter them on the balance sheet. We will obtain the same results from consolidation and aggregation only if the consolidated entity uses the same valuation procedures for productive instruments that the original entities used.

Since we use market values for the consolidated entity as well as the original entities, the consolidated balance sheets will be the same as the aggregate balance sheets. The proprietor will have the same assets, liabilities, and net wealth no matter which procedure he uses.

The consolidated balance sheets of a closed entity (society) will have no financial instruments, and will show only productive instruments and net wealth, as in Chapter 4. The productive instruments will be the sum of the productive instruments of the entities comprising the society, and the net wealth will be the sum of the net wealths of the households, provided that all economic instruments are carried at market by all entities.

2.2 Consolidated Product and Income.

The measurement of consolidated product and income starts from the consolidated balance sheets, and then considers flows between the consolidated entity and other entities. Flows between the two original entities are not accounted for, in the same way that exchanges between members of a household are not accounted for.

As before, all we need are the exchanges of productive and financial instruments which we may call "mixed" transactions, transfers, and consumption, unless we want to attribute income to specific instruments. This gives exactly the same results that we get by adding the two entities, providing that the balance sheet for the consolidated entity is the aggregate of the two original balance sheets.

This is particularly important when we recognize that there are non-economic considerations which influence the definition of an entity. The proprietor may be one or two (or more) "entities," depending upon legal and other considerations. One of the important characteristics of our accounting procedures is that the measurement of income is independent of the definition of the entity.

We could also create sub-accounts to allocate the value added and income to individual economic instruments. This allocation, however, has arbitrary elements.

In our example, the consolidated accounts which were presented in Chapter 4 suggest that the society produces $10,900 of consumer goods and capital goods, but no labor. These balance sheets and productive flow accounts have entries only for consumer and capital goods. This is consistent with GNP value added accounting, which allocates all value added to business firms, and the goods and services they produce.

Chapters 5 and 6, however, suggest that the household generates $9,500 of productive value added by producing labor services, and the firm produces $1,400 of consumer and capital goods. This raises the question of accounting for labor in a consolidated entity, which we mentioned in Chapter 4.

If there are flows of labor within a consolidated entity, we can account for this by creating sub-accounts. We can use sub-accounts to generate any internal flows we think will be useful for decision making or for descriptive purposes. The only constraint is that the net productive, financial, and transfer incomes measured in the consolidated accounts above must remain unchanged.

The proprietor of our consolidated entity could, for

example, break it into two accounting centers in the same way
that we broke Crusoe into two parts in Chapter 2, and create
sub-accounts that are exactly the same as those of Chapters 5
and 6. The firm accounted for by the proprietor need not be
legally incorporated as a separate entity. The proprietor may
think that he can make better decisions about how to employ his
labor and his financial assets if he keeps separate accounts for
his household activities and his firm activities, and exchanges
both productive and financial instruments between the accounting
centers.

If he does this, he will conclude that the household
produced $9,500 of labor services, and the firm produced $1,400
of other productive instruments, provided that his estimate of
the value of labor services is the same as the market value
which we have been using. He will also conclude that he earned a
financial income of $1,400 on the $8,500 which he has lent to
his firm, if his estimate of the share value coincides with the
market value we have been using. This information will be useful
to him in deciding whether he should sell his labor services
elsewhere and find another use for his financial assets.

The GNP accounts also employ an allocation similar to this,
called "National Income by Distributive Shares," rather than
value added. They would show $9,500 of wages, $300 of personal
interest received from the firm, and $1,200 of (corporate)
profits before tax. These profits would be broken down into $200
of dividends and $1,000 of retained earnings. The total income

would therefore be $11,000, rather then $10,900. The difference
of $100 arises because the GNP income measurement includes the
$100 interest paid by the household on its account payable as
part of household income, and as the purchase (consumption) of a
service by the household. The GNP accounts would show $9,100 of
consumption and $1,900 of net investment, while we measure only
$9,000 of consumption and the same net investment.[1]

There is an important difference in outlook between our
measurements and the national income by distributive shares. We
are saying that the household produced labor services, and the
firm processed these services into consumer and capital goods,
and had a net product of only $1,400. The national income
accounts look at income generated, rather than product. They say
that households earned wages, and the corporation earned profit,
a word which we have not yet tried to define.

Chapter VIII

Accounting Principles

This chapter is concerned with accounting principles, although they are brief, in keeping with Paton and Littleton's warning to would-be accounting theorists [32, page 4]:

"The term 'standards' is used advisedly. 'Principles' would generally suggest a universality and degree of permanence which cannot exist in a human-service institution such as accounting. In this monograph, accordingly, the term 'principles' is used sparingly and the idea of useful standards is emphasized."

I quote this in full for two reasons: 1) it brings out the difference between the "accountant" and the "economist." As an economist, my interest in "standards" is minimal. I do not care if an accounting statement is "auditable," or if an asset is "measurable" with sufficient "reliability." I am primarily interested in the principles and concepts which guide the preparation of the statement, and the estimate of asset value.

2) It brings out the misuse of the word "principles" in common accounting usage. GAAP are not generally accepted principles. They are generally accepted practices. There is no such thing, for example, as a realization "principle." If it were a principle, we would violate it only when we did not have the information required to follow it. GAAP permits violations because its abandonment produces better estimates of income. It is a "rule of thumb" which is relatively easy and inexpensive to use, and which usually produces "reasonable" results.

I can find only one true "principle" in GAAP: aggregate

debits must always equal aggregate credits. This principle #1 continues to be the cornerstone of my accounting scheme.

All other GAAP are rules of thumb which are abandoned in "special" cases when they produce "unreasonable" results. In my view, the special cases should determine the principle, rather than to be permitted as exceptions. If the "realization" principle does not produce "good" estimates of revenue for long-term construction projects, it is a bad principle, even it is an adequate rule of thumb in many situations. It should, as a matter of principle, never be used, because it is not theoretically correct. We can justify its use on a cost-effectiveness basis: the improvement resulting from a more principled estimate would not be worth the cost.

I start on the premise that the initial purpose of accounting is to measure wealth, income, and product. Wealth measures the stock of economic resources under the control of (owned by) an accounting entity. Income measures what the entity has gotten from the economy. Product should measure what the entity has contributed to, or done for, the economy. Economists have generally agreed on the meaning of the concepts of "wealth" and "income." As we have seen, there is disagreement about the meaning of "product." I have adopted the "capitalist" definition which identifies "marginal product" as "product," and as the contribution of the entity to society.

There is no objection in principle if the accountant also wants to provide information which is "useful," but this should be regarded as the icing on the cake. The fundamental problem is to "measure" ("describe") the important characteristics ("attributes") which have been identified by economists. This is why the "core" accounting statements were the balance sheet and the income statement, and more recently, the "Funds Statement." The recent trend toward almost unlimited "disclosure" outside the framework of the traditional statements can also be viewed as an attempt to describe more fully the activities of the firm.

The economic instruments which comprise "wealth" must therefore be "elements" of the balance sheet, as conceived by the FASB [16]. In a Crusoe society, these are also a) productive resources, or b) financial instruments.

One of the major problems in more complicated models is whether we can measure wealth by breaking the total into components, and valuing the components. Since many models do not have the property that the value of the whole is the sum of the values of the parts, we cannot formulate a general accounting principle concerning the proper definition of the "elements" of a balance sheet.

The FASB's concurrence with the tradition that "elements" should be "recognized" only if they have "attributes" which are "measurable" with "sufficient reliability" [15, Highlights] is totally unacceptable either in "principle" or in "practice." Failure to recognize is the equivalent of recognition at a zero value. The accountant should be required to make the best estimate that he can,[1] with appropriate "disclosures."

Probably the most important component of wealth which is not included on the grounds of "measurablilty" is human capital. The issue here is twofold. 1) In many models, slavery is illegal so that no market price can exist. 2) In almost all models, the production of human capital is strongly influenced by non-economic factors. The "cost" price is therefore likely to be different from the "use" value, making estimation that much more difficult and unreliable.

Theory tells us, however, that human capital is important in consumption decisions. A "principle" which said that only "marketable" instruments are to be included in accounting estimates would therefore not satisfy the requirements of economic theory, and should be rejected, even if the "practice" is usually to refuse to estimate human capital, as we did in Chapter 2. We shall find, for example, in Chapter 10, that we cannot account properly for government taxation whithout explicit consideration of human capital.

Nevertheless, economists do not include the value of "purely" non-economic variables which admittedly have important influences on human welfare, such as love and marriage, in their estimates of national income and wealth. This does not deter courts, however, from assessing damages for "loss of consortium," or economists from analyzing marriage as an economic phenomenon. There is apparently no principle involved in the exclusion of any variable which influences welfare.

This has implications for GAAP. Accountants know that there

is frequently more than one "price" in a market, in the sense that there are entry prices, exit prices, replacement costs, and so on. The study of a Crusoe economy sheds no light on the question of which price ("attribute") is the most appropriate in the measurement of wealth, since there is only one price in the Crusoe model. We have as yet no "principle" which suggests that one estimate is better than another. We do, however, have a goal, which is the measurement of wealth.

We can suggest, however, two "guidelines" for measurement. The first is that the value of an economic instrument cannot be estimated by estimating income, and inferring value, although this might more properly be a principle of economics rather than of accounting. It is worth mentioning, however, because GAAP so frequently tries to infer value from income, which is my definition of "matching." There is no way, in principle, to measure income except as an "unexplained" change in value.

The second "guideline" is that two identical items cannot contribute different "values" to the wealth of an entity. Whatever estimation procedure is used must apply to all identical economic instruments. A share of GM stock bought in 1987 cannot possibly have a different value from a share bought in 1937, from the point of view of measuring the wealth of the entity which holds both shares, no matter what they might have cost. Similarly, a share of GM issued in 1987 cannot have a different value to GM from a share issued in 1937.

Principle #2 is that only natural persons, or entities

which account for groups of persons (states, nations), have wealth or income. Business firms therefore must have balance sheets which balance with zero net wealth, and therefore they will show zero income.

One might argue that this is also a principle of GAAP, since there is never an entry for "Net Wealth" on a firm's balance sheet. I do not consider this to be a GAAP principle for two reasons. 1) GAAP clearly measures the income of a firm. Since there is agreement that income is the increase in wealth plus consumption, and also agreement that firms cannot consume, GAAP must assume that firms have wealth. 2) The discussion of "Owners' Equity" frequently suggests that it should be interpreted as net wealth, so that firms can have income.

We also propose a principle #3 that financial instruments must add to zero in a closed economy, even though Barro and others have suggested that government debt might generate "real" wealth [2]. We shall return to this question in Chapter 10.

This is an important principle, since it requires both the debtor and the creditor to carry financial instruments at the same (absolute) value. If we have trouble valuing financial instruments, as noted above, this principle may be very difficult to implement.

This principle has two corollaries: accounting entities must be defined so that no economic instrument is either the asset or the equity of two entities. Contingent liabilities, and joint liabilities, present impossible problems.

A second corollary is that we can consolidate entities without having to make special adjustments with respect to financial instruments which are assets for one and equities for another of the entities to be consolidated. The books will continue to balance, and the income of the consolidated entity will equal the sum of the incomes of the original entities, if we simply "remove" the offending financial instruments.

Principle #4 is that every transaction can be treated as if it were a purchase of an economic instrument for "medium of exchange," and the sale of another instrument for "medium." Even gifts can be treated in this way. If a firm receives a gift of "cash," it records the sale of shares (with no change in the number outstanding), and the purchase of cash.

My final principle #5, and one of the most important from the point of view of accounting practice, is that income arises from changes in value which are not "explained" by exchanges, or by gifts, which the economist frequently calls "transfer payments" since they transfer wealth and income from one entity to another. "Accruals" do not "explain" changes in value. If interest accrues on a financial instrument, this is not an "exchange" or a "gift." The change in value caused by the accrual of interest is therefore "unexplained," and is income. "Matching" is unnecessary. Income is never generated by an arms-length market exchange. All such exchanges are "fair." The trick is not to "match" revenues with expenses, but to determine when the value of an economic instrument has changed.

Chapter IX

Money, Banks, and Financial Institutions

In the Crusoe model, we assumed that the only financial instrument was the share which the firm issued to Crusoe when the firm was organized. This required us also to assume that any "medium" accumulations by the firm had to be immediately returned to Crusoe, and that any "medium" shortages had to be borrowed from Crusoe. In the real world, transactions costs, risk, and uncertainty make this procedure uneconomical.

Firms usually pay dividends quarterly, and sell new shares at infrequent intervals. Other financial instruments are developed to "store" value. Some of these are usually called "money," and money becomes both a store of value and a medium of exchange. From our point of view, we do not need to specify which financial instruments are "money." We simply observe that there are financial instruments called "currency," "demand deposits," "savings deposits," "certificates of deposit," "accounts payable," "bills," "bonds," "notes," and so on. All of these instruments are stores of financial value. They differ in liquidity, risk, and yield.

Our model still requires that net flows of "medium" be zero for each accounting entity at every point in time. If an entity has excess "medium," it must immediately buy a financial instrument. Since currency and demand deposits are usually used "pay" for economic instruments, the initial accumulation of "medium" is usually spent on one of these instruments, which are frequently referred to as "money." The transactions costs

involved in converting "medium" into either of these instruments
are very low. These instruments also have very high liquidity,
low risk, and low yield. The entity can then analyze its
portfolio and exchange financial instruments, if this is in its
self interest. If "payment" is made by "credit," the "medium" is
obtained by selling a "note" or "account payable," and is used
to purchase another economic instrument."

This means that we still regard "medium" as having no
"physical" form. It cannot be accumulated, even for an instant.
It is always used to buy an economic instrument, the moment it
is "received." It is acquired by the sale of an economic
instrument. If an individual eats lunch and pays $5 in currency,
we "account" as if the individual sells $5 of currency (a
financial instrument), and purchases $5 of "medium," which he
immediately uses to pay the restaurant. The restaurant receives
$5 of "medium" and immediately uses it to buy currency. If
"payment" is made by credit card, the customer purchases
"medium" by selling a "note" to the restaurant, and buys lunch.
The restaurant sells the note to VISA, and uses the "medium" to
pay some transactions costs, and buy a bank balance. If
"payment" is made by check, the customer buys "medium" by
selling the restaurant a financial instrument called "bank
deposit," which he has previously bought at his bank. The
restaurant sells it to his bank, and his bank sells it to the
customer's bank.

We first consider accounting for demand deposits at

comercial banks, and then consider other financial institutions.

We treat the debt of the bank to the deposit-holding entity as a financial instrument which has a market value like any other financial instrument. The bank carries the instrument as a negative value (credit), while the customer carries it as a positive value (debit). The application of our principles and procedures to a financial sub-account for "Cash" suggests that cash generates value added and financial income just like any other financial instrument.

If we think from the point of view of the customer, a withdrawal from the bank or a payment of currency reduces the value of the instrument (credit), while the receipt of currency or the deposit of a check in the bank increases the value of the instrument (debit). Any change in value not explained by the observed flows is financial value added, and generates income.

The same is true for the bank, except that all of the signs are changed.

As a practical matter, the biggest problem is that banks frequently render productive services (e. g., clearing checks) without formally charging for the service. This means that financial and productive activities are confused, and it becomes difficult to distinguish productive and financial income.

Accounting for the bank customer.

In this section, we account for a bank customer. For accounting purposes, the data which we need are opening and final values of the financial instrument involved, and flows between the entities and other entities.

We start on the assumption that there is no currency, only bank deposits. The customer, which may be either a household or a firm, is called "A". He has a bank balance of $500 at t_0 and $300 at t_1. We interpret these balances to be market prices. During the year, he makes payments of $15,000 and receives payments of $14,700. These balances and flows are part of the accounting data base.

The payments which he makes can be for any purpose. He can pay for consumer goods, make payments on accounts payable, pay interest, pay dividends, pay for labor services, buy bonds or shares. In accounting for his "monetary" activities, we do not need to know what he got in return for his money. Similarly, the receipts can be from any source, sales of productive resources or financial instruments, receipt of interest or dividends, etc.

We account for the value of a financial instrument. The financial instrument is a bank account or bank deposit. It is sold to A by the bank. He carries it on his balance sheet as an asset (debit). He buys and sells this instrument, like any other, by using "medium of exchange."

The usual terminology is that A deposits money or a check in his account. We look upon this as a use of "medium of exchange" to purchase a financial instrument. Such an exchange (flow, financial transaction) should increase the value of the financial instrument, bank deposit, which he holds. "A" therefore uses the $14,700 which he receives from sales of other instruments (productive and financial) to buy additional bank deposits. The purchase of "bank deposit" is recorded in the "Flow of Bank Deposit" account as a debit. The sale of the other instrument is recorded as a credit to the flow account which is keeping track of the value of the other instrument.

If we were keeping an account for "medium," we would record the purchase of the deposit as a debit to the "store" account and a credit to the "medium" account. The sale of the "store" instrument would require a credit to the "store" account and a debit to the "medium" account. In practice, we bypass the "medium" account, and simply debit "store" and credit "other instrument," since we know that the "medium" account will always be in balance.

Similarly, the withdrawal of $15,000 from the bank to pay for purchases is the sale of a financial instrument (bank deposit). This should reduce the value of the instrument on A's books. We debit the "Flow of Bank Deposit" account, and credit another flow account.

We create a financial sub-account to keep track of the value of the financial instrument, bank deposit.

Flow of Bank Deposit

From t_0 B.S. $ 500.
Purchases (sales of other instruments)   14,700.
Value added (close to Financial Flow)   100.
      To t_1 B. S. $ 300.
      Sales (Purchases of Other Instruments)   15,000.

According to the information in the data base, A started with a financial instrument (balance) valued at $500 and bought an additional $14,700, which "should" increase the value to $15,200. In our terminology, he used "medium" to buy "store." The common terminology is that he "deposited" currency or a check. He then sold (withdrew) $15,000 worth of the instrument, so the value "should" be $200. The value of the instrument (bank balance) is, however, $300, which is an unexplained increase of $100 in the value of of the instrument, and is financial value added. When it is closed to the Financial Flow account, it will be recorded as $100 of (positive) financial income.

As with any other financial instrument, we need not know why the market value of the deposit is larger than "expected." We can assume, for purposes of discussion, that the bank credited interest to the account. This should not be interpreted, however, as the payment of interest by the bank. There was in fact no transaction and no payment by the bank to A.

The bank balance in the bank statement is properly viewed as an announcement by the bank that the market value of the instrument (deposit) has increased (because interest has accrued). There is no active secondary market for bank deposits. This is because the bank stands ready to buy and sell at the same price. The bank balance is an offer by the bank to (re)purchase the instrument at the stipulated price. The bank also stands ready to sell an identical financial instrument to any entity at the same price. The bank has therefore effectively fixed the price of the instrument, by announcing identical bid and asked prices. No entity would pay more, or sell for less.

The fact that the bank has "explained" the increase in value as accrued interest is not important to the accountant who is measuring past values. It may well be important to an entity which is contemplating the purchase of a deposit at the bank, because it gives some information about what may happen in the future to the value of deposits purchased from the bank. Predicting the future, however, is not a function of the economic accountant.

The bank has not paid the interest. There has been no observed flow, exchange, or transaction between the bank and A. The bank has sent A a statement offering to buy the financial instrument at a specified price. Since no sale has taken place, there is no transaction to record.

If the bank were actually to "pay" the interest, this would "explain" a decrease, not an increase, in the value of the deposit. This is most easily seen if we think in terms of a savings deposit. The accrual of interest increases the balance of the deposit, i. e., increases its market value. If the bank then "pays" the interest by transfer into a checking account, the bank will reduce the balance (price) of the savings account and increase the balance (price) of the checking account. The accrual of interest causes the market to increase the price of a financial instrument. The payment of interest reduces its price.

This also illustrates correctly the meaning of the statement that shareholders do not care whether "earnings" are retained or paid out in dividends. The bank has announced that it has earned financial income of $100 for A. This has increased the value of A's bank deposit. If this is the end of the story, then the bank has "retained" the earnings. If A wishes to consume the earnings, he simply sells some of his financial instruments by writing a check for consumer goods. If the bank pays out the interest and A does not wish to consume the earnings, he simply buys additional financial instruments by depositing the "money" in the bank.

The same principles would apply to shares of firms if there were no transactions costs, and if the firm calculated its earnings so that they reflected changes in the market value of shares. These are the assumptions of finance theory on which the "irrelevance" of dividend policy[1] is based. The market value of the share should reflect its "earnings." If the earnings are paid out in dividends and the shareholder does not want to consume, he can buy additional shares with the dividend. If the earnings are retained and he wishes to consume, he can sell some shares.

In the real world, the reported (GAAP) "earnings" do not usually reflect changes in share value, and there are transactions costs and taxes. With bank accounts, "earnings" do reflect market value, there are no transactions costs, and the "interest" is usually taxable to the deposit holder whether it

is realized (withdrawn) or not. All of the assumptions of
finance theory are satisfied, and the "irrelevance" of dividend
policy theorem holds in the real world.

No additional difficulties arise if there is currency as
well as bank deposits. We treat the currency as a financial
instrument which is bought and sold with "medium of exchange."
If we keep a separate sub-account for "Flow of Currency Value,"
we expect this account to balance with no closing entry for
"Value Added." The treatment of the bank deposit flow account
would be exactly as above.

The only complicating factor is that the bank performs
productive services for its customers, and does not bill for
many of them explicitly. This makes it difficult to measure
production and consumption, and also confuses productive and
financial activities. We return to this issue after we discuss
other financial institutions.

Accounting for the bank.

As with all financial instruments, the bank's accounting
for A's deposits is the mirror image of A's accounting. All of
the numbers are the same, but the signs are reversed.

Flow of A's Deposit Value

To t_1 B.S.	$ 300.	
Purchases (Customer Withdrawals)	15,000.	
From t_0 B. S.		$ 500.
Sales (Customer Deposits)		14,700.
Value Lost (Close to Financial Flow)		100.

From the bank's perspective, it started the year with a financial instrument valued at -$500. The bank has sold deposits short, and records a negative quantity and value. The sale of a bank deposit is the same as the sale of any financial instrument. The quantity is negative for the seller and positive for the buyer.

During the year, the bank sold an additional $14,700 of deposits, and (re)purchased $15,000. The value "should" be -$200 on the basis of these observed flows. The value is -$300, which is an "unexplained" decline of $100 in the value of a financial instrument. This is negative value added, and generates negative financial income when the "Bank Deposit" account is closed to the "Financial Flow" account.

In traditional accounting, the bank will achieve the same result, but by a somewhat different route. It will "recognize" the accrual of interest by debiting an "interest expense" account and crediting the customer deposit account. These are in fact exactly the same entries which we make, except that we call the "interest expense" negative financial income.

The other difference is that the traditional accountant would say that the bank had "paid" its customer the $100 of interest. We insist that the "expense" is the accrual, not the payment, of interest. The "payment" of interest with respect to a bank deposit is not a well-defined idea. If someone opens an account with $1,000, earns $100 interest, and withdraws $200, it makes no difference to anyone whether the remaining $900 is called principal, or includes any part of the interest earned. The "expense" to the bank, and the financial income to the depositor, occur when interest accrues.

The unusual feature of a bank and other financial institutionsis that they expect to earn income from financial activities rather than from productive activities. On the basis of their recorded purchases and sales of productive instruments, we would expect banks to have negative productive income, although this might become positive if they accounted properly for the productive services rendered. Even if productive income were positive, it would be small compared to income generated by financial activities. Banks expect to generate most if not all of their income by borrowing money at low interest rates and lending at higher rates. This could not happen in a world of certainty where there can be only one interest rate, which is why we did not introduce banks in Part 2.

The expectation is that the negative financial income generated by their deposits (borrowings) will be more than offset by positive financial income generated by their loans and other financial assets. This net financial income generated by their normal business activities is transmitted to shareholders, as with any other firm.

Other financial institutions.

The development of financial instruments is accompanied by the development of financial institutions, which perform two functions. 1) They buy financial instruments, "repackage" them, and sell other financial instruments.   2) They reduce risk by providing insurance.

We do not consider brokerage firms to be financial institutions.   They "make" markets. The fact that stock brokers make markets for financial instruments while real estate brokers make markets for productive instruments does not change the nature of the brokerage business. Resources are required to match buyers and sellers, no matter what the instrument being traded. Brokers are no different from farmers, for accounting purposes.

1) The typical financial institution which "repackages" financial instruments is a mutual fund.   The fund buys financial instruments issued by other firms (or governments), and sells its own "shares."   Its objective is risk reduction through diversifiation.   It uses resources to "manage" the fund, so that the shareholders get a return which is less than the average return on the fund's holdings.

As an example, assume that the fund earns $1,000 on its loans, pays $900 to shareholders, and pays $100 for productive instruments, with no change in the market value of any financial instruments, and without owning any productive instruments.   Our accounting would show productive income of -$100, and financial income of $100, for a net income of zero.

This is not a good description of the economic contribution of the fund. Shareholders pay the $100 management fee because they think that they will be better off if they do so rather than to manage their own portfolios. The productive instruments used by the fund are not wasted, they are increasing welfare. The problem is to estimate the value of the services performed by the fund. The solution is to assume that the productive instruments used by the fund are as productive as they would be if they were used by another firm.

From the economic standpoint, the "correct" procedure would be for the fund to charge its customers explicitly for all productive services rendered. Presumably, these services are now paid for by a reduction in the dividend paid by the fund. Put differently, if the charges were made explicitly, the dividend paid by the fund could increase dollar for dollar. The fund shareholder would then record a higher financial income than he does at present, and also would record the purchase and consumption of productive services from the fund.

In effect, the fund is paying some return in "money," and some in kind, which confuses financial and prouctive activities. It understates the true financial return on the financial instruments, and also understates consumption and the use of productive resources.

We therefore estimate the value of the services performed at $100, since this is the opportunity cost of the resources. We assume that shareholders are buying these services in a free market, and would not buy them if they would bring a greater return in some other use.

This means that the fund is performing productive services

for its shareholders, as well as financial services. However, the fund does not sell the services to shareholders directly, and collect a fee for services rendered, the way a broker does. We therefore must construct "fictitious" transactions to correct for this deficiency. We assume that the fund returns the full $1,000 to shareholders, and that they buy $100 of productive services from the firm. We record no net productive income, and no net financial income.

The balance sheet will show $10,000 of financial assets, at market value, and $10,000 of equities. Without the adjustment, the assets would earn 10%, and the equities would pay (earn) 9%, as if somehow there were a difference in risk. With the adjustment, all financial instruments yield (on average) 10%, and shareholders purchase $100 of services from the fund. We can also say that the shareholders earn 10%, and take 9% in financial returns, and 1% in services.

This is the result of assuming that the fund owns no physical productive assets, which is usually the case. Mutual funds usually employ a management "service" which owns the equipment, so that all fund assets are financial.

Institutions which provide fire or automobile or other term insurance are selling "pure" risk reduction, without diversifying financial assets. Insurance (and annuity) policies such as whole life policies, which accumulate a "reserve," provide both pure insurance and financial diversification.

"Pure" insurance involves the payment of a premium to

ensure that certain "losses" will be compensated. In principle, the premiums cover the losses plus a transactions fee to cover the cost of finding and organizing a large number of entities which want the same kind of protection. The pooling of risk is a purely financial activity, but the insurance company is also selling productive services, in the same way that the mutual fund does.

We have the same kind of problem that we had with mutual funds, in that the productive services rendered by insurance companies are not billed directly. Assume that the company collects $1,000 in premiums, and pays $900 in claims, and $100 for productive services. Our accounting would show financial income of $100 and productive income of -$100. A better description of the events would assert that $100 of the premium payment was for (productive) services rendered, so that both financial and productive income would be zero.

Insurance companies, however, have shareholders and physical assets (offices, computers), which must also be taken into account. They own productive instruments as well as financial instruments. We must therefore assume that the productive instruments are earning their opportunity costs, and that the company has a net product equal to the marginal product of its productive instruments.

This is the general principle for accounting for financial institutions. The problem is that they provide productive services but do not charge for them directly, i. e., they provide them "free" as part of their financial activities. Their purchases of productive instruments therefore exceed their sales, and our (unadjusted) accounting would show that they have negative product and productive income. We therefore "adjust" their accounts to show productive income equal to the value of the marginal product of the productive instruments which they own. Since we must now consider risk explicitly, we cannot assume that there is a single, "known" real rate of interest. We therefore assume that the risk-adjusted rate of return on productive assets equals the "average" (expected) return to shareholders.

We must therefore record a sale of productive services large enough to generate the desired productive income. With "pure" insurance, we subtract the (adjusted) purchases of productive services from the premiums, and lower the financial receipts of the firm. With "pure" diversification, we add the the adjusted purchases to the financial payments from the financial institution to their customers.

Banks are primarily diversifiers, as well as providers of productive services. Their major function is diversification, so that individuals (and firms) who buy the financial instruments which they "issue" (demand and savings deposits, certificates of deposit, etc.), reduce their risk. The risk is now reduced still further by insurance (FDIC), so that the risk to most bank creditors is virtually zero.

They sell some of their productive services directly, e.

g., charges for returned checks and overdrafts. However, they also frequently disguise their productive services as financial services. They frequently do not charge for check clearing, or for the cost of making loans. Our principles tell us that we should inflate the financial payments which banks make to "depositors," and record sales of productive services to "depositors." The sales should be large enough so that the bank's productive income equals a risk-adjusted return on its productive assets (instruments).

This differs somewhat from the GNP accounting adjustment for banks. The assumption in the GNP accounts is that all bank financial income "flows through" to "depositors." "Depositors" then buy enough services from the bank to make productive income equal shareholders' return, rather than a risk-adjusted return on productive assets.[2] The two adjustments would produce the same result only if shareholder equity were equal to the bank's productive assets, and there is no reason to expect such an equality. Our adjustment permits the bank to "invest" some of the shareholders' "funds" in financial instruments, and thereby get a return generated by financial activity rather than productive activity. Similarly, some of the depositors' "funds" may be used to buy productive instruments, so that depositors may also get a return generated by productive activities.

The GNP accounting scheme concludes that banks generate no net financial income on the basis of their diversifying activity. If they pay depositors less interest than they collect, they make up the difference by providing productive services of equal value. Our scheme also concludes that banks generate very little net financial income from diversification activities. The "fact" which both schemes reflect is that almost all of the spread between the borrowing rate and the lending rate is made up by providing depositors with productive services, which the depositors would have to purchase elsewhere to obtain the same risk reduction from another institution.

A mutual fund generates financial income for its shareholders by purchasing shares of other companies. There is no reason to assume that a bank cannot do the same thing. The difference between a bank and a mutual fund is that a bank guarantees a specified return on some of the instruments which it sells, while the mutual fund has no fixed-return creditors. This does not imply that a bank cannot engage in financal diversification for its shareholders as well as its fixed-return creditors. There is no reason to assume that bank shareholders' financial income is derived entirely from productive income, rather than to recognize that some of their income may be derived from financial activities, as with mutual funds.

Theory suggests that depositors think that the services are worth the price they pay (the reduction in _financial_ return), just as any other purchaser of resources thinks that this is the best use of his purchasing power.

This requires that we also modify the accounts of "customers" of financial institutions. If the institutions

perform productive services, these are purchased by customers,
which reduces their productive income if they are firms, and
increases their consumption if they are households.   The
financial income of customers must also be increased to reflect
the "true" interest which the institutions are paying on the
financial instruments which they sell.

In conclusion, there is a large number of financial
instruments available as a store of value.   They vary in
liquidity, risk, and return. Only "currency" bears no interest,
no risk, and has 100% liquidity. Even demand deposits have a
small risk, although the FDIC makes this minimal, but they are
less liquid than currency.

Chapter X

Accounting for Government

1.   Introduction

This chapter considers accounting for government. There are
two important objectives: 1) to describe accurately the state of
the economy, and 2) to permit comparisons of income and wealth
through time.

I do not think that current accounting practices describe
the economy accurately.   One of the important considerations is
to measure wealth in such a way that households can use wealth
as a constraint in making savings-consumption decisions. Current
accounting practice   fails   to do this because government
"entitlements" are not included in household wealth.   For
example, social security entitles many households to retirement
payments. They must consider the present value of these payments
as part of their wealth if they are to make rational decisions.

The general principle is to consider government taxes and
payments as if they were financial instruments.   This idea is
implied in many discussions of the influence of government on
the economic system.[1] The emphasis, however, is on fiscal policy
and macroeconomic models, not on accounting.   This chapter is
concerned with the accounting problems which are encountered
when future taxes are capitalized by government as assets, and
by taxpayers as liabilities,   and when future government
subsidies are capitalized by government as liabilities and by
the public as assets.   For example, the social security taxes
which government will collect should be capitalized (discounted)

as government assets, and as taxpayer liabilities. The   future
social security payments should be capitalized as government
liabilities and household assets.

This principle is recognized in discussions of public
finance. Social security taxes and payments are sometimes
projected for as much as fifty years to determine if the system
is solvent. Economists summarize such projections by taking
present values. If the present value of the (future) payments
exceeds the present value of the (future) taxes plus the
accumulated surplus, the system is insolvent, and additional
taxes or reduced benefits are inevitable. From the point of view
of the social security administration, the future taxes are
assets, and the future payments are liabilities. Good accounting
practice will record these assets and liabilities on the balance
sheet, so that the statements correctly reflect the financial
position of the social security administration.

I shall also adopt the principle that financial assets are
matched by financial liabilities, even though formidable
implementation problems are encountered.   In the case of the
social security tax, the government would have to consider the
present value of all future tax collections as assets. Some of
these taxes will be paid by people who are not yet born. It is
not clear just who should carry these taxes as liabilities on
their balance sheets, even in a world of certainty.[2] Similarly,
some corporate income taxes will be paid by firms which do not
now exist. The government would not act responsibly if it did

not plan for these receipts, i. e., if it did not consider the present value of these receipts to be assets. It is not clear where the offsetting liability should be found. My principles, however, tell me that each financial asset must be matched by a financial liability, and I proceed on this basis.

Comparisons of wealth between years are also distorted in conventional accounting, because the taxes and benefits are not capitalized. Consider real estate. Assuming no shifting, the imposition of a real estate tax does not change its marginal productivity, but reduces its market value by the capitalized amount of the tax.[3] The imposition of a real estate tax would therefore reduce real wealth by the capitalized amount of the tax, according to conventional accounting practice.

If the capitalized tax is correctly carried as an asset by government and a liability by the landowner, the land must be carried at its productive value, rather than its market value. This means that the land is "valued" according to the present value of its future marginal products, whether there is a real estate tax or not. This correctly measures the contribution of land to the (future) utility of consumers. The economic contrubution of the land is not changed if the tax is not shifted. Comparisons are distorted if its balance sheet value is reduced. The correct measurement for purposes of comparing real real estate wealth at two points in time is to value real estate by discounting its future marginal product, and reducing the wealth of the landowner by carrying the capitalized tax as a

208   Accounting for Government

financial liability.

Our accounting, which I call "social" accounting, uses
these two principles: 1) government taxes and payments are
capitalize and treated as assets and liabilities, and 2)
productive instruments are carried at the present value of
future marginal products. In addition, I retain the idea that 3)
business firms have no net wealth or income.

On a purely logical basis, it is not clear to me why
application of the first two principles is consistent with the
third. My starting point, which I use as a model, is the real
estate tax. In this case, capitalizing taxes (principle 1) adds
to liabilities, and adding the tax liability to the productive
value of the land a) brings the land value to its productive
value (principle 2), and b) balances the books (principle 3).
Since this is "obviously" the correct way to handle a real
estate tax, I am encouraged to attempt to reconcile these three
principles with other kinds of taxes.

There are two parts to the valuation of productive
instruments at "productive" value: the determination of marginal
product, and the determination of the discount rate. I adapt my
definition of the real interest rate from Solow [37, Chapter 1],
and find that income taxes "distort" the nominal interest rate,
in the sense that they create a difference between the "true"
real rate and the nominal rate. The Appendix to this chapter
discusses the idea of the real interest rate more fully. I find
that the use of the real interest rate to discount both

productive and financial flows (taxes) restores the balance in the firms' balance sheets.

Some of the taxes which I consider apparently have the effect of "transferring" some human capital wealth from households to firms. This means that the analysis of this chapter considers human capital and the production of leisure, topics which we have abandoned since Chapter 2.

This chapter will probably be of more interest to economists than accountants, since accountants who take the decision-making approach will find the idea of the real rate of interest uninteresting. The nominal rate is clearly correct for private decision-making.

There is one point, however, which should interest accountants. "Matching" requires the allocation of taxes to time periods, and leads to the question of when an expected future tax payment becomes a liability. My answer is simple. Taxes laws are financial instruments, and the future payments should be capitalized as liabilities when the law is passed. The real estate tax provides a convincing example. The future real estate taxes become a liability when the land is purchased. The firm assumes the tax liability when it buys the land, just as it assumes the liability for the future interest and principal repayments when it sells a bond. If the tax is recognized as a liability, then the productive value of the asset must also be recognized to keep the books in balance.

The case for capitalizing other future taxes is less

compelling,[4] but is worth considering. Anything which reduces
the reliance of accounting on "matching" must be a step forward.

I confine my more formal analysis to some highly
restrictive assumption about government activity:

1) All government activities are financial. They pass tax
laws and collect the appropriate taxes.   Similarly, they pass
appropriation bills and make the appropriate payments.   However,
all appropriations are subsidies, paid to households.

There are no transactions costs.   No resources are used in
legislating, collecting taxes, or paying subsidies.   The
government neither buys nor sells any productive instruments.

2) The government has no net wealth. This means that the
present value of the future taxes (government assets) must
exactly equal the present value of future payments (government
liabilities), plus the government debt.

This is not a "balanced budget" ammendment, but a "balanced
wealth" ammendment. Annual surplusses or deficits are permitted.
If the economy will grow in the future enough to cover present
deficits (supply-side economics), we are not required to
increase taxes or reduce expenditures.   If the economy will not
grow fast enough, we are required to increase taxes or reduce
expenditures.   In the real world, of course, the future is
uncertain. One way to interpret the present (1988) fiscal
situation is to suggest that most people think that the
government accounts are not in balance, and that changes will be
required. We are not bankrupt because the power to tax becomes

an asset in an uncertain world. This creates uncertainty, and a large volume of lobbying as various groups jockey for position.

Sections 2 through 6 of this chapter consider accounting for specific kinds of taxes, from the point of view of descriptive accuracy. Section 7 considers the problem of comparison of national income and wealth through time.

2. Real Estate Taxes

2.1 Conventional Accounts

We distinguish between "pure" land, defined as the "original and indestructible powers of the soil," and "improvements." In this section, we assume a tax assessed only on land with a market value of $800, and that the tax is 5% of market value. All land is owned by firms, so the tax of $40 is paid by firms.

If the market interest rate is 20%, the market value of the land will be 80% of its productive value. The land will have to have a large enough marginal product to provide a 20% return on market value to shareholders, and a 5% return to government. It will have to "earn" a dividend of $160 and a tax of $40, for a total productivity of $200 per year, and a capitalized productive value of $1,000. If there were no tax, and taxes were not shifted, its marginal product would be the same, and the land would have a market value of $1,000, instead of $800.

Firms have "other" capital valued at $9,500 at t_o, for a total capital value of $10,300. At t_1, "other" capital rises to $10,500, because of investment. The firm buys 5,500 hours of labor @ $1.00, and sells $6,600 of consumer goods. It pays $40 in taxes, and must pay $1,060 in dividends to keep its cash balance at zero.

Households have available 16,000 of labor. They sell 5,500 in the market, and use 10,500 in the "cottage." Cottage labor is also valued at $1.00, and is used to produce leisure of equal value. The leisure is consumed immediately when it is produced. Households therefore have human capital of $80,000, which is the present value of $16,000 of wages per year, discounted at 20%.

The government collects $40 in taxes per year. It has $50 of debt outstanding at t_o, and borrows an additional $20 during the year. Government therefore pays interest of $10 at t_1, and subsidies of $50, so that cash income and outgo are both $60. After t_1, government pays $14 in interest and $26 in subsidies. All government bonds are owned by households.

Table 10-1: Sector Cash Flows, Real Estate Tax

	Households		Business		Government	
	In	Out	In	Out	In	Out
Wages	$5,500			$5,500		
Dividends	1,060			1,060		
Consumer Goods		$6,600	$6,600			
Taxes				40	$40	
Subsidies	50					$50
Bond Interest	10					10
Bond Sale		20			20	
TOTALS	$6,620	$6,620	$6,600	$6,600	$60	$60

We first draw up "conventional" balance sheets, which reflect market prices and neglect the present values of taxes and subsidies, but record the value of government bonds, which are $50 at t_o and $70 at t_1.

CONVENTIONAL BALANCE SHEETS (BUSINESS)

	t_o	t_1
Assets		
Land	$800.	$800.
Other Capital	9,500.	10,500.
TOTAL	$10,300.	$11,300.
Equities		
Shares	$10,300.	$11,300.

CONVENTIONAL BALANCE SHEETS (HOUSEHOLD)

Assets		
Shares	$10,300.	$11,300.
Bonds	50.	70.
Human Capital	80,000.	$80,000.
TOTAL	$90,350.	$91,370.
Equities		
Net Wealth	$90,350.	$91,370.

CONVENTIONAL BALANCE SHEETS (GOVERNMENT)

Assets		
None		
Equities		
Bonds	$50.	$70.
Net Wealth	-50.	-70.

The conventional balance sheets show a national net wealth of $90,300 (=$90,350 - $50). This includes government net wealth of -$50, which is difficult to interpret.

Conventional accounts record income of $18,100 at t_1. Business income is always 0. Government pays $10 interest and $50 in subsidies, and collects $40 in taxes at t_1, which produces a deficit (negative income) of $20, which is met by borrowing. At t_1, households get $5,500 in wages, $1,060 in dividends, $10 in interest, $50 in subsidies, $10,500 in cottage wages, and a $1,000 capital gain on shares, for a total income of $18,120. National income is only $18,100, however, because of the $20 government deficit. An income of $18,100 with net wealth of $90,300, is not consistent with a 20% real interest rate.

2.2 Social Accounts

Social accounts treat taxes, bonds, and subsidies as if they were financial instruments. The present value of future taxes, discounted at the real rate of interest, is a government asset, and a liability for the individual who is required to pay the money to the government. We are not concerned with the tax "burden," but only with the tax payer. Bonds are government liabilities and household assets. The present value of future subsidies is a government liability, and a household asset.

These financial instruments are the only entries on the government balance sheet, since government undertakes no productive activities. We also assume that the government, like the business sector, has zero net wealth. This is obvious if we

assume no cash balances, as we always do. Government receipts
and expenditures balance each year. Tax receipts always equal
subsidies plus net payments (interest plus debt repayment or
less new borrowing) to bondholders. If all receipts are
capitalized as assets, and all payments are capitalized as
liabilities, assets will equal liabilities as long as the same
discount rate is used in all capitalizations.

If the government holds cash balances, we must introduce
uncertainty or transactions costs to explain why the government
is foregoing potential interest, just as in the private sector.

We also record the productive value of resources, rather
than market value, when these differ. The productive value of
the land is $1,000. The marginal product of the land is $200
annually, of which $160 goes to shareholders in dividends, and
$40 goes to government in taxes. The purchaser of land gets a
packge, an asset whose productive value is $1,000 and a tax
liablity whose present value is -$200. The market price of the
package (the price of the land plus the tax liability) is
therefore $800.

Conventional accounts record only the (net) market value.
Our accounts record the tax liability of the landowner (firm),
and a tax asset for government. We balance the books by
recording the productive value of the land, instead of its
market value. Conventional accounts confound productive and
financial activities, whereas our accounts are more informative
by separating productive and financial activities.

SOCIAL BALANCE SHEETS (BUSINESS)

	t_0	t_1
Assets		
Land	$1,000.	$1,000.
Other Capital	9,500.	10,500.
TOTAL	$10,500.	$11,500.
Equities		
Taxes	$200.	$200.
Shares	10,300.	11,300.
TOTAL	$10,500.	$11,500.

SOCIAL BALANCE SHEETS (HOUSEHOLD)

Assets		
Shares	$10,300.	$11,300.
Bonds	50.	70.
Subsidies	150.	130.
Human Capital	80,000.	80,000.
TOTAL	$90,500.	$91,500.
Equities		
Net Wealth	$90,500.	$91,500.

SOCIAL BALANCE SHEETS (GOVERNMENT)

Assets		
Taxes	$200.	$200.
Equities		
Subsidies	$150.	$130.
Bonds	50.	70.
TOTAL	$200.	$200.

Net wealth accrues entirely to households, and is $90,500 at t_0 and $91,500 at t_1. Income is 20% of net wealth.

We measure income as $18,100 at t_1, but our allocations to the sectors are different from the conventional accounts. We treat the sudsidies as financial instruments. Subsidy income for households is therefore $30, even though subsidy cash payments are $50. The decline in the value of the subsidy asset from $150 to $130 is a negative capital gain, and negative financial income for the asset holder. Net financial income is always 20% of the initial capital value. In this case, the principal value is $150 at t_0, and the income at t_1 is $30.

Our treatment also implies that government, like business, has no net income. All assets earn 20%, and all liabilities cost 20%. Only entities with net wealth can have net income, and government has no net wealth in our model.

Wealth is supposed to measure the ability of the society to produce income. The land has a marginal product of $200 annually, and "produces" $200 of income. Other capital which produced a similar income would be valued at $1,000. The tax distorts the market price of land by preventing the price from reflecting the productivity. Our accountng removes this distortion and measures the land at its productive value.

Our procedure also measures both productive and financial income more "realistically" than conventional accounting. Households will make the wrong consumption-savings decisions if they do not recognize that the increased government debt will

lead to lower subsidies in the future. Their net financial
assets do not rise $20 when they buy government bonds, because
this is necessarily offset by a reduction in the present value
of subsidies.

3. Personal Income Taxes

3.1 Conventional Accounts

We now assume that the only tax is a personal income tax of
30%, levied on the pre-tax market income of persons. The tax
base includes market wages, but not the "cottage" labor income
used to produce leisure, or the change in the value of human
capital. It includes dividends, interest, and capital gains on
shares and bonds. It does not include subsidies.

We assume that business firms have $10,500 in physical
capital and shares at t_o, and invest another $1,000 during the
year. The market interest rate is 20%, and the pre-tax wage rate
is $1. Net dividend payments are $1,100: the "earnings" of
$2,100 less the $1,000 which is retained to finance investment.
Market consumption is $6,600. Market wages are $5,500, with
10,500 hours of leisure. Government debt is $50 at t_o, and $70
at t_1. The tax base is the $5,500 in wages, the $2,100 in
dividends plus capital gains, and the $10 interest, for a total
of $7,610. The tax payment at t_1 is therefore $2,283.

Cash flows aggregate to zero for each sector. Government
collects $2,283 in taxes and $20 from the sale of bonds. It pays
$10 interest and $2,293 in subsidies. Households receive $1,100
in dividends, $5,500 in wages, $10 in interest, and $2,293 in

subsidies,   for   a   total   of $8,903.   They   pay $6,600   for

consumption, $20 for bonds, and $2,283 in taxes, for a total of

$8,903.   Firms sell $6,600   of consumer goods, and pay $5,500 in

wages and $1,100 in dividends.   These   flows   are summarized   in

Table 10-2.

Table 10-2: Sector Cash Flows, Personal Income Tax

	Households		Business		Government	
	In	Out	In	Out	In	Out
Wages	$5,500			$5,500		
Dividends	1,100			1,100		
Consumer Goods		$6,600	$6,600			
Taxes		2,283			$2,283	
Subsidies	2,293					$2,293
Bond Interest	10					10
Bond Sale		20			20	
TOTALS	$8,903	$8,903	$6,600	$6,600	$2,303	$2,303

The major problem in generating   "conventional"   accounts is

to determine the interest rate at which   future   wages should be

discounted in valuing human capital.   The nominal and real rates

of interest are 20%.   The   "private" after-tax rate of interest,

however, is 14%.   An individual who purchases shares   receives a

20%   pre-tax   return,   but   only a 14%   after-tax   return.   The

appropriate rate for households to use in allocating consumption

over time to maximize welfare is   14%.   This is because the rate

at   which   households   can   substitute   consumption   at t_1 for

consumption at t_o is 14%, even though the nominal   interest rate is 20%.

If the tax structure causes households to discount at a lower rate than the nominal rate, this should lead to tax shifting. Households can be expected to save less if their return is 14% than if it is 20%, thereby receiving less income in the future, and paying lower taxes. In addition, leisure is not taxed. Its private opportunity cost falls relative to other consumer goods, which should also lead to tax shifting.

The price of shares is "distorted," in much the same way that the price of land was distorted by the real estate tax. The market price of a share is the present value of the pre-tax dividends less the present value of the tax liability which accompanies the share. However, the household uses a 14% discount rate, instead of a 20% rate, so that the market price also equals the present value of the pre-tax dividends discounted at the nominal interest rate of 20%.

Consider, for simplicity, a share which will pay $20 per year forever, before tax. This capitalizes to $100 at the nominal interest of 20%. The household, however, nets only $14 after tax, which also capitalizes to $100 at the after-tax rate of 14%. To the household, the pre-tax dividend of $20 has a present value of $20/.14 = $142.86. The tax of $6 has a present value of $6/.14 = $42.86. The package which is sold in the market therefore has a present value of $100.

For private decision making, households will value cottage labor at the after-tax wage rate of $.70, instead of the market wage, which represents another distortion, and should lead to additional tax shifting. This suggests that we should measure the price of leisure as $.70 in measuring the price index. Our objective is to measure utility to households, and the after-tax wage measures the (relative) utility of leisure.

For private decision making, households will calculate the value of human capital by discounting after-tax (full) wages (16,000 * $.70 = $11,200) at the after-tax interest rate (14%), rather than by discounting nominal (full) wages ($16,000) at the nominal interest rate (20%). Both calculations come to $80,000, since the (tax) reduction in wages is exactly offset by the reduction in the discount rate.

In general, however, the private present value of human capital will be influenced by the imposition of the tax, since the tax is not on total labor income (wages plus capital gain), but only on wages. Our tax scheme taxes the capital gain as well as dividend income from shares, but does not tax the capital gain component of labor income. A tax on total income does not change the present value of the future flows: the before-tax flow discounted at the nominal rate of interest, rn, equals the after-tax flow discounted at the after-tax rate of interest, (1-t)rn. A tax which exempts capital gains increases the private present value of human capital if there are positive capital gains. The present value of human capital is the same with and without the tax in our example because there are no capital gains to tax: the wages are a constant flow forever. If the wage rate were to rise through time, the after-tax present value would be greater than the before-tax present value.

We present conventional balance sheets for business and households:

CONVENTIONAL BALANCE SHEETS (BUSINESS)

	t_0	t_1
	Assets	
Physical Capital	$10,500.	$11,500.
	Equities	
Shares	$10,500.	$11,500.

CONVENTIONAL BALANCE SHEETS (HOUSEHOLD)

	t_0	t_1
	Assets	
Shares	$10,500.	$11,500.
Bonds	50.	70.
Human Capital	80,000.	80,000.
TOTALS	$90,550.	$91,570.
	Equities	
Net Wealth	$90,550.	$91,570.

These balance sheets would be appropriate for private decision making if they also recorded the present value (discounted at 14%) of the future subsidies. The tax liability is accounted for, but the benefits are not.

3.2 Social Accounts

Social accounts record the present values of future flows, discounted at the real interest rate. In determining the future we assume that t_1 represents the start of a steady state. Taxable income at t_2 is therefore $5,500 in wages plus $2,300 in dividends and $14 in bond interest, for a total of $7,814. Taxes are $2,344.20 at t_2 and thereafter.

Table 10-3: Cash Flows in Second Period, Personal Income Tax

	Households		Business		Government	
	In	Out	In	Out	In	Out
Wages	$5,500			$5,500		
Dividends	2,300			2,300		
Consumer Goods		$7,800	$7,800			
Taxes		2,344.20			$2,344.20	
Subsidies	2,330.20					$2,330.20
Bond Interest	14					14
Bond Sales	0.	0.			0.	0.
TOTALS	$10,144.20		$7,800.00		$2,344.20	

The present value of the taxes is $2,344.20/.2 = $11,721 at t_1, and ($11,721 + $2,283)/(1.2) = $11,670 at t_0, if we discount at 20%. We use 20% as the real rate even though the Appendix to this chapter indicates that the real rate is ambiguous.

The value of human capital depends on how we value leisure. If we use the $.70 value from the utility function, the flow is $12,850 annually, with $5,500 from the market, and $7,350 from the cottage, and the value of human capital is $64,250. If we use the value of $1 from the production function, the flow is $16,000 and the capitalized value is $80,000. We first use the $1 value, and then investigate the use of $.70.

The social business accounts are the same as the
conventional accounts presented earlier. The personal and
government accounts are:

SOCIAL BALANCE SHEETS (HOUSEHOLD)

	t_0	t_1
Assets		
Shares	$10,500.	$11,500.
Bonds	50.	70.
Subsidies	11,620.	11,651.
Human Capital	80,000.	80,000.
TOTALS	$102,170.	$103,221.
Equities		
Taxes	$11,670.	$11,721.
Net Wealth	90,500.	91,500.
TOTALS	$102,170.	$103,221.

SOCIAL BALANCE SHEETS (GOVERNMENT)

	t_0	t_1
Assets		
Taxes	$11,670.	$11,721.
Equities		
Bonds	$50.	$70.
Subsidies	11,620.	11,651.
TOTALS	$11,670.	$11,721.

All sectors receive 20% income on all economic instruments
(except net wealth). Only households have net income, which is
20% of net wealth, or $18,100 in the first year, and $19,100
thereafter. Personal tax payments are $2,283 at t_1, but social

accounting treats the tax liability like a financial instrument,
and includes the capital gain of -$51 as "tax" income. Personal
tax income is therefore -$2,283 - $51 = -$2,334, which is 20% of
the t_o value of the tax liability (-$11,670).

In both the household and the government accounts, tax
income (-$2,334) plus bond income ($10) plus subsidy income
(cash receipts of $2,293 plus a capital gain of $31, for a total
of $2,324) add to zero. This follows from the assumption that
the government has no net wealth. All personal income is
generated by shares and human capital if households pay all of
the taxes, own all bonds, and receive all subsidies.

Net personal income therefore equals market wages ($5,500)
plus cottage wages ($10,500), plus a capital gain of zero on
human capital, plus financial income of $2,100 (a dividend of
$1,100 plus a capital gain of $1,000), for a total of $18,100.
This is also national income, since government and business have
no (net) income.

The alternative is to value leisure at $.70, according to
the utility function. This reduces household wealth to $74,750,
and households and national income are $14,950, which is 20% of
the reduced wealth. However, the price level is not the same as
if leisure is valued at $1.00. We must make a price level
adjustment, if we compare the two balance sheets. This is
discussed in Section 7, where we consider comparisons through
time.

Since only household accounts are affected, we present

nominal and real household balance sheets, with leisure at $.70:

NOMINAL SOCIAL BALANCE SHEETS (HOUSEHOLD)

	t_o	t_1
Assets		
Shares	$10,500.	$11,500.
Bonds	50.	70.
Subsidies	11,620.	11,651.
Human Capital	64,250.	64,250.
TOTALS	$86,420.	$87,471.
Equities		
Taxes	$11,670.	$11,721.
Net Wealth	74,750.	75,750.
TOTALS	$86,420.	$87,471.

The leisure = $.70 household balance sheet differs from the
leisure = $1 balance sheet in that the ratio of physical to
human capital is larger in this case. The marginal product of
the physical capital is entirely market goods, which are
relatively more expensive. The marginal product of human capital
is partly market goods, and partly leisure, which is lower in
(relative) price.

In summary, income taxes distort the price of leisure. The
shadow price using the production function is $1, while the
shadow price from the utility function is $.70. If we use the $1
price from the production function, the real rate of interest is
20%. If we use the $.70 value for leisure from the utility
function, the real interest rate becomes ambiguous, although 20%

still seems to be the "best" rate. This implies that the price level falls, if market goods are stabilized at $1.

With the personal income tax, there is no difference between conventional and "social" national wealth if we value leisure at $1, even though conventional accounts discount at 14%, while social accounts discount at 20%. Social accounts, however, still reflect the economic situation more accurately by capitalizing subsidy income and tax liabilities, and by associating all wealth and income with households.

4. Corporate Income Taxes

We now assume that the only tax is a corporate income tax of 40%. The tax base is corporate productive income, so that bond interest is not deductible if firms issue debt.

We continue to assume that business productive income is $2,100 during the first year, and $2,300 thereafter. First year taxes are $840, dividends are $260, and $1,000 is retained for investment. Thereafter, taxes are $920 and dividends are $1,380. The nominal market interest rate is 12%, so that the return on physical capital must be 20%, following the argument of the last section. The market price of shares is $10,500 at t_0 and $11,500 at t_1. The tax deprives persons of the opportunity to transfer consumption through time at the real 20% rate, which was also the case with the personal income tax.

Government bonds yield 12%, and sell at par. Government debt is $100 at t_0 and $150 at t_1. Government collects $840 in taxes and $50 from bond sales at t_1, and pays $12 interest and

$878 in subsidies. Thereafter, tax collections are $920, interest is $18, and subsidies are $902.

Households receive $5,500 in wages, $260 in dividends, $12 in interest and $878 in subsidies at t_1, for a total of $6,650. They spend $6,600 on consumer goods and $50 for bonds, for a net cash flow of zero. Thereafter, they collect $5,500 in wages, $1,380 in dividends, $18 in interest and $902 in subsidies, and spend $7,800 on consumer goods. Consumption of leisure is $10,500 at all times.

Business sells $6,600 of consumer goods at t_1, and pays $5,500 in wages, $260 in dividends and $840 in taxes. Thereafter, sales are $7,800, and payments are $5,500 in wages, $1,380 in dividends and $920 in taxes. We summarize in Tables 10-4 and 10-5.

Table 10-4: Sector Cash Flows, Year 1, Corporate Income Taxes

	Households		Business		Government	
	In	Out	In	Out	In	Out
Wages	$5,500			$5,500		
Dividends	260			260		
Consumer Goods		$6,600	$6,600			
Taxes				840	$840	
Subsidies	878					$878
Bond Interest	12					12
Bond Sale		50				50
TOTALS	$6,650		$6,600		$890	

Table 10-5: Sector Cash Flows, Year 2, Corporate Income Taxes

	Households		Business		Government	
	In	Out	In	Out	In	Out
Wages	$5,500		$5,500			
Dividends	1,380		1,380			
Consumer Goods		$7,800	$7,800			
Taxes				920	$920	
Subsidies	902					$902
Bond Interest	18					18
Bond Sale						
TOTALS	$7,800		$7,800		$920	

Conventional accounts discount the future at the nominal interest rate of 12%. We omit government accounts, because there are no problems which we have not already discussed. The conventional business accounts would be exactly the same as the conventional business accounts with personal income taxes (p. 222). Household accounts are:

CONVENTIONAL BALANCE SHEETS (HOUSEHOLD)

	t_0	t_1
	Assets	
Shares	$10,500.	$11,500.
Bonds	100.	150.
Human Capital	133,333.	133,333.
TOTALS	$143,933.	$144,983.
	Equities	
Net Wealth	$143,933.	$144,983.

Conventional accounts discount the labor services at 12%, since this is the nominal interest rate. This looks like a huge increase in the quantity of human capital and real wealth as compared to other cases, but is seriously misleading. The flow of labor service remains at $16,000. The real interest rate is unchanged. The decline in the nominal rate increases the present value of future flows. The national income is $18,100, ($18,150 of household income less the $50 government deficit), and national wealth is $143,833 (household wealth of $143,933 less government debt of $100), for a rate of return of 12.6%, which is also misleading.

Social accounts discount all future flows, including wages, at the undistorted real rate of 20%, to determine the "social" value of shares, taxes, bonds, and subsidies.

SOCIAL BALANCE SHEETS (BUSINESS)

	t_0	t_1
	Assets	
Physical capital	$10,500.	$11,500.
	Equities	
Taxes	$4,533.	$4,600.
Shares (Social value)	5,967.	6,900.
TOTALS	$10,500.	$11,500.

SOCIAL BALANCE SHEETS (HOUSEHOLD)

Assets

Shares (Social value)	$5,967.	$6,900.
Bonds (Social value)	43.	90.
Subsidies	4,490.	4,510.
Human Capital	80,000.	80,000.
TOTALS	$90,500.	$91,500.

Equities

Net Wealth	$90,500.	$91,500.

In this case, the productive value of the physical capital
equals its market value. If the tax is on productive business
income, as we have assumed, firms must earn 12% for shareholders
and 8% for government. In making investment decisions, firms can
either discount the productive flows at 20%, or discount the net
(after-tax) cash flows to shareholders at 12%. In determining
the t_1 social value of physical capital, we discount the
productive flows of $1,100 (productive income is $2,100, less
the "purchase" of $1,000 of productive capital) at t_1 and $2,300
thereafter at 20%, to obtain $10,500, which is also the market
value. The net cash flow to shareholders is $260 at t_1 and
$1,380 thereafter. Discounted at the nominal rate of 12%, this
also gives $10,500.

The "distortion" comes in the market value of shares.
Government has in effect confiscated 40% of the shares. The
dividends are lower than they "should" be, but the market price
is unchanged, because the market rate of interest falls to 12%.

The real interest rate is 20%. If households reduce consumption by $100, they buy $100 of shares and firms invest $100, which increases future consumption by $20 annually. Shareholders (savers) get $12 of this consumption, and the rest goes to the government, and then to subsidy recipients and bondholders. This distortion presumably reduces savings and leads to tax shifting.

The social value of shares is less than the market value by the present (social) value of the taxes. The social value of the productive assets equals the market value, but the government is taking 40% of the income generated by the resources. This reduces the social value of the shares by the social value of the tax liability.

Households are compensated for this decline in social share value by the financial instruments, bonds and subsidies, generated by government. Household net social wealth is the same as in other examples. Tax shifting can be expected to reduce savings and investment, and perhaps increase the real rate of interest.

Private decision-making, however, cannot be based on either the social or the conventional accounts. Individuals must use the market interest rate of 12%, rather than the social rate of 20%, in decision-making because this is the rate at which they can exchange consumption through time. This means that the social accounts are inappropriate for private use. Conventional accounts are also inappropriate, however, because they do not account for the subsidies. They therefore underestimate private wealth for decision-making purposes.

The private accounts add the present value of future
subsidies, discounted at 12%, to the conventional
accounts:

PRIVATE BALANCE SHEETS (HOUSEHOLD)

	t_o	t_1
	Assets	
Shares	$10,500.	$11,500.
Bonds	100.	150.
Subsidies	7,495.	7,517.
Human Capital	133,333.	133,333.
TOTALS	$151,428.	$152,500.
	Equities	
Net Wealth	$151,428.	$152,500.

Private decision-makers should maximize welfare at t_o,
subject to the constraint that the present value of future
consumption, discounted at 12%, will be $151,428.   This permits
them to consume $17,100 at t_1, and $18,300 annually thereafter,
which is the observed consumption pattern. (Households consume
$6,600 of market goods at t_1, and $7,800 thereafter.   They
consume $10,500 of leisure annually).

This consumption pattern is also permitted by the social
accounts, since it has a present value of $90,500 at t_o and
$91,500 at t_1, if discounted at 20%.   It would, however, not
maximize welfare if households were constrained by the social
accounts.   The tax will change the optimal consumption pattern,

and there will be shifting.

It should also be noted that the social household balance sheet at t_1 is exactly 60% of   the   private household balance sheet at that date, because t_1 is the   start of a steady state. The steady flow is capitalized at 20% to get social values and at 12% to get private values.   The   relationship   is   more complicated at t_0, since it is not a steady state.

5.   Social Security Taxes

5.1 Taxes Paid by Employees

We now assume a 10% tax on wages, paid by households.

The numerical example is similar to the preceding ones. Market wages are $5,500 at t_0, and the tax liability and human capital are calculated on the assumption that this will continue forever.   As with the (general) income tax, the price of leisure is distorted.   Its value in production is $1, while its value in consumption is $.90.   Physical   capital is $10,500 at t_0 and $11,500 at t_1, and earns a 20% return.   Market consumption is therefore $6,600 at t_1, since net dividends are $2,100 less the investment of $1,000, and market wages are $5,500.   The flow of taxes to the government is balanced by a flow of interest and subsidies from the government.   We need not keep track of bonds and subsidies separately, since we know that the present value of the sum always adds to the present value of the taxes.

The results are essentially the same as with the personal income tax.   If we value leisure at $1, social accounts measure national income and wealth at $18,100 and $90,500, which is the same as with conventional accounts, although wealth is redistributed, and new financial instruments are created. If we value leisure at $.90, human capital declines, as with the income tax.

As with the personal income tax, balance sheets with leisure @ $.90 show a larger fraction of investment in physical capital. The leisure @ $.90, social balance sheets are:

NOMINAL SOCIAL BALANCE SHEETS (HOUSEHOLD)

	t_o	t_1
	Assets	
Shares	$10,500.	$11,500.
Bonds and Subsidies	2,750.	2,750.
Human Capital	74,750.	74,750.
TOTALS	$88,000.	$89,000.
	Equities	
Taxes	$2,750.	$2,750.
Net Wealth	85,250.	86,250.
TOTALS	$88,000.	$89,000.

5.2 Taxes Paid by Employers.

We now assume a 11.111% tax on market wages, paid by employers. The change in tax rate is employed to keep the tax payments the same. The marginal product of labor is $5,500, of which $550 goes to the government in taxes, and $4,950 goes to households, for a tax rate of (1/9) on market wages (and 10% on marginal product). The market wage rate is $.90, while other market prices are as before. The value of leisure is distorted.

It is valued at $9,450 in consumption, and $10,500 in production.

The private value of (marketed) human capital is less than its productive value. The effect of the tax is to transfer some of the human capital to firms, in the sense that firms no longer pay households for the productive value of services rendered. The previous taxes did not have this effect because firms only paid taxes on the marginal product of capital. Social security taxes require payment of taxes on the marginal product of labor, and profit-maximizing firms will pay wages which are less than labor productivity.

If we value leisure at $1.00, the social balance sheets are:

SOCIAL BALANCE SHEETS (BUSINESS)

	t_0	t_1
	Assets	
Physical capital	$10,500.	$11,500.
Human capital	2,750.	2,750.
TOTALS	$13,250.	$14,250.
	Equities	
Taxes	$2,750.	$2,750.
Shares	10,500.	11,500.
TOTALS	$13,250.	$14,250.

SOCIAL BALANCE SHEETS (HOUSEHOLD)

	t_0	t_1
	Assets	
Shares	$10,500.	$11,500.
Bonds & Subsidies	2,750.	2,750.
Human Capital	77,250.	77,250.
TOTALS	$90,500.	$91,500.
	Equities	
Net Wealth	$90,500.	$91,500.

Social national wealth and income are the same as always. The value of human capital is also the same, except that the tax has transferred $2,750 of the human capital from households to firms. The households are compensated by $2,750 of financial assets (subsidies and bonds). The firms are penalized by a financial liability for taxes which exactly offsets the human capital which they receive. The consolidated balance sheet is exactly the same as when the tax is paid by households.

Social income at t_1 is 20% of the t_0 wealth of $90,500. Households get $4,950 in wages, $2,100 from shares, $10,500 in cottage labor income, and $550 in bond and subsidy income, for a total income of $18,100. Investment is $1,000, and consumption is $17,100.

If we value leisure at $.90, as in consumption, we get the same kind of results as with the personal income tax. The distinctive feature of the social security tax is the transfer of human capital from households to firms.

6. Excise Taxes

The last tax we shall consider in an excise tax, imposed on a single product (industry), and payable by firms.

I assume that taxes and subsidies are expected to be $200 per year, forever. Nominal market consumption is $6,800 at t_1 and $7,000 thereafter. Leisure consumption is $10,500 every year, wages are $5,500, and nominal physical capital and share values rise from $10,500 at t_0 to $11,500 at t_1. Dividends are $1,100 at t_1 and $2,300 at t_2.

Table 10-6: Sector Cash Flows, Excise Tax

	Households In	Households Out	Business In	Business Out	Government In	Government Out
Wages	$5,500			$5,500		
Dividends	1,100			1,100		
Consumer Goods		$6,800	$6,800			
Taxes				200	$200	
Subsidies		200				$200
TOTALS	$6,800		$6,800		$200	

Conventional business balance sheets will show assets and equities of $10,500 at t_0, and $11,500 at t_1, as in Section 3 (page 222). If we assume a nominal interest rate of 20%, social balance sheets will have to record a $1,000 tax liability, and the problem is to discover corresponding assets.

The solution is to note that both labor and capital in the taxed industry must have marginal products which exceed those in other industries, and which exceed the private return to wage earners and shareholders. Labor must be productive enough to cover the wage of $1 plus the excise tax, which I shall assume to be 50% of "cost." Labor in the taxed industry must therefore have a productive value of $1.50 per hour. Similarly, capital must earn 30%, instead of 20%.

If taxes are $200, "costs" must be $400, divided between wages and a 20% dividend to shareholders, assuming that the taxed industry produces no untaxed goods, and does not invest.[5] For example, if wages are $300, the dividend must be $100, so that physical capital is $500. However, labor must have a marginal product of $450, and capital a marginal product of $150, so that the industry can pay taxes of $200.

The productive value of the capital must therefore be $250 higher than its market value, bringing the total productive value of physical capital to $10,750. As with the social security tax, we capitalize the value of the "taxed" marginal product of labor, and assign this as human capital to firms. However, we do not subtract this from the household value of human capital, since market wages are still $5,500.

National wealth is therefore $91,500 at t_0, and national income at t_1 is 20% of this wealth, or $18,300. National income accrues to households, and is $1,100 dividends, $1,000 capital gain, $200 subsidy, and $16,000 wages. At t_2, income will be 20% of $92,500, or $18,500, consisting of $2,300 dividends, $200 subsidy, and $16,000 wages. These measurements are independent of the way the tax liability is allocated to physical and human capital.

The social balance sheets are:

SOCIAL BALANCE SHEETS (BUSINESS)

	t_o	t_1
Assets		
Physical Capital	$10,750.	$11,750.
Human Capital	750.	750.
TOTALS	$11,500.	$12,500.
Equities		
Taxes	$1,000.	$1,000.
Shares	10,500.	11,500.
TOTALS	$11,500.	$12,500.

SOCIAL BALANCE SHEETS (HOUSEHOLD)

	t_o	t_1
Assets		
Shares	$10,500.	$11,500.
Subsidies	1,000.	1,000.
Human Capital	80,000.	80,000.
TOTALS	$91,500.	$92,500.
Equities		
Net Wealth	$91,500.	$92,500.

7. Comparisons of Real Social Income and Wealth

The previous sections have been concerned with developing a balance sheet which reflects economic reality, and which shows more reasonable government accounts. We have assumed profit maximizing firms for the purpose of measuring the marginal productivity of labor and capital with different tax schemes. We have not used economic theory to estimate tax shifting, i. e., the changes in prices and quantities brought about when households and firms optimize after taxes have been imposed.

Measures of real income and wealth correct nominal accounts for changes in prices so that meaningful comparisons can be made through time, or between different economies at the same time. Price indices measure the change through time in the cost of a fixed market basket, and the indices are influenced by tax shifting, as well as other events which change relative prices.

In this section, we look at some shifting possibilities, and show that the social accounts which we have developed give reasonable results when we use some very simple shifting assumptions. This does not, to be sure, demonstrate that our results are also reasonable with more complicated shifting. However, an accounting scheme which gives unreasonable results in simple cases is very unlikely to give reasonable results in more complicated cases.

The fundamental problem is that we have no criteria for assessing the reasonableness of results in complicated cases. We are therefore forced to rely on simple cases where we have a chance of assessing reasonableness. My judgment is that the social accounts give better comparisons through time, and therefore are preferrable to conventional accounts for both descriptive and comparative purposes.

The standard comparison is with a "no-tax" case, constructed on the assumption that the quantities produced

without a tax would be the same as the quantities with the tax,
and on various simple assumptions about the prices which would
prevail with no tax. The "reasonable" result is therefore to
measure real national income and wealth as the same with or
without the tax.

The difficulty, of course, is that theory tells us that
quantities change when relative prices change. Theory then tells
us that real income and wealth should usually fall as a result
of the tax, but does not tell us how large the fall should be.

7.1 Real Estate Taxes.

The real estate tax provides the clearest argument.   The
simplest assumption is that there is no shifting: prices and
quantities produced and consumed are exactly as they would be
without the tax. The market price of the land will fall by the
capitalized value of the tax. No other prices need be affected,
and the consumer price index stands at 1.00.

In this case, social accounts are clearly more reasonable
than conventional accounts. If we compare an economy with a real
estate tax to an economy without a tax on the no-shifting
assumption, our accounts say that real national wealth and
income are the same with and without the tax. Conventional
accounts say that real national income is unchanged, but that
the tax destroys some real wealth. There has, by assumption,
been no decline in the ability of the resources to produce
future income and utility. It is not reasonable to say that real
national wealth has declined.

If the tax is really on "pure" land, economic theory suggests that the tax cannot be shifted, in the sense that the market value of the land should be reduced by the capitalized value of the tax. Theory suggests, however, that there will be changes in relative prices associated with demand shifts caused by the redistribution of wealth and income which were presumably the purpose of the tax. In addition, the tax is likely to include improvements as well as pure land, in which case theory suggests that shifting is to be expected.

The simple assumption of no shifting is therefore almost surely unrealistic. In the real world, even real estate taxes cause changes in relative prices, output, and consumption. We may reasonably expect, however, that these adjustments will be relatively small. Furthermore, conventional accounting would give "wrong" results if there were no shifting, and is unlikely to produce "correct" results in real-world situations. Social accounting gives the correct results with no shifting, and is therefore likely to do better in the real world.

7.2   Personal Income Tax.

The "no-shifting" assumption in this case would mean that market prices and quantities of consumer goods would be unchanged by the tax. The wage rate would presumably be $1 in keeping with the prices of consumer goods. Leisure would therefore be valued at $1. National wealth would rise to $91,500 at t_1 from $90,500 at t_0, and national income would rise to $18,300 from $18,100. Since these coincide with the conventional

figures, conventional accounting gives the "correct" comparison
with the no-tax no-shifting case.

If we value leisure at $1 for social accounting purposes,
the social accounts give the same measurements as the
conventional accounts, and the same comparisons. The valuation
of leisure at $.70, however, presents problems. National wealth
is only $74,750 at t_o, and rise to $75,750 at t_1. We can
concentrate on wealth because income is always 20% of wealth and
both figures move in the same way.

These figures are in nominal dollars, however, and need to
be corrected for price level changes, since the relative price
of leisure is lower with the $.70 value. If we use the no-tax
case as 100, we get a price index of 81.58 (= $17,100/$13,950)
if we use the t_1 market basket of consumer goods, and an index
of 82.79 (= $15,150/$18,300) if we use the t_2 basket. Real
social national wealth is therefore $91,629 at t_o and $92,855 at
t_1 using the t_1 market basket, and $90,292 at t_o and $91,500 at
t_1 using the t_2 market basket.

These results are difficult to interpret. The use of base
year weights makes the price index look higher at t_2 than at t_1
even though there are no price changes between t_1 and t_2, which
is a common problem with the implicit GNP deflator. The t_2
market basket gives the "correct" wealth at t_1, but all other
measurements are difficult to assess. The fundamental problem
may be that we are assuming that leisure is valued at $1. with
no taxes and $.70 with taxes, when market consumption is the

same in both cases, as is the split in activity between market
labor and cottage labor. The slopes of the indifference curves
should be the same in both cases, and there should be only one
shadow price for labor. The "simple" assumption of no shifting
apparently contradicts utility maximizing. Optimal behavior
requires shifting, since the relative price of leisure
consumption falls relative to market consumption as a result of
the tax.

My conclusion is that valuation of leisure according to the
production function ($1) is better for comparative purposes than
valuation according to the utility function ($.70), since it
side steps this problem. If we use the $1 for social accounting,
we get the same comparative results that we get with
conventional accounting, although we still get better
measurements of household income and wealth using social
accounts.

7.3 Corporate Income Tax

The no-shifting assumption with a corporate income tax
leaves the price index at 1.00. Social accounts give the same
measurement of national wealth and income that we would get if
there were no taxes and no shifting, which is not an
unreasonable conclusion. If there is no shifting, dividends are
reduced 40%, and the income and wealth are redistributed, and we
have pretty much the same situation as with the real estate tax.

Conventional accounts, however, discount at 12% instead of
20%, which leads to a huge increase in human capital. National

wealth therefore rises, even though national income and consumption do not increase. Social accounts are clearly superior if there is no shifting, since they give a better measure of wealth, and the same measurement of income.

Theory tells us to expect some shifting, however. The rate at which consumers can exchange consumption through time is 12% with the tax and 20% without it. Savings (consumption) patterns should therefore change, as we noted when we presented private balance sheets (page 233).

7.4 Social Security Taxes

The no-shifting assumption suggests that nominal wage costs to firms will be reduced by the amount of the tax that is paid by firms. Prices and quantities of market consumer goods need not change. The no-tax no-shifting national income and wealth are the same as with the conventional accounts. The "market consumption" price index is 1.00. The "full consumption" price index depends on whether we value leisure according to its productive value ($1) or its utility value ($.90).

The only difference between this and the personal income tax case is that the market interest rate is the same as the social interest rate of 20%, since social security taxes are not imposed on the marginal product of capital.

The only question is the valuation of leisure. The discussion in connection with the personal income tax is apparenty unchanged. Valuation according to the productive value gives the same results as the conventional accounting. Valuation according to utility produces unreliable results.

7.5 Excise Taxes

In this case, both conventional accounts and social accounts measure national income as $18,300 at t_1, although there is the usual difference in that conventional accounts measure government income as equal to the deficit, while social accounts measure government income as zero. Social accounts, however, measure national wealth as $1,000 more than conventional accounts at both t_0 and t_1.

There are two "simple" no-tax no-shifing alternatives. In both cases quantities are unaffected. In one case, the tax is shifted forward, so that the no-tax price is lower than the taxed price. In the other case, the tax is shifted backwards so that prices of consumer goods are the same with and without tax.

Consider first backward shifting. National income and wealth would be exactly the same as with social accounts. There would be no changes in the price level, and social accounts would give the "correct" answer: if there is no shifting, the tax does not affect national wealth or income. Conventional accounts show a decline in national wealth, with no decline in income, and give an inferior comparison.

Forward shifting means that no-tax accounts would show an income of $18,100 at t_1, and national wealth in conformity to the conventional accounts. A price-level correction would be required, however, so that neither the conventional nor the social accounts would measure real national income and wealth as equal to the no-tax figures.

I conclude again that social accounts are better for comparative purposes.

8. Discussion

The conclusion is that social accounts always provide a better description of the economic situation because they capitalize government taxes and subsidies, in addition to bonds.

They also usually give better comparisons of national income and wealth over time, at least on simple shifting assumptions. The superiority is clearer in the measurement of national wealth than national income. The real estate tax, for example, gives the same measurement of national income on both social and conventional accounts, but conventional accounts suggest that the tax would destroy real national wealth even if the tax were not shifted and there were no changes in economic activity.

Even in the measurment of income, however, social accounting gives a better picture of the distribution of income by assigning all income to households, and insisting that government has no net income.

In the real world, government does not confine itself to taxing and subsidizing. It also purchases goods and services, provides subsidized goods and services to both persons and firms, and uses resources to administer its programs. Finally, there are times when it appears that the government balance sheet does not balance.

I would argue that the assumption of no net wealth for government is the only viable one. In a world of certainty, the government would be bankrupt if it had negative net wealth, and citizens would no doubt insist on tax reductions if it had positive net wealth. In an uncertain world, there may be times when the laws on the books generate positive or negative net wealth for government. However, I interpret this to mean that the laws will be changed in the future, not that the imbalance in the government accounts is permanent.

There does not seem to be any alternative to accounting for government productive activities in the same way that we account for business, with the added assumption that the goods and services provided are worth exactly what they cost, as in long-run competitive equilibrium. This is essentially what is done in conventional accounting, except that the value of productive resources owned by government is not carried on the balance sheet, as it should be. Conventional accounts will have to be supplemented by 1) projections of tax receipts and subsidy payments, and 2) estimates of the market value of government owned productive resources, if we are to construct social accounts of the kind envisioned here.

Appendix

The Real Interest Rate

We adopt the definition of the social real rate of interest used by Solow [37, Chapter 1]. This appendix draws heavily on Solow's monograph. The real social rate is the rate at which society can transfer real consumption through time. If there are no taxes, and the rate of inflation is zero, this is the increase in income (product) divided by the investment required to generate the extra income, and equals the nominal rate of interest. This appendix considers the effect of a personal income tax on the social real rate, as opposed to the private real rate.

The problem becomes more complicated if the interest rate changes through time, since income changes even when investment is zero. It is necessary first to determine what income would have been with no investment, and then define the social real rate of interest as the increase above this hypothetical level divided by last year's net investment.

We therefore follow Solow's suggestion and assume that the society has a planned or expected growth path, and investigate the additional (as compared to the plan) future consumption which is made possible by the sacrifice (as compared to the plan) of current consumption. In principle, we can either 1) take all of the additional consumption in the next period, or 2) take the additional consumption as a constant flow forever. If the rate of interest is stable through time, these two calculations lead to the same interest rate. If the rate of interest fluctuates, these rates differ. However, the one-year rate is the appropriate discount rate in capitalizing future flows. Hicks [20, Chapter 14] suggests that the perpetual rate should be used in defining income, but we are using the more conventional concept of income which says that wealth should be maintained, rather than perpetual consumption.

The one-year rate (1+rr) is the increase in income caused by the sacrificed consumption, divided by the sacrificed consumption. The society could restore itself to the planned path by consuming the extra income, and the original sacrificed consumption, in the year after the sacrifice. As we shall see, one of the peculiarities of our model is that "investment" and "sacrificed consumption" may not be the same thing.

Our model is similar to the one used in the text of the Chaper. K_0 ($10,500) is the value of initial capital. The nominal interest rate is rn (20%). Human capital (HK) is measured by discounting the future wage flows, including both market wages (MW) and cottage wages (CW), at the (yet to be determined) real rate of interest, rr. The total labor hours available are H = 16,000. There is a personal income tax of t (30%), imposed on market wages, dividends, interest, and capital gains on shares. There is no tax on cottage labor, or capital gains on human capital. There is no government debt. Personal tax paid equals personal subsidies received, and these flows can be ignored since they cancel out. It would complicate the analysis, but not change the outcome, if government had debt.

The opportunity cost of leisure is "distorted." The market wage is $1, and the production function says that $1 of market goods are sacrificed for each hour of leisure consumed. However, the opportunity cost (shadow price) of cottage labor (leisure) is only $(1-t)(\$1) = \$.70$, if we value leisure using the utility function, since households get an after-tax market wage of only $(1-t)$. Our procedure is to determine the real interest rate if the opportunity cost of leisure is $(1-t)$, from the utility function, and then assume $t = 0$ to determine the real interest rate if the opportunity cost is taken from the production function.

The formal model has two decision (independent) variables per year. At t_0, the society has inherited physical capital, K_0, and households decide a) how much labor time to spend in the market (MW_1), which determines cottage time and leisure consumption (CW_1), and b) how much to spend on market consumption (MC_1), which determines investment in physical capital (K_1). Human capital (HK) is the discounted value of the future wages, MW + CW. Income (Y) equals consumption (MC + WC) plus investment $(K_1 - K_0) + (HK_1 - HK_0)$, and also equals the interest on the physical capital plus the interest on the human capital. We include the changes in human capital as investment and income because households must include human capital as wealth if they are to make optimal decisions. As we shall see, however, the fact that we have no explicit mechanism for

investing in human capital by sacrificing consumption, as we
have with physical capital, creates some anomalies in the model.

At t_1, households again decide on market labor activity
(MW_2), and market consumption (MC_2), for year 2. Eventually, the
model assumes a steady state. In the year in which the steady
state is inaugurated, either MW or MC can be determined
independently, and the other is determined so that investment in
physical capital is zero. Subsequent years duplicate the last
year, which also makes investment in human capital equal zero.

For simplicity, our numerical example assumes that the
steady state is inaugurated at t_2, which means that either MW_2
or MC_2 is determined so that $K_2 = K_1$.

(1) $CW_i = (1-t)(H - MW_i) = 11200 - .7MW_i$

$MW_i + CW_i = (1-t)H + t(MW_i) = 11200 + .3MW_i$ for all i

Cottage income equals leisure consumption, and is the cottage
wage rate (1-t) times the number of hours available ($H - MW_i$).

(2) $K_i = (1+rn_i)K_{i-1} - (MC_i - MW_i)$ for all i

$K_1 = 12600 - MC_1 + MW_1$

K_i increases by the difference between $(rn_i)K_{i-1}$ and
dividends. The return to shareholders must be $(rn_i)K_{i-1}$, and is
the sum of dividends and capital gain (increase in K). The
dividend is the difference between sales (MC_i) and wage payments
(MW_i), since there are no cash balances. Alternatively, the firm
"produces" $(rn_i)K_{i-1} + MW_i$, of which MC_i is consumer goods, and
the rest is investment.

The assumption of a steady state implies that $K_2 = K_1$:

(3) $K_2 = (1+rn_2)K_1 - MC_2 + MW_2 = K_1$

$MC_2 = (rn)K_1 + MW_2 = MW_2 + (rn)[(1+rn)K_o - (MC_1 - MW_1)]$

$= MW_2 + 2520 - (.2)(MC_1 - MW_1)$

From (1), the cash flow to labor at t_2 [$MW_2 + CW_2 = (1-t)H$ + tMW_2] is $11,200 + .3MW_2$, and is assumed to continue forever as a steady state. To obtain HK_1, we capitalize $MW_2 + CW_2$ at rr, the unknown real rate of interest.

(4) $HK_1 = [H - t(H - MW_2)]/rr_2$

To obtain HK_o, we use (1) again, and get the present value of $MW_1 + CW_1$, followed by $MW_2 + CW_2$ as a perpetuity.

(5) $HK_o = [(1-t)H + t(MW_1) + HK_1]/(1+rr_1)$

If the real interest rate does not change ($rr_2 = rr_1$), then

(6) $HK_1 - HK_o = t(MW_2 - MW_1)/(1+rr)$

Income is consumption plus investment, which also equals the return on capital:

(7) $Y_i = MC_i + CW_i + K_i + HK_i - K_{i-1} - HK_{i-1}$

$= rn_i K_{i-1} + rr_i HK_{i-1}$

This model has the usual properties. Financial income equals the interest on financial (and physical) capital. Labor income equals the interest on human capital, to which we add the interest on physical capital to get total income.

There are some unusual characteristics, however. If the tax rate is zero, human capital is simply the capitalized value of the available hours. If the tax rate is positive, then the wage rate for market labor is larger than the wage for cottage labor, and human capital rises as labor is shifted from the cottage to the market. According to (4) and (5), HK_1 depends on MW_2, and HK_0 depends upon both MW_1 and MW_2.

If $t > 0$, the one-year real rate is ambiguous. We can sacrifice either leisure consumption or market consumption, and the bonus future consumption can also be either leisure or market consumption. Solow's real rate equals the rate of return on physical capital (rn) if and only if the sacrificed consumption and the bonus consumption are of the same kind, or if the the bonus consumption is in proportion to the sacrificed consumption of each kind.

Assume that rn=.2 and K_0 = \$10,500. We should discount wages at the unknown real rate of interest. We start by discounting wages at 20%, and call this rhk, the interest rate on human capital. The initial plan, which is summarized in the first two lines of Table A1, calls for MW_1 = MW_2 = \$5,500 and MC_1 = \$6,600. This implies that HK_0 = HK_1 = \$64,250. Furthermore, Y_1 = \$14,950, and K_1 = \$11,500, for investment of \$1,000. If we now set MC_2 = \$7,800, we find Y_2 = \$15,150 and K_2 = K_1 and HK_2 = HK_1, as required. Investment of \$1,000 increases income (product) \$200, for a return of 20%.

Suppose now that people alter the plan by consuming \$100 fewer market goods at t_1 (MC_1 = \$6,500), and taking the "gain" by increasing future market consumption as a perpetuity. This is summarized as alternative A (rows 3 and 4) of Table A1. MW_1 and MW_2 remain at \$5,500, while MC_2 rises by \$20 to \$7,820, and Y_2 also rises by \$20 to \$15,170.

Table A1. Wages Discounted at 20%

	CW	MC	TC	Y	K_{-1}	HK_{-1}	rhk	rr
Plan, t_1	7,350	6,600	13,950	14,950	10,500	64,250	.2	
Plan, t_2	7,350	7,800	15,150	15,150	11,500	64,250	.2	
A, t_1	7,350	6,500	13,850	14,950	10,500	64,250	.2	
A, t_2	7,350	7,820	15,170	15,170	11,600	64,250	.2	.2
B, t_1	7,350	6,500	13,850	14,945	10,500	64,225	.2	
B, t_2	7,364	7,800	15,164	15,164	11,600	64,220	.2	.14
C, t_1	7,280	6,600	13,880	14,950	10,500	64,250	.2	
C, t_2	7,364	7,800	15,164	15,164	11,600	64,220	.2	.2
D, t_1	7,280	6,600	13,880	14,955	10,500	64,275	.2	
D, t_2	7,350	7,820	15,170	15,170	11,600	64,250	.2	.286

The sacrifice of $100 of market consumption at t_1 increases future income and consumption by $20, for a real interest rate of 20%, which is also the nominal rate (rn) and the rate at which we discounted wages (rhk). Investment at t_1 is defined as income minus consumption, and is $1,100. Investment increases by the amount of the sacrificed consumption.

The next alternative, B, supposes that people sacrifice market consumption but decide to take the extra consumption as leisure, rather than in the market. This means that the first year of alternative B is the same as the first year of alternative A. They differ in the second year, however. Alternative A maintains CW as planned in year 2, and takes its reward in MC. Alternative B restores planned MC in year 2, and gets the benefits of larger CW. Physical capital maintenance (Equation 3) requires that MW_2 be reduced by $20 to $5,480, so that leisure consumption (CW_2) rises by $14, to $7,364, compared to the plan. This is a real rate of only 14%, since the sacrifice of $100 in year 1 increases income by $14 in year 2.

We must keep referring to the plan because alternative B still shows a 20% return on "investment" undertaken in year 1. Even though sacrificed consumption is $100, "investment" only increases by $95, because the changed behavior causes a revaluation of human capital and income in both years. HK_0 is $25 under plan at $64,225, because of the change in MW_2, so that Y_1 is $5 less than planned, at $14,945. HK_1 is $30 less than plan at $64,220, and K_2 is $100 above plan because of the sacrificed consumption, causing Y_2 to be $14 [= 20% of ($100 - $30)] under plan. Alternative B therefore shows investment of $1,095 in year 1, and an increase in income of $219, for a return of 20%.

The real rate of interest, as defined by Solow, is only 14%. The "facts" that income is lower in year 1 under the revision than it would have been under the plan, and that human capital has similarly been changed from the plan, are totally irrelevant. Consumption possibilities are all that matter. We sacrificed $100 of market consumption (as compared to the plan, not as compared to the previous year), and income is $14 larger than it would have been had we stuck to the plan. This is a "real" return of 14%.

We get similar results if we revise the plan in year 1 by
working an additional 100 hours in the market and consuming $70
less leisure. Alternative C takes additional leisure in year 2,
and continues MC as planned. We reduce market labor by $20 to
$5,480, and increase leisure conumption by $14, for a return of
20%. It also shows $1,070 of investment, so that additional
investment and sacrificed consumption are equal.

Alternative D returns to the planned leisure consumption of
$7,350 in year 2, and increases market consumption to $7,820,
which is $20 over plan. This gives us a real rate of return of
28.6%, since the sacrifice of $70 of leisure consumption permits
us to increase market consumption $20. Again, the rate of return
on investment, measured from alternative D, is 20%. HK_o is $25
larger than plan, so that Y_1 is $5 above plan. HK_1 reverts to
plan, so that the revised data show negative investment of $25
in human capital, with net investment at $1,075, so that extra
investment is $5 larger than sacrificed consumption. Revised Y_2
is $215 above the revised Y_1, for a return on "investment" of
20%.

Finally, it is possible to reduce consumption by reducing
both market and leisure consumption. This has the same effect as
two changes: first reduce market consumption, and then reduce
leisure consumption. We therefore obtain a 20% real rate if we
recoup the sacrificed market consumption in the market, and
recoup the sacrificed leisure consumption in the cottage.

We should also investigate the influence of the rate used

to discount wages, rhk, on the measurement of the real interest
rate, and we summarize the results in Table A2. In this example,
we discount wages at 30% instead of 20%. The "real" plan is the
same as before. We have changed ony the discount rate on human
capital. HK is obviously much lower if we discount at 30% rather
than 20%. However, nothing else changes in year 1 becauswe have
assumed that neither market labor nor interest rates change from
year to year. We then consider alternative B, where we sacrifice
market consumption (MC_1) and increase leisure consumption (CW_2).
While there is a slight change in Y_2, as compared to Table 2
when rhk=.2, there is no change in the real rate of interest,
which continues to be 14%.

Table A2. Wages Discounted at 30%

	CW	MC	TC	Y	K_{-1}	HK_{-1}	rhk	rr
Plan, t_1	7,350	6,600	13,950	14,950	10,500	42,833	.3	
Plan, t_2	7,350	7,800	15,150	15,150	11,500	42,833	.3	
B, t_1	7,350	6,500	13,850	14,945+	10,500	42,818	.3	
B, t_2	7,364	7,800	15,164	15,164	11,600	42,813	.3	.14

The one-year real interest rate is independent of the rate
at which we capitalize wages. This is because HK_o is
recalculated when we change MW_1 or MW_2. It therefore makes no
difference to the measurement of the real rate of interest,
whether we capitalize wages at the real rate, or at any
arbitrary rate (which does not even have to be constant from
year to year), although the rate at which we capitalize wages

does influence the measurement of wealth and income.

The model forces all sacrificed consumption into physical capital. There is no way to "invest" in human capital by sacrificing consumption. Since the real rate of interest measures the increased consumption made possible by sacrificing current consumption, it is related to the productivity of physical capital, but not to the productivity of human capital.

This also explains why the real rate is always rn (20%) if we value leisure at $1, according to the production function, which effectively means that t = 0.

It therefore makes sense to use the nominal return on physical capital as the real rate. 1) The opportunity cost of leisure is distorted. If we value leisure according to the production function, the real rate is the nominal rate. 2) Even if we value leisure according to the utility function, the real return will equal the return on physical capital if the society reaps the reward in the same kind of consumption that is sacrificed. 3) To the extent that investment in human capital is governed by economic forces, we should expect the rate of return on investment in human capital to approximate the return to physical capital, so that we should discount returns to human capital and physical capital at the same rate.

Uncertainty

Additional problems arise if there is uncertainty, and we are not permitted to recalculate the balance sheets on the basis of information obtained after the balance sheet is prepared. The

balance sheet drawn up at t_o depends on estimates of MW_1 and
MW_2, and cannot be changed if it develops that our estimates
were inaccurate.

As an example, assume that we expect MW to be $5,500
forever. We would measure human capital at t_o as $64,250, and
market capital as $10,500. Income at t_1 should therefore be
$14,950, with leisure consumption of $7,350. If market
consumption is $7,600, then K_1 would also be $10,500, and a
long-run equilibrium would exist.

Assume that we observe MW_1 = $5,600, CW_1 = $7,280, and MC_1
= $7,600. This will make K_1 = $10,600, and Y_1 = $14,970, if we
believe that market wages will revert to the "normal" level of
$5,500. Earnings on shares will be $2,100 as always, and labor
income will be MW_1 + CW_1 = $16,030. There will be no capital
gain for labor, since the t_1 value of human capital will still
be $64,250. The t_o value of human capital was in fact $64,275,
but the balance sheet drawn up at t_o recorded $64,250, and we
are not allowed to change the balance sheet. The $25 capital
loss will not be included in income, and Y_1 will be measured as
$14,980 (instead of its "true" value of $14,955). This also
means that investment will be measured as $100 (instead of its
"true" value of $75).

At t_1, we will have $10,600 of market capital and $64,250
of human capital. If expectations are correct, Y_2 will be
observed as $14,970. The $100 investment at t_1 will result in a
lower income in Y_2 than in Y_1. Note that the "true" values give

the "correct" result.   "True" income is $15 higher at t_2 than at t_1, and "true" investment at t_1 is $75, for a 20% return.

The conclusion should still be, however, that the real rate is 20%. The real rate is not necessarily the market rate, nor is it the "observed" return.   We are engaged in a theoretical exercise.   We are asking the rate at which society can exchange consumption in one year for consumption in another year.   Taxes distort private decision-making, and uncertainty distorts measured values.   "True" measurements, however, reveal that the real rate is 20%, even though households use 14%, and national income figures may show almost anything.   The best accounting measurements which we can make require that we use the best possible estimate of the real rate, which is 20%.

We should also note that we have investigated a very narrow kind of uncertainty.   The market rate of 20% is not subject to uncertainty, nor is the wage rate. The only uncertainty comes in estimating the split between cottage and market labor.   Other kinds of uncertainty would surely make it more difficult to estimate the real rate.

Chapter XI
Business Accounting

Accounting in a Crusoe economy is based upon equation (9), Chapter 2, which also has important implications for "real-world" accounting. Our previous discussions of equation (9) emphasized the idea that it implies that the discounted value of the future returns to shareholders will equal the market value of the productive assets. We also made the usual assumption that the market price of shares equals the discounted value of future cash flows to shareholders. This implies that the firm's balance sheet will show zero net wealth if all economic instruments are valued at market price. Since we were assuming that there were well established markets for all economic instruments, we based our accounting system on market prices and market transactions.

Traditional business accounting (GAAP) generally does not value economic instruments at market for balance sheet purposes, but usually relies on historical (cost and revenue) information, although it also emphasizes the idea that an asset is a "service potential," which suggests that its value ought to reflect its future benefits, rather than its historical cost.

It would be possible to base Crusoe accounting on either a historical (past transactions) basis, or on a service-potential (future) basis, as well as the market (price) basis previously discussed. This chapter first develops the theory of historical and service-potential accounting, and then turns to a discussion of GAAP, and some possible modifications which would be more in keeping with the theories presented here.

1. Historical (Cost-Based) Accounting

A. The Crusoe Case.

We start the firm at t_o by recording sales of shares and purchases of productive instruments. Since we follow our usual practice of distinguishing between "medium of exchange" and "store of value," net cash flows are zero at any point in time. A balance sheet which reports equities equal to historical cash inflows, and assets equal to historical cash outflows (costs) will therefore balance. At t_o there is no difference between market prices and historical costs, so that a historical balance sheet coincides with the market-price balance sheet which we have previously discussed.

The balance sheet need not list the items purchased. We can lump all assets together, or we can disaggregate and identify classes of assets, which would presumably be the capital goods which enter the production function. Unlike GAAP, however, we do not need to decide whether the item purchased qualifies as an asset, or is an expense. Every purchase is part of the cost of one of the classes of assets we identify.

Historical accounting then measures the interest "cost" of the equity capital at the nominal interest rate, rn. At t_1, this is added to both equities, and to assets at cost. Equities therefore measure the amount the firm "owes" its shareholders. An alternative interpretation is that it measures the amount which must be returned to shareholders to justify the faith which shareholders put in the firm when they bought the shares.

Shareholders expected a return of rn when they bought the shares. The firm "owes" them this return, i. e., has an obligation to provide this return for them.

In addition, all purchases of productive instruments are added to assets, and sales are subtracted. The fundamental idea of cost-based accounting is that all purchases are costs, and they are all capitalized. Since sales are negative purchases, they must also be negative costs, which we call cost recoveries. This procedure measures assets at unrecovered cost. If sales exceed purchases, unrecovered costs decline. If purchases exceed sales, they increase.

Finally, sales of shares are added to shareholders equity, and purchases (counting the payment of dividends as a purchase of shares) are subtracted. Since net cash flows are always identically zero, this process leaves the books in balance, and the process can be repeated annually.

In general, the book value of historical cost (HC) of productive instruments at time t is

$$HC_t = HC_{t-1} (1 + rn_t)$$

$$+ (Purchases_t - Sales_t) \text{ of productive instruments.}$$

The book value of historical equity (HE) is:

$$HE_t = HE_{t-1} (1+rn_t)$$

$$+ (Sales_t - Purchases_t) \text{ of financial instruments.}$$

These book values must be equal because net cash flows must be zero at any time, t. (We have our usual problem with signs. The equation for financial instruments should subtract sales and add purchases, just as the equation for productive instruments does. It would then be true that $HC_t = -HE_t$.)

The cost of productive instruments includes interest on the money borrowed to acquire the instruments. The benefits which the firm expects to get increase because capital has a marginal product if it is properly employed. A Crusoe economy is always in long-run equilibrium, so that shareholders always actually receive the return which they expect when they purchase shares. The balance sheet prepared by using market values is always identical to the one based on historical costs.

There is one problem, however. If the firm has more than one type of physical capital, for example buildings, plant, and iventory, there is no way for historical cost accounting to allocate the costs to the different assets with knowing either a) market prices, or b) shadow prices. The problem arises because we must assign cost recoveries (sales) to individual assets, and there is no theory which permits us to do this if there is more than one class of capital goods.[1] This need not pose a problem for finished goods inventory, for which a market price is known. It may well be a problem for other assets for which there are no markets.

This also means that we have difficulty allocating the interest cost to individual assets. The aggregate procedure defined above works as long as the system in in equilibrium. Disaggregation, however, is not possible on the basis of cost data alone. Prices, or at least shadow prices, must be available for disaggregation, even in the Crusoe case.

B.   A more general case.

   In the real world, uncertainty, transactions costs, and the absense of constant returns to scale, give rise to problems which are not present in a Crusoe economy. We observe more than one kind of financial instrument (debt as well as shares), and the different instruments yield different interest rates. The counterpart of this is that assets also have different yields (marginal products), or a different probability that they will generate enough sales to recover all of the costs incurred in their acquisition. It also becomes rational for firms to have financial assets as well as financial equities (debt and shares).

   In this section, we consider the problems which arise because there is uncertainty, and different assets are in different risk classes. Different assets therefore have different yields, and different liabilities and shares have different costs. We also introduce problems created by transaction costs and interaction.

   We start with two problems 1) should all of the interest costs, including the cost of equity capital, be capitalized, or should some be expensed, and 2) should assets be charged costs at a rate equal to the average cost of capital for the firm, or at a rate which varies from asset to asset?

   Both Anthony [1, Chapter 7] and FAS 34 [14, paragraphs 38 - 50] consider the possibility of capitalizing all interest, and decide that this is not appropriate. FAS 34 is simply not prepared to consider such a radical inovation. Anthony recommends treating a return on equity as a cost, but exempts some "cost objectives" from getting an assigned interest cost.[2]

Both Anthony and FAS 34 also advocate using the average cost of capital in assigning interest costs to cost objects, except in rare cases where it is possible to associate particular assets with particular borrowing.

Our theory requires 1) capitalizing all interest, and 2) assigning interest cost to assets on the basis of the rate of return which the firm should get from the assets, rather than on the basis of the average cost of capital.

The simplest case to consider is an all equity mutual fund which incurs no transactions costs or overhead, and which owns two zero-coupon bonds. GAAP, FAS 34, and probably Anthony, would advocate recognizing interest revenue on each bond at its own interest rate, as it accrues. This increases assets and shareholders' equity. The increase in equity is income. If there are no surprises, the asset value will also equal the market value of the assets, although unexpected changes in interest rates could cause a difference between market value and book value.

I argue that this is an unwarranted deviation from historical cost-based accounting. There is no justification for abandoning the realization principle and recognizing interest revenue. The correct accounting procedure is to determine the

cost of equity capital, which the capital asset pricing model[3]
tells us is the weighted average of the yields on the two bonds
held as assets. We can determine the total interest cost by
multiplying the equity capital by the cost of equity capital.

We then allocate the interest to the two assets on the
basis of their yields.   The end result, as Anthony apparently
understood,[4] is identical to GAAP. Each asset is valued at cost
plus accumulated interest. Equity increases by accrued interest.
The only difference is in interpretation.   GAAP interprets all
increases in equity not associated with increased shareholder
investment as income.   We agree with Anthony and interpret a
normal rate of return on equity as a cost, which is also
consistent with economic theory.

If we follow Anthony and do not assign interest cost to
financial assets, we will still arrive in the same place. He
will presumably recognize the (unrealized) interest income, and
then charge the interest on equity capital as an "expense:"

Interest expense   XXX

Shareholders' Equity   XXX

The expense will reduce income to zero, which is what we want
when the return on equity equals its interest cost, and total
assets and equities are the same as for GAAP.

The argument for assigning interest cost to assets on the
basis of their returns is that this is the cost of the capital
which was borrowed to acquire the asset. Both Anthony [1, p. 84]
and FAS 34 [14, paragraph 51] agree that a specific interest

cost associated with the asset would be proper if we could
determine the cost of the capital borrowed to acquire the asset,
but they consider this to be too difficult to determine. The
capital asset pricing model (CAPM), however, provides a
theoretical basis for determining the cost of the borrowed
capital, if the assets acquired are independent of each other in
the sense that the cash flows associated with each asset do not
depend upon whether the other asset is acquired or not.[5]

This condition is highly restrictive, but is satisfied by
our mutual fund. The yield on either bond does not depend upon
whether or nor we own the other. (The yields on the two issues
may be correlated, but this is another issue. We cannot change
either yield by our purchases or sales.) If we assume that the
bonds yield 10% and 5%, CAPM tells us that the cost of equity
capital will be 10% if we own only the first bond, and will drop
to 7.5% if we purchase an equal dollar amount of the second. The
(marginal) cost of equity capital for the first is 10%, while
the marginal cost of equity capital is 5% for the second. CAPM
also tells us that we get the same result if we buy the 5% bond
first and the 10% second, or if we buy them simultaneously. The
results are also the same if we sell any of the bonds.

In general, CAPM tells us that the average cost of the
borrowed funds will equal the average rate of return on the
assets, even if some borrowing is debt and some equity. The
acquisition of a new asset therefore has a marginal cost of
capital equal to the yield on the asset, no matter whether the

marginal borrowing (actually) associated with the asset   is debt
or equity.   The only restriction is that   the   asset   yields be
independent,   as   noted before.   We   do not   have   to   associate
particular assets with particular borrowing.

We   run into formidable theoretical   problems if there   are
transactions   costs,   joint costs, economies   of scale,   or other
interaction between assets.

Suppose   that   we   buy   a   bond   for $100 which   pays $10
annually, and can   be sold for $100 at any   time.   If there are
brokerage   fees of $1 upon purchase and sale, the yield is 7.92%
if we sell at the end of the first year,[6] 8.95% if we sell after
two years, 9.57% after   five years, 9.81% after eight years, and
9.9% if we hold it forever.   There is no unique yield associated
with   the asset, and the cost of capital to the firm will depend
upon how long the market expects the firm to hold the asset.

Strictly speaking, joint costs and other dependency between
assets   make disaggregation   of   assets   impossible.   We cannot
account for individual assets   in the way GAAP   does.   If we use
different kinds of equipment to produce a product,   or advertise
the product, we cannot argue that the cash flows associated with
one   asset   do   not depend   upon   whether   or not we own another
asset.   In terms familiar to CAPM, each asset must   belong to a
risk class which determines   its expected yield.   The risk class
for a particular asset, however, is not the same for all   firms,
or at all times.   It depends   on   the way the asset is used, and
upon the other assets which are employed jointly.

We therefore think of a firm as a group of projects,[7] and the shareholders as owners of a portfolio consisting of the firm's projects. A project can be productive or financial. A financial project is the purchase of a financial asset, or the issue of a financial liability. Ideally, each productive project has a production function of the type discussed in Chapter 2. If we can disaggregate the firm into projects of this type, each cash flow can be associated with a project, and the projects are independent because the production functions are independent.

As a practical matter, we will almost surely be faced with the alternative of either no disaggregation, or disaggregation which involves projects which are not entirely independent. The salary of the CEO is unlikely to be allocable to any project. It should be emphasized, however, that the disaggregation does not influence the measurement of total assets or total income, providing we follow historical cost-based accounting as we have defined it. All interest costs will be capitalized. Shareholders' equity will always increase by the interest on equity capital, whether this is called income or not.

This suggests disaggregation by division, or profit center. The purpose of disaggregation is to provide information about sources of income, not to measure income.

The procedures outlined above differ from GAAP in very important ways. All transactions are "fair." Every purchase except purchases from shareholders (treasury shares or dividends) increases one asset, measured at cost, and either reduces another or increases a liability. No income is ever recognized when a transaction takes place. Purchases from shareholders reduce equity and assets, again with no income. Sales of productive instruments reduce assets (at cost) by the amount of the sale, and increase another asset, and do not generate income or influence shareholders' equity. Sales of financial instruments held as assets are no different from the sales of productive instruments. Sales of financial instruments which become liabilities increase assets and liabilities. Sales of shares increase assets and equity. No purchase or sale can generate income, or loss.

All "income" is generated by "accruals," and the only accruals are interest costs. Pure economic profit is always zero, since interest on equity capital is a cost. Since we define income as the unexplained change in value, all equity holders, including shareholders, get an income equal to the normal interest cost which is accrued to their accounts.

This gives correct results in a long-run equilibrium, where there is no pure economic profit. In the real world, we must find a way to discover which firms are in fact earning a normal return, which are earning less, and which are earning more. Our historical cost-based accounting accepts the "null" hypothesis that all firms are earning a return which is normal for their risk class. We must provide the possibility of finding evidence which causes us to reject the null hypothesis. We return to this problem in Section 5.

2. Service-Potential Accounting

The basis of service-potential accounting is that the value to the holder (user) of any economic instrument is the present (discounted) value of the future benefits which the instrument will generate for its owner. This is the generally accepted valuation of financial instruments, in the financial literature, and can also be applied to productive instruments.

The basic procedure is therefore to determine the future cash flows, and discount them at the nominal rate of interest to obtain a present value. The major problem is the same as with the historical basis, which is to associate future productive flows with particular capital assets. Future financial flows are easily identified with particular financial instruments, so that the present value of each instrument can be estimated.

Costs are not considered. They are irrelevant because they are "sunk," and have no bearing on the future. Service potential looks only to the future, and never looks back. There is no way to reconcile this approach with GAAP. Forecasting is at the heart of the procedure, and is obviously unreliable in an uncertain world. In the Crusoe case, however, he must forecast if he is to make rational decisions, and our initial accounting is based on the assumption that he forecasts correctly.

One of the important implications of equation (9), Chapter 2, is that correct forecasting will lead to discounted values which equal market values. The valuation of shares is necessarily a discounting of forecasts of the future. The flows to shareholders are generated by productive activities, which is another way of saying that they are the service potential of the assets. The discounted value of the future flows equals the value of both shares and assets, in the Crusoe case.

In a Crusoe economy, service-potential accounting will be identical to market-value accounting, and to historical cost accounting. In terms of economic theory, the historical cost determines the competitive supply, and the service potential determines the competitive demand. The equilibrium market price is determined jointly by supply and demand. In the real world, long-run competitive equilibrium is never observed, and the accountant must select a single procedure, or a compromise which he thinks best reflects the economic situation.

In the real world, the present value of the service potential of the assets is the value of the equities. Shareholders and potential shareholders must somehow forecast the future, and estimate the value of equities and assets. Some real-world differences between cost-based and service-potential accounting are discussed in the Appendix to this chapter.

3. GAAP

It is important to understand the short-comings of traditional business accounting (GAAP), in accounting for even the simplest cases.

Assume that Crusoe starts a firm at t_o by borrowing $1,000 from Crusoe and purchasing capital goods. The nominal and real rates of interest are 10%, and there is no inflation. At t_1, the firm borrows an additional $500 to buy labor from Crusoe, and sells nothing. At t_2, the firm sells Crusoe $1,760 of finished product, buys no new resources, pays Crusoe a "dividend" of $1,760, and goes out of business.

We have presented three ways of accounting for these events:

1) Historical (cost-based) accounting records costs and debt of $1,000 at t_0. The costs accumulate at 10% during the year, because this is the interest on the equity, and the equity debt to Crusoe accumulates at 10% because this is the nominal interest rate. Prior to the borrowing and purchase of labor at t_1, the firm therefore has assets and equities of $1,100. The firm also has productive income of $100, since this is the unexplained increase in asset value, and financial income of -$100, since this is the unexplained increase in shares. We call this income, since this is the more common usage, although it is not "pure" economic profit, since it represents a normal return on capital.

After the borrowing and purchase of labor at t_1, costs and shares rise to $1,600. The costs and shares accumulate to $1,760 before the transactions at t_2. The firm therefore has $160 of productive income, and -$160 of financial income. The transactions at t_2 reduce the unrecovered costs and the unrepaid borrowing to zero.

2) Service-potential accounting is easier to understand by working backwards. The moment before the transactions at t_2,

the present value of the benefits to be received from the physical assets is $1,760, and the present value of the financial repayments to Crusoe is also $1,760.

If we go back to t_1, after the transactions, the present value of the benefits and the shares fall to $1,600. Before the transactions, the present value of the benefits and shares are both $1,100. Finally, if we go back to t_0, the present values fall to $1,000.

Since the service-value balance sheets are identical to the historical balance sheets, the service-value basis also gives the same measurements of income as the historical basis.

3) Market price accounting gives the same values as the service-value basis. The market value of the shares must be the present value of the flows to be received at t_1 and t_2. The market value of the assets must equal the value of the shares, or the markets would not be in equilibrium.[8] If balance sheet values are the same, the income measurements must be the same.

All of our accounting procedures show productive income of 10% per year, and financial income of -10% per year. Productive resources earn their marginal product of 10%, and financial instruments earn the interest rate of 10%, in each of the two years.

GAAP would find it almost impossible to agree with our results.

The t_0 balance sheets could well agree with ours. The sale of $1,000 of shares would be recorded at market. All of the

capital could probably be written up as an asset, even if it
were necessary to label some of it "Organization Costs."

The situation at t_1, however, is chaotic.   The GAAP
accounant would face three problems on the asset side of the
balance sheet: how much depreciation should be charged against
the capital purchased at t_0, how much of the labor purchased at
t_1 should be capitalized (or how much should be expensed), and
how much interest can be charged on construction work in
progress. Without debt, no interest can be capitalized. Even if
there were debt, the interest on equity could not be
capitalized. Even if he decides for zero depreciation and 100%
capitalization of labor costs (each of which is unlikely), there
is no way that he can record productive assets of $1,600 at t_1.

This is important in understanding GAAP. The idea of
historical cost is totally confused with the idea of an asset.
If we interpret that the balance sheet value is a cost, we must
also interpret interest as a cost.   In fact, it is conservative
to overestimate costs, and GAAP systematically underestimates
interest costs of productive assets. This happens because GAAP
measures historical costs, and then calls them "assets." The
idea of an asset, as is clear from most accounting texts, is
inherently forward looking. "Assets" are most frequently defined
as "service potentials," which means that assets are concerned
with the future, not the past.   It is conservative to
underestimate assets if they reflect future benefits.   It is
conservative to overestimate assets if they reflect past costs.

The difficulty, of course, is that the balance sheet value is related to the measurement of income. If GAAP were to record productive assets of $1,600 at t_1, this would increase equity by $100, and this increase in equity would be interpreted as income, instead of as an increase in the amount (debt) which the firm owes its shareholders. The traditional accounting interpretation of an (unexplained) increase in equity is that the firm owes the shareholders additional money because it has "earned" the money for its shareholders. The correct interpretation, if we use a historical cost basis, is that the firm owes its shareholders additional money because interest has accrued on the debt, whether or not there have been earnings.

The recording of income is usually considered to be "unconservative," when no transactions have been recorded to justify the increased asset value at t_1. On the other hand, the absence of sales at t_1 does not necessarily imply an absence of income. Shipbuilders, for example, are permitted to record revenues in advance of sales. These revenues would have to generate financial assets (receivables) of equal value, since cash cannot be debited when the revenue is recorded.

GAAP therefore would almost certainly record some expenses at t_1, although the amount would be left to the whim of the accountant (or management), and undervalue productive assets. An arbitrary quantity of the anticipated t_2 sales might also be recorded as revenue at t_1, with a corresponding increase in financial assets. By coincidence, it would be possible for revenue to exceed expenses by $100, so that income might accidentally be measured properly. In this case, the underestimate of productive assets would be compensated by an overestimate of financial assets, and shareholders' equity would be correctly measured. This coincidence, however, is very unlikely.

Barring this coincidence, GAAP will not produce the same balance sheet at t_1, nor the same income at t_1 or t_2 that we get using our procedures. It should be emphasized that only coincidence could produce the correct results. There are no principles in GAAP which would consistently reach the correct results in examples of this kind.

From the point of view of accounting theory, this means that GAAP are fatally flawed. They do not produce the correct results even in the most ideal conditions. It does not make sense to use accounting principles or practices which do not work in such a simple case. The minimum requirement of "good" accounting principles is that they should produce correct results when applied to simple problems.

This also illustrates an important point in the measurement of income and wealth. Accountants frequently say, for example, that LIFO inventory accounting produces a better measurement of income in inflationary periods than FIFO inventory accounting, but a worse measurement of balance sheet value (wealth).

The idea that there may be a conflict between the measurement of income and wealth is a half-truth. If wealth is correctly measured at the beginning of the accounting period, there can be no conflict between the measurement of income and wealth. In our example, we assumed that the t_o balance sheet was correct. The t_1 measurements will therefore have the property that the error in the measurement of income will equal the error in the measurement of wealth. If t_1 wealth and income are incorrectly measured, as they almost certainly will be if GAAP is used, then it is possible to measure t_2 income correctly and t_2 wealth incorrectly, or vice-versa, and a conflict between the measurement of income and wealth can develop.

Another point which is frequently emphasized in accounting literature is that the question of income measurement is "only" ("merely") one of timing. Even GAAP measures aggregate income over the two years as $1,760 - $1,500 = $260. Our procedures say that income is $100 in the first year and $160 in the second. GAAP divides the $260 between t_1 and t_2 in an unpredictable way.

The obvious question is what difference it makes how the income is allocated between the two periods. The answer must be considered in two parts: what difference does it make to the firm, and what difference does it make to the shareholders.

1) The firm. The conventional finance literature and most accounting suggest that the firm makes no decisions on the basis of balance sheet assets, and income figures. The firm makes investment decisions on the basis of predicted cash flows and interest rates.

If this be true, the only possible influence of the

income measurement on the operations of the firm is via the tax structure. From the point of view of theory, there should be no association between tax reporting and accounting measurements of income. Requirements in the tax laws that firms use the same measuements for financial reporting that they use for tax purposes are clearly improper. The government can not require firms to pay taxes on their own estimates of their income. It passes laws defining procedures for determining the base of a tax called an income tax. The tax base can properly be called taxable income, but is unlikely to bear any relationship to economic income, and firms should be permitted to measure economic income without interference from tax legislation.

2) The shareholders. In a Crusoe economy, with good markets and certainty, Crusoe would pay no attention to the balance sheets or income statements of the firm. He would measure his income and wealth, and make his consumption decisions based upon the market price of his shares.

The question therefore must be the purpose of financial statements in the real world, where markets may be imperfect (or non-existent), and uncertainty prevails.

The traditional answer in the accounting literature is that shareholders need information for "investment" purposes, i. e., for purposes of determining their optimal portfolio of wealth holding.[9] The discussion of Chapter 2 suggests that shareholders need the information for purposes of making consumption decisions.

From the point of view of consumption decisions, the market price of the shares measures the potential current consumption, no matter what the quality of the market. Most shareholders, however, do not liquidate all their shares and spend the proceeds on consumption. They are interested in the consumption pattern through time which will be made possible by their shares. In a Crusoe economy, the share price properly measures the present value of future consumption possibilities. In the real world, share prices may reflect short-run considerations, and fluctuate to a much greater extent than do the future consumption possibilities. The consumer is therefore interested in the long-term investment value of the shares, rather than in the current price.

This is probably also the concern of many shareholders. Speculators do not need information about the long-term prospects of the firm, but the long-term share holder may expect to learn something about the firm's prospects from its financial statements. The timing of income is important for consumption decisions even if the total income reported over the lifetime of the firm is correct, particularly if the timimg errors stretch over decades rather than years.

If shareholder-consumers are interested in the long-term prospects, the service-value approach would appear to be most appropriate, and accountants should explicitly recognize that their purpose is to generate statements which reflect the future, not the past.[10]

4. Objective of Accounting

The earlier chapters suggest that the ideal accounting scheme would be based on current market prices.   In the real world, there are serious problems:

First, we do not know what to do with transactions costs. This leads the FASB to identify three "current" price concepts: "current cost," "current market value," and "net realizable (settlement) value" [15, paragraph 67], which differ primarily in the different handling of transactions costs.

Second, asset aggregation is not precisely defined. Assets can be aggregated, more or less arbitrarily, into "composite" assets.[11] The market value of the "composite" may be larger or smaller than the values of the individual assets.

Third, there is no reason for the balance sheet to "balance" without an entry for net wealth, no matter how "current" market value is defined, or how the assets are aggregated for valuation purposes, unless we lump all of the assets together and value the firm.

This is critically important for accounting theory.   GAAP never values shareholder equity at market.   Even if all assets and all other equities were valued at market, shares would be recorded so that the balance sheet would not require an entry for net wealth.   If we accept the idea that shares are not significantly different from other equities, and should be valued at market, we must face the problem making assets equal equities.

FASB has taken the traditional route of insisting that financial accounting is not designed to measure the value of a business enterprise.[12] I interpret this to mean that the total assets are not supposed to represent the market value of those assets, if they were sold as a going concern. This implies that assets should not be aggregated to the point where there is only one of them, but gives no guidance as to the proper level of aggregation.[13]

From the point of view of economic theory, there is no way to value the individual assets of a firm to obtain the value of the firm, unless we make very highly restrictive assumptions like those of Chapter 2. Furthermore, the level of aggregation influences the market value of assets, no matter which of the three valuations is used.

Economic theory tells us that the balance sheet should balance if the assets and equities both measure the value of the firm, and that it cannot be expected to balance if we value assets individually. Outside entities could obtain the firm's assets by purchasing all of its equities. The assets cannot therefore be worth more than the equities, or some entity would aquire the assets and liquidate them. If the assets were worth less than the equities, it would be profitable to buy the assets and sell equities.[14]

Accountants have therefore set for themselves a theoretically impossible task - to value individual (groups of) assets, and make the balance sheet "balance." This can, of course, be done arithmetically by not valuing shares, but there are no principles which can guide the accountant in his aggregation or valuation of the assets. Endless and fruitless arguments about the choice between entry values and exit values are inevitable, since there is no theory to provide an answer.

The solution must be to change the objective of accounting. The objective should be to value the firm as a whole, and then try to make "useful" guesses or estimates about the sources of the value in terms of groups of assets, which I have called "projects." We must start with a meaningful whole, and try to break in into parts, rather than to start with the parts and try to add them to get a meaningful whole. Even the FASB admits that the whole is meaningless if we sum the parts. Since the valuation of the parts is sufficiently stylized that there is no uniform interpretation for the parts either, we should abandon the traditional procedure and try to value the whole firm.

This approach strongly suggests that the emphasis should be on the valuation of shares. The shareholders are going to get the benefits of the future services of the assets held, less whatever payments are required to liability holders. The present value of the shares should be the present value of the assets less the present value of the liabilities.

One approach frequently advocated by economists is therefore to use the market value of shares on the balance sheet [5, page 132-36]. Practical difficulties arise, however, because shares may not be traded in active markets, and active markets may not properly reflect the present value of future flows because 1) the future flows are uncertain, and 2) the market price may be influenced by short-term speculative considerations. Most accountants therefore believe that market price is frequently not an accurate measure of the future returns to shareholders.[15] The tradition is therefore to base accounting on historical costs.

5. Modified Hisorical Cost Accounting

As we have seen in Section 1 on this Chapter, historical cost accounting can be applied in a Crusoe economy. It can also be adapted to the real world, provided that some important, possibly radical, adjustments are made.

First, the idea of matching must be abandoned. If a cost is incurred to acquire a productive instrument, this should be recorded and capitalized as an asset. No depreciation expense should ever be recorded, although "transfers" of the asset value from one asset "aggregation" (or project) to another are harmless, and therefore permitted. The point is that "expense" reduces assets and income. "Transfers" of value from one asset classification to another do not change total assets or income.

This does not mean that "accruals," as they are usually defined [16, paragraphs 134-42], are prohibited. The problem is that "accruals" (which for my purposes include "deferrals") include two entirely different kinds of events. Purchases on account are defined as accruals, apparently because no "cash" has changed hands. However, a transaction has taken place, and a

legal liability has been incurred. We describe the event
properly by recording a cash purchase, followed by a sale of a
financial instrument for cash.[16] The proper recording of
transactions is an integral part of historical cost accounting.

Depreciation, interest, and taxes, however, are accruals
(deferrals) of an entirely different nature. No transaction with
an outside entity occurs when these entries are made. The
transaction occurs when the asset is purchased, and this is
recorded. The depreciation of a fixed asset, or the interest
accrued on a financial asset, do not record transactions, but
record events which the accountant believes to have taken place,
and records in the interest of "matching."

Most accruals (deferrals) which do not record transactions
should not be recorded.

The exception is the second required adjustment to
historical cost accounting. Interest on all equities, including
shares, must be accrued periodically.

The last important modification is to introduce "projects"
as the cost "objects," rather than "individual" assets.

The fundamental theory comes from the theory of finance and
investment decisions.[17]

Only cash flows are considered when making investment
decisions, or valuing shares. There is no depreciation, or any
other kind of "matching." In principle, I would argue that cash
flows should be "constructed" when purchases or sales on account
are anticipated, as noted above, but this refinement is

frequently ignored in practice, presumably on the grounds that the difference would be immaterial and that forecasting at that level of detail is too costly and unreliable.

All of the required "matching" is accomplished by the discouting process. If we buy a plant in year 1 and sell its output over the next ten years, we must discount the revenues, but we need not depreciate the plant. If the present value of the cash receipts exceeds the present value of the cash outlays, the project is "profitable," and should be undertaken.

As we have seen, historical cost-based accounting can accomplish the same objective by charging an interest cost on all borrowed funds (equities).[18] The two major difficulties in implementing these proposals are 1) the determination of the interest rate to charge on shareholders' equity (the cost of equity capital), and 2) the determination of the appropriate evidence that cost recoveries have exceeded, or fallen short of, costs incurred.

1) One of the important reasons why the FASB rejected imputing an interest cost to shareholders' equity is because "the cost of equity capital is not reliably determinable." [14, paragraph 49] The idea that a cost should be estimated at zero because no other estimate is "reliable" is very difficult to accept. The FASB appears to believe that they are not estimating the cost, but ignoring it. This is not logically possible. If there is a cost of equity capital, and the FASB agrees that there is, then refusing to estimate it because the estimate

would be unreliable is logically equivalent to estimating the cost to be zero. The FASB has said [15, Highlights] that reliable information is "representationally faithful, verifiable, and neutral." A zero estimate is certainly verifiable, but is clearly biased downward, is not representationally faithful, and is therefore highly unreliable.

Anthony's solution is certainly better than the FASB's ostrich-like posture. He suggests, in effect, that the FASB should promulgate rules like: "Noncyclycal, non-regulated industries should use a cost of equity capital of 9 to 10%." [1, page 71] While such rules would be difficult to formulate, and they would no doubt have to be revised periodically, such rules would have to be better than using an estimate of zero. The costs would be as verifiable as the present estimate of zero, and might be representationally faithful and neutral.

2) "Pure" cost-based accounting explains all changes in account values on the basis of transactions, except interest accruals. The credit entries to the equity accounts generate negative financial value added equal to a "normal" return for equity holders. The debit entries to assets generate positive value added, corresponding to the marginal product of productive assets, or an interest return on financial assets. We must therefore modify our accounting when we find convincing evidence that returns are not normal.

GAAP almost never estimates returns to be normal, because 1) interest is not charged on shareholders' equity, and 2) revenues and expenses are measured in arbitrary ways.

The appropriate idea of an expense in cost-based accounting should be that the accountant has evidence that the cost involved will not be recovered in the future. Put slightly differently, assets are costs which have not been recovered, but which we expect to recover. The "standard" procedure assumes that no mistakes have been made, and that all costs will eventually be recovered. We require "expenses" (or "losses") to measure negative mistakes. Similarly, "revenues" ("gains") also measure mistakes, but favorable ones: we are going to recover our costs, and more.

GAAP, however, construes both revenues and expenses more broadly. Expenses imply that certain costs will not be recovered in the future, but they do not imply that they have not been recovered in the past, or during the current accounting period. Similarly, revenues do not imply an excess of recovery over cost: they simply measure recovery. Revenue less expense measures income. Gains and losses are "net," and so are more consistent with a cost-based approach.

Consider the treatment of sales of inventory on account. GAAP first attempts to determine the cost of acquiring the particular items of inventory sold. The absence of theoretical foundation for this cost allocation has been amply demonstrated by Thomas [42 and 43], among others. This amount is called an expense, on the grounds that these particular costs cannot be recovered after the inventory has been sold. Next, GAAP seeks to

estimate   the future by measuring revenue as the   amount of cash
which the firm will eventually realize from the receivables.[19]

This problem   illustrates the importance of   the definition
of the "project" for which we account. If the production and the
decision to make the sale on account, instead of for cash, are
part of the same "project," there is no need for an entry at
all: the   cost   recovered by   the sale of merchandise is
immediately "reinvested" in a financial asset,   accounts
receivable.   The   only theoretical justification for   the GAAP
treatment of revenue would be that we are accounting for two
projects: a productive project which sells inventory, and a
financial project which buys accounts receivable (lends money)
from customers.   The separation of these activities into two
projects can be criticized on the grounds that the projects are
not independent: the terms of the loan influence the volume of
sales. It may therefore better accounting to consider only one
project, even though I have previously argued that it is
desirable to separate productive and financial activities.

If we account for two projects, we must credit the
productive project for the amount which we lend to customers,
and debit the financial project for the same amount. We have
recovered costs from one project, and incurred equal costs in
connection with another project.   The total cost basis for the
firm is unchanged. The identification of projects may add to our
understanding of what is going on, and we may even argue that
the financial project is less risky than the productive project,

and should therefore be charged for interest at a lower rate. The total unrecovered cost of assets, however, would be independent of the partitioning of the firm's activities into projects.

Part of the problem arises because GAAP does not credit the project for cost recovery equal to the sales receipts, however measured. The credit to inventory (cost recovery) is "balanced" by a debit to cost of goods sold expense, not by a debit to "cash" or "accounts receivable."

The major problem, however, is that GAAP attempts to disaggregate to a level which is much too small to be supported by the available evidence. GAAP examines each sale to determine if the firm is earning a normal return, and brings evidence to bear which is theoretically unacceptable. The cost allocation procedures have no economic foundation. "Projects" of much broader scope must be identified if we are to have any chance of determining "profitability." Accountants have been trying to estimte cost of goods sold for centuries. The best they have been able to come up with is a laundry list of "acceptable" procedures. As Thomas has so eloquently argued [42 and 43], the time has come to abandon this effort and look for alternatives.

Objective evidence that a firm is earning more or less than a normal return is not easy to come by. There appear to be two kinds of evidence which might be used, one which resembles "standard costing," and the other which looks at market prices. The two approaches could be used simultaneously.

a) <u>Standard Costing</u>. The basic idea is for the firm to project cash flows for each project (however defined) when it is undertaken, following familiar capital budgeting and investment decision procedures. The discount rate would be a measure of the normal return on projects in this risk class. The presumption is that the firm will not undertake any projects whose present value is negative. We should also probably constrain the initial projections to show a normal return on investment, since this is the "null" hypothesis. These projections would be "standards" which would be used for post-auditing, and for determining whether the firm was earning more or less than a normal return.

Negative variances could be interpreted as evidence that the firm will not recover all of its cost, and lead to a writing down of the project's assets, and the recognition of a loss. Alternatively, the firm might argue that the cost recoveries have been postponed rather than lost forever, and therefore revise its estimates of future recoveries upward.

Positive variances could similarly be the cause to write up the assets, if projections justify the expectation that the larger-then-expected early recoveries are not likely to be at the expense of future recoveries.

We would also want to require that no project should have negative assets, unless projections call for large costs at the end of the project. Negative assets could arise only if past recoveries exceeded costs.   For the overwhelming majority of projects, costs exceed recoveries in the early years, and recoveries exceed costs in later years. The exception that gets the most attention is mining operations where the landscape must be restored after the operations are completed.

b)   Market Prices. The major evidence of variance from normal returns would have to come from markets, however, and market values would supercede values determined on the basis of standards.

Many financial instruments held as assets could be treated as separate projects and valued at market, if prices are available. This does not mean that a rise or fall in market value will always be interpreted as a deviation from a normal return. Each financial asset belongs to a risk class and has a risk-adjusted expected return. The return consists of cash (interest or dividends) and capital gain (loss). If the cash plus capital gain differs from the expected return, then a gain or loss should be recorded. The market value represents the opportunity cost to the firm at any time, and its use is therefore consistent with cost-based accounting. In effect, we assume that the firm liquidates its holdings annually, and then repurchases its existing portfolio, without transactions costs. The market price is then the appropriate cost basis at any time.

Other assets or projects may well be much more difficult to value at market, because of interaction and the absence of markets. An arms-length offer for any group of assets (project) should serve as a basis to revalue those assets upward. It could also serve as a signal for downward revision unless there is good evidence that the offer is too low. The more serious problem is whether the revaluation should come at the expense of other projects, or shareholders' equity.

Similarly, market transactions involving similar projects undertaken by other firms could be used as a basis for revaluation. The cost of an appraisal based on this kind of market evidence, however, might prove to be greater than its benefits.

Evidence of the market valuation of liabilities and shareholders' equity should also be used. There is no excuse for carrying shares issued at different times at different book values. No matter what criticisms may be made of the workings of the stock market, the issue of new shares by a firm must be taken as convincing evidence of the value of every outstanding share. Old shareholders must consider the issue price to be the opportunity cost of holding their shares. The firm should not, according to accepted economic and finance theory, issue new shares unless it expects to earn enough to provide both old and new shareholders with a "normal" return on their shares, valued at issue price.

Similar reasoning suggests that shareholders' equity should be revalued whenever treasury shares are acquired. Management is presumably saying that they think their shares to be undervalued in the market, and that this is a good investment for their shareholders.

In both these cases, the revaluation of shares will require

the revaluation of assets. If management thinks the shares to be valuable enough to repurchase, or to issue, they should be required to explain which assets (projects) are going to provide the expected return to shareholders.

Market prices of shares, if available, should also be used even when new shares are not issued, or treasury shares sold. The argument that the market may reflect short-term considerations which are transitory should not be an excuse for huge and long-run differences between market and book values. Economists have developed various techniques for the measurement of permanent income as distinguished from nominal income[20] which could also be adapted to the estimation of long-run share value as compared to nominal or transitory share value.

These suggestions may well be "conservative" in their measurement of income, in the sense that fluctuations in income could be smaller than with GAAP. Income would equal a "normal" return on shareholders equity unless convincing evidence called for a change. The evidence would either be deviations of observed flows from expectations, or market prices which differ from expectations.

Appendix

This appendix considers the circumstances under which the historical cost-based (accumulation) approach will generate the same balance sheet values as the service-potential (discounting) approach. We need not consider income measurement explicitly, since identical balance sheets must generate identical income.

We explore the arithmetical, rather than the theoretical, properties of the capital asset pricing model (CAPM), which has been developed in corporate finance to explain share prices.

CAPM says that the risk associated with each share on the stock market can be measured by a variable $\underline{B}_i$. The discount rate $(\underline{dr}_i)$ on the share is a linear function of the B_i for the share, according to the "security market line" (SML):

$$dr_i = re + (rm - re)B_i,$$

where $\underline{re}$ is the discount (interest) rate on risk-free securities (usually taken to mean 90-day bills), and $\underline{rm}$ is the average discount rate in the stock market.

The $\underline{B}_p$ for a portfolio of shares is the weighted average of the $\underline{B}$ values of the shares which constitute the portfolio, where the weights are the the proportion of the portfolio value $(\underline{V}_p)$ associated with each share $(\underline{V}_i)$:

$$V_p = \text{Sum } V_i$$
$$w_i = V_i/V_p$$
$$B_p = \text{Sum } w_i B_i$$
$$dr_p = re + (rm - re)B_p$$

The accounting approach is based on the idea that a firm

undertakes "projects," each of which involves a risk which can be measured by a $\underline{B}$. The shareholder is considered to be the owner of a "portfolio" of "projects." We can calculate the $\underline{B}_p$ for the shareholder by averaging the $\underline{B}_i$ for the projects (portfolio), and get the appropriate discount rate on the shares by using the decurity market line.

These projects may be exclusively "productive," and involve only the purchase and sale of productive instruments, or be exclusively "financial," and involve only the purchase and sale of financial instruments, or may involve both productive and financial instruments. Every cash flow of the firm must be associated with a project, except the flows between the firm and its shareholders. These flows are treated as a residual, and the shareholders are the owners of a portfolio which consists of the projects undertaken by the firm. While the theory of CAPM requires that the flows to the projects be independent, the arithmetic holds no matter how the projects are defined, so long as we know the $\underline{B}$ for each project for each year, and the flows to be assigned to each project.

The cash flows to shareholders must make the net cash flows of the firm zero. This means that we are, as usual, thinking in terms of the flow of "medium of exchange," rather than the flow of "store of value." The exchanges between "store" and "medium" can be treated as a separate financial project with its own risk, or they can be treated as a part of a larger project.

Service-potential accounting discounts the future cash

flows associated with each project at the appropriate discount rate, i. e., the rate determined from the SML, using the $\underline{B}$ for the project. It should be emphasized that this is a purely arithmetical statement. We assume that the future flows are known, and that the $\underline{B}$'s are also known, and use the CAPM to determine the discount rate for each project and for the shares.

The balance sheet values for each project are the discounted values of the future cash flows associated with the project. The flows to shareholders are discounted at the rate associated with the portfolio to obtain the share value, and the balance sheet is in balance with no entry for net wealth.

It should be emphasized that the discount rate on shares changes annually because the weights for the projects change annually, even if the $\underline{B}$'s for the projects do not change from year to year. However, the arithmetical statements all hold even if the $\underline{B}$'s for the projects also change annually. Finally, it should be noted that there are no restrictions on the $\underline{B}$'s, and that the valuations of the projects are signed. Inflows of medium to the firm are taken as positive, outflows as negative. The present values may therefore be negative or positive. Weights may be positive or negative, in determining the $\underline{B}_p$ to be used to discount flows with shareholders. The $\underline{B}$'s for the projects are not restricted to be positive, even though CAPM suggests that no interest rates below the risk-free rates should be observed.

For example, a firm may issue bonds, and consider them as a

separate project. The weight to be associated with the B_i
associated with the bond will therefore be negative, since the
bond contributes a negative value to the portfolio held by
shareholders. A negative B would be required if "cash" (store of
value) were considered to be a separate project, rather than to
assign cash balances to other projects. In this case, we would
require a zero interest rate, and work backwards with the
security market line to determine $B = re/(re-rm)$. Demand
deposits, if considered as a project, would also require a
negative B if the interest rate were less than re.

The historical cost-based procedure records balance sheet
values at "cost." Cash flows out increase the cost basis, and
cash flows in reduce the cost basis. In addition, an interest
cost is accrued, equal to the initial cost-basis multiplied by
the interest rate associated with the project for the period, as
determined by the B and the security market line.

The historical cost procedure produces the same results as
the service potential (discounting) procedure if each project
undertaken by the firm has a zero present value when it is
undertaken. This follows directly from the well known fact that
the present value can be calculated either by discounting the
future flows or accumulating past flows, providing that the
present value at t_o is zero.[21]

This implies that the firm is in equilibrium, in the sense
that the Crusoe economy is in equilibrium. Each project must in
fact earn a "normal" rate of return, where the "normal" rate is

defined as the rate with is appropriate for the risk, in accordance with CAPM.

This is not "unreasonable" if we think in terms of financial projects. If the firm buys or sells financial instruments, theory suggests that the present value of the future flows should equal the price. In the case of fixed-rate instruments, it seems sensible to start with the interest rate implied by the market, and work back to the B for the project, rather than to start with the B and work back to the discount rate, as we have been suggesting. While transactions costs present difficulties with any financial instrument, the major difficulty, as we have previously noted, is to justify the extremely low interest rate associated with store of value, on the basis of CAPM.

Serious problems arise, however, in connection with productive projects. It rarely happens that firms expect such projects to earn the "normal" rate of return when they are initiated. Furthermore, problems arise in connection with taxes, in light of the Modigliani-Miller [30 and 31] approach to the valuation of the firm.

The Modigliani-Miller approach, which is consistent with CAPM, suggests that the value of a levered firm equals the value of the equity firm, plus the present value of the future tax saving which is associated with the fact that interest is a deductible expense. The theory says that the discount rate on the tax savings should be lower than the discount rate on the tax payments and the other flows associated with the project, since there is less (or no) risk associated with this flow.[22]

This is an important idea. Tax payments are associated with the productive flows, and presumably have approximately the same risk. The interest tax saving, however, is a sure thing, provided only that the carry-back and carry-forward regulations permit the firm to find some taxable income against which to offset the interest charge. This suggests that different flows associated with the same project may have different risk, and should be discounted at different rates. This suggests the possibility of breaking a "grand" project into "sub-projects," each with its own $\underline{B}$ and discount rate.

The major difficulty is that a "sub-project" consisting exclusively of interest tax savings cannot have zero present value when the project is undertaken, since all of the flows to the project are in the same direction (inflows to the firm). The cost-baased accumulation procedure will then not give the same balance sheet values as the discounting procedure even for the grand project, let alone the sub-projects, even if the the present value of the grand project is zero. This is because the accumulation procedure does not weight the sub-projects in the same way that the discounting procedure does.

Consider a simple example. A firm consists of two productive projects, A and B, each of which has one outflow (cost) at t_o, and one inflow (cost recovery) at t_1, and two financial projects, bonds which are sold at t_o and repaid at t_1,

and "interest tax savings," which bring an inflow at t_1. Each of
these projects has a risk class with an associated discount
rate. Shareholders provide the residual cash flows.

The flows and discount rates are:

FLOW DATA

	Cost at t_0	Recovery at t_1	Discount Rate
Project A	$101.60	$120.00	20.0%
Project B	202.40	260.00	30.0
Bonds	176.00	193.60	10.0
Tax Saving	0.00	4.40	10.0
Shares	128.00	190.80	49.1

In keeping with the usual finance assumptions, the flows to
projects A and B are assumed to be net of the corporate income
taxes which would be paid by an all-equity firm. Notice that the
discount rate on the tax savings is less than the discount rate
for the productive projects. The discount rate on shares is
an implicit rate calculated by dividing the return to
shareholders at t_1 ($190.80) by their t_0 investment ($128.00).
The tax saving is calculated by using an income tax rate of 25%.
The interest payment at t_1 is 10% of $176, and the saving is 25%
of the interest payment.

We present two balance sheets at t_0, first on a cost basis,
and then by discounting the t_1 flows:

BALANCE SHEETS (t_o)

	Cost Basis	Discounted
Assets		
Project A	$101.60	$100.00
Project B	202.40	200.00
Tax Saving	0.00	4.00
TOTALS	$304.00	$304.00
Equities		
Bonds	$176.00	$176.00
Shares	128.00	128.00
TOTALS	$304.00	$304.00

We can reconcile the cost basis with the discounted basis if we assume that 40% of the tax saving is associated with project A, and 60% with project B. This suggests that we think in terms of only the two productive projects, and assign the tax savings to these projects.

If we want to use a cost basis, the problem is to allocate the interest cost at t_1 to the two projects. We define the interest cost as the $17.60 on bonds plus the dividend of $62.80, which gives $80.40, although we could reduce this by the tax saving of $4.40 to get $76.

If we allocate 40% of the tax saving to project A, the return becomes $121.76. The interest charge must be $20.16, which is 19.8% of the t_o cost basis, if we are to get agreement between the cost basis and the discounted basis at t_1. Similarly, we must allocate $60.24 of interest to project B, which is 29.8% of the t_o cost basis.

The 19.8% interest rate is a weighted average of the interest rate on project A (20%) and the interest rate on the tax saving (10%), where the rates are proportional to the present values at t_o. The trouble is that there is no way to determine the weights without calculating the present values, which effectively means that we are abandoning the cost basis for the discount basis. Put differently, there is no way to determine the weights even if we assume that we "know" the t_o cost data and the five discount rates from the "Flow Data."

Cost-based accounting is therefore on a firm theoretical basis only if each "project" has a zero value, as in the Crusoe economy. If received finance theory is correct, it cannot be used in the presence of an income tax subsidy, even in equilibrium.

FOOTNOTES

Chapter II

1. A "synthetic" variable is the accounting equivalent of a "statistic." Just as a "statistic" is any number calculated from the observations in a statistical sample, a "synthetic" variable is any number calculated from the "observed" accounting data. In Hirshleifer's terminology [21, p. 37], it is a "fiction," or "mental construct," rather than an "observation."

2. This production function is essentially the same as that used by Hirshleifer [21, Chapter 6]. He uses only one consumer good, instead of two, and the quantity of labor service is not determined by the maximizing process, although labor is a variable in his production function.

3. This point was made by Samuelson [35, p. 233, footnote 30].

4. Lerner [26, p. 250] notes that "The inconveniences of falling prices can be avoided by a positive rate of interest on money."

5. The nominal interest rate will be negative if Crusoe prefers more deflation than is provided by the shadow prices.

6. Professor Mathur has observed that the assumption of constant returns is unnecessarily restrictive. Homogeneity (of any degree) is all that is required.

7. The determination of the interest rate and the magnitude of the firm's liability to its shareholders at t_1, are the central problems of financial accounting in the "real" world. The cash flows are known, at least after the fact. The interest charge, and the value of the remaining debt, must be estimated.

8. We could assume that Crusoe made decisions about x_o, y_o, and L_o at t_{-1}. He would then make decisions about x_1, y_1, and L_1. at t_o. The analysis would not be changed in any significant way.

9. See, for example, Becker [3, Chapter 6].

10. It seems more reasonable to assume that the firm plans a year ahead, even though we have assumed that Crusoe does not. This inconsistency does not affect the analysis.

11. Crusoe does not know (or care about) the price of capital, and so must project until the end of his time horizon. If the firm did not know the price of t_1 capital, it would also have to project as far as Crusoe does.

12. We consider the net marginal product of capital in Section V.

13. One of the problems in the real world is that data on household inventories are difficult to obtain. Accountants, therefore, usually assume that inventories are zero (except for homes), and that consumption takes place whenever a household makes a purchase. We assume that inventories of consumer goods are zero for our example. In principle, household inventories should be treated in the same way as firm inventories.

14. At this point, we do not specify whether the shadow prices are for t_o or t_1. This is discussed later.

15. It is also interesting to consider what happens if 1) Crusoe performs two different kinds of labor, perhaps fishing (L), and cooking (J), such that $L_i + J_i + R_i = M$, and 2) each of these variables enters separately into the utility and

production functions, so that Crusoe is not indifferent between time spent fishing and cooking, and the activities may have different productivities.

Assume that utility is a function of $\underline{x}$, $\underline{y}$, $\underline{L}$, and $\underline{J}$, and that $pn_1^L > pn_1^J$. We then define

(22a) $dU = v_x*dx + v_y*dy + v_L*dL + v_J*dJ$

   $D_i = v_x*x_i + v_y*y_i + v_L*L_1 + v_J*J_1 + v_L*M$,

for i=0,1. We conclude

(24b) $NC_1 = x_1*pn_1^X + y_1*pn_1^Y + R_1*pn_1^L + J_1*(pn_1^L - pn_1^J)$,

   $= M*pn_1^L + K_0*pn_0^K*(1+rn_1) - K_1*pn_1^K$.

Crusoe's "full earnings" are the earnings he would receive if he spent all his time, M, at his most remunerative activity, $\underline{L}$. He then consumes R_i hours of full leisure at the full price pn_i^L, and consumes J_i hours of more pleasant work (semi-leisure) for which he only pays $(pn_i^L - pn_i^J)$, and works L_i hours at his most remunerative employment.

16. This is quite different from the approach taken by Fisher and Shell [17, pp. 1-7]. They argue (correctly) that our problem has no theoretically correct solution, and propose a different interpretation of real consumption.

17. This definition is taken from Hicks [20, p. 172].

18. See Hirshleifer [21, p.36].

19. This is the position taken by Irving Fisher [18, p. 11], and Frank Knight [25, pp. 45-46].

20. Hicks [20, Chapter XIV] suggested this definition, and also suggested defining income as the maximum possible consumption

which can be maintained as a perpetuity. He preferred the
perpetual consumption formulation because he thought that wealth
might change beause of a change in the interest rate, even
though the perpetual consumption did not change.

21. The difference between (27) and (28) is small in my
example, but could be large.

It is also possible to develop $(1+rr_1)$ as a weighted
average of the own rates of interest of the consumer goods.

(27) implies

$$(1+rr_1) = [x_1*pn_1^X*(1+rx_1)+y_1*pn_1^Y*(1+ry_1)+R_1*pn_1^L*(1+rL_1)]/ RC_{1,1}$$
$$= 1.143,$$

while (28) implies

$$(1+rr_1') = [x_0*pn_1^X*(1+rx_1)+y_0*pn_1^Y*(1+ry_1)+R_0*pn_1^L*(1+rL_1)]/ RC_{0,1}'$$
$$= 1.144.$$

The weights are the relative importance of the commodities,
measured either in terms of relative values at t_1, or of
relative values of t_0 quantities in t_1 prices. As in the case of
measuring inflation, there is no theoretical preference for
either set of weights for measuring the real interest rate.

22. This idea is quite common in the literature. For example,
Ruggles [34, p.9], says "In broader terms any process that
creates value or adds value to already existing goods is
production." Relative value is clearly implied, and anything
which changes relative value qualifies as a "process."

23. Stigler [41, p. 129] suggests that marginal product can be
defined by holding constant either 1) "the quantity and form of

the constant factors," or 2) the "economic quantity (or value)" of the constant factors. He seems to prefer the value approach which we adopt. Hirshleifer [21, p. 158] uses the physical product approach in analizing (essentially) our model. The GNP accounts also use the physical product approach.

There are other differences between Hirshleifer's interpretation of the model [21, pp. 180-193] and ours. The most important is that Hirshleifer measures income in terms of what would happen if K_1 were the same as K_0. He assumes a production function, and defines income and product in terms of what this function says would happen if $K_1 = K_0$. Hirshleifer requires information to measure income which we assume to be unavailable, since there is no way to estimate the properties of Hirshleifer's production function from our data base.

24.   The propriety of using only one general price index for adjusting historical values is common in accounting. See Sterling [39, pp. 344-349].

25.   They introduce an "inventory valuation adjustment" to remove increases in inventory values recorded by firms.

26.   This is consistent with Hirshleifer [21, Chapter 6], who assumes that the price level is constant if the price of consumer goods is constant and the price of capital changes.

It is also consistent with Solow's approach [37, Chapter 1]. He treats the creation of capital as a sacrifice of consumer goods, and the return to capital as the increased availability of future consumer goods. The clear inference is that only consumer prices are relevant.

27. From equation (7).

28. This can be illustrated with a simple example that has two
kinds of capital, J and K, one consumer good, x, and no labor.

Two Capital goods

t	x	pn^X	K	pn^K	J	pn^J	1+rn
0	100	1.0	100	0.9	100	1.0	
1	110	1.0	110	1.0	110	0.9	1.679

The rate of inflation, rf_1, is zero on either formula (27) or
(28). At t_1, real (and nominal) income and product are $129,
consumption is $110 and investment is $19.   In addition, rr_1 =
rn_1 = rx_1 = .679, rK_1 = .511, and rJ_1 = .865.

The "physical" approach says that a (t_0) dollar's worth of
K_0 has a   net   marginal product of $pn_1^K * rK_1/pn_0^K$ ($.568), and
should therefore increase t_1 product by this amount, while an
extra dollar's worth of J_0 should increase t_1 product by
$pn_1^J * rJ_1/pn_0^K$ ($.778).   Crusoe could   increase his t_1 product by
$pn_1^J * rJ_1/pn_0^J$ - $pn_1^K * rK_1/pn_0^K$ ($.21)   for   each   dollar   of
resources shifted from K_0 to J_0 at t_0. Since his   consumption
could remain unchanged at t_0 and rise at t_1 without changing
capital quantities at t_1, he would be better off than before,
which contradicts the welfare maximizing assumption.

Our model says that the marginal product of a t_0 dollar's
worth of K_0 is rr_1 ($.679). Exactly the same is true for J_0, and
no gain is possible by shifting resources between K_0 and J_0 at
t_0. This will also hold if there is inflation, since the value

of both marginal products will be inflated by $(1+rf_1)$.

In our model, real investment in $\underline{K}$ is $K_1*pn_1^K -$ $K_0*pn_0^K*(1+rf_1)$ ($20), and real investment in $\underline{J}$ is $J_1*pn_1^J - J_0*pn_0^J*(1+rf_1)$ (-$1), for a net investment of $19. If we use pn_1 instead of $pn_0*(1+rf_1)$ to measure "real" quantities, we would get real investment in $\underline{K}$ of $(K_1 - K_0)*pn_1^K$ ($10), and real investment in $\underline{J}$ of $(J_1 - J_0)*pn_1^J$ ($9). In this special case, the totals agree, but the subtotals do not. The subtotals can agree only if $pn_1^K/pn_0^K = pn_1^J/pn_0^J = (1+rf_1)$, which requires 1) that the own rates of interest on $\underline{K}$ and $\underline{J}$ be equal, $rK_1 = rJ_1$, and 2) that capital goods change in price at the same rate as consumer goods.

29. The GNP accounts maintain the equality between income and product by not counting the increase in Crusoe's financial wealth as personal income. Instead, they treat retained earnings of firms as part of national income. They thereby avoid the question of the appropriate deflator to use in measuring Crusoe's financial gains.

Chapter III

1. My approach has, of course, been considered by accountants, but usually rejected. For example, Ijiri [24, p. 8], says: "If necessary, wealth accounts could be prepared by taking inventories of all assets and liabilities of an enterprise at a given point in time, and by applying whatever prices may be available and appropriate at that time, without knowing the past records of the enterprise." He concludes the paragraph, however,

by saying: "There is no way that such an approach can be taken in the case of capital accounts." The capital accounts to which he refers are the owners' equity accounts.

Chapter VII

1. This was the original treatment in the national income accounts [11, pp. 52-54]. More recently, interest payments by households have been isolated from "consumption" expenditures, and treated as a separate category of "expenditure" of income, rather than as a "reduction" of income.

Chapter VIII

1. The idea that accountants should ignore information because the entity for which they are accounting was not directly involved in the transaction is common in the literature. For example, Littleton [27, p. 197] says, apparently as a matter of "principle," that firms should confine themselves to "inside" information, and ignore "outside" information in preparing their financial statements. I cannot make sense out of such a principle. I see no reason why any potentially useful information should be rejected.

Chapter IX

1. For a good discussion of the "irrelevance" theorem, see [9, pp. 476-89].

2. The GNP imputation is explained by the National Income Division, Office of Business Economics, Department of Commerce [11, pp. 40-41]. Another good source of information about the national income accounts is Ruggles [34]. His discussion of bank

imputations (pp. 56-58) is, however, not entirely consistent with the Nation Income Division explanation.

Chapter X

1.   Barro [2] presents a good discussion of the problem. He assumes that the future taxes which must be required to finance government bonds are negative wealth, in effect treating them as financial instruments. He then considers the question of whether the negative wealth exactly offsets the bond asset, or whether there is an increase (loss) of net wealth. My assumption is that no net wealth is created or destroyed.

2.   Barro's discussion of this kind of problem [2, pages 1098-1110] might provide the basis for a more sophisticated accounting treatment.

3.   The idea that the tax reduces the market value of the land is commonplace in economics and public finance. See, for example, Rosen [33, pages 265-66, 482-83]. I am not aware of any discussions which consider explicitly recording the land at productive value and the capitalized tax as a liability. It is, however, implied in Marcus [28], where he suggests the possibility of selling the land separately from the tax liability, in much the way that mineral rights are frequently sold separately from other land rights. If the tax were assumed by somebody other than the landowner, the landowner would have an asset equal to the productive value of the land, and the tax "owner" would have a liability equal to the present value of the taxes. The government would then have to record a tax asset, or

financial instruments would not add to zero.

4. References are difficult to find. The treatment is implied
by Staubus [38, p.337], where he suggests that all negative cash
flow "potentials" are liabilities. Bodenhorn [7] capitalizes all
future payments as liabilities. In that paper, however, I
consider both the future wage payment and the future social
security tax to be liabilities. In this chapter, the future tax
is treated as a liability even though the wage on which it is
based is not a liability.

5. There is no theoretical basis for dividing the liability
between human and physical capital if a firm produces both taxed
and untaxed goods. There is really no way of deciding how much
labor to allocate to each product, as I argued earlier. The same
is true of capital. I am not sure what useful purpose is served
by tax allocation, when other allocations are so suspect.

Chapter XI

1. This is one aspect of the allocation problem which Thomas
discusses [42 and 43]. As always, his conclusion that
allocations have no theoretical foundation is correct.

2. I do not understand Anthony's reasoning: "If one takes the
view that nonmenetary assets are essentially unexpired costs,
and that the function of accounting is to match these costs with
the appropriate revenues, then interest cost probably should be
associated only with nonmonetary assets. If no such distinction
between monetary and nonmonetary assets is drawn, an argument
can be made for assigning some interest cost to monetary assets,

although such a practice may well have no material effect on net income." [1, p. 86] Since I do not know what distinction between monetary and nonmonetary assets he is suggesting, I can not follow the argument.

3. See, for example, Copeland and Weston [9, pp. 185 - 204]. The shareholders of the mutual fund en effect hold a portfolio consisting of the two financial instruments. The risk associated with the portfolio is a weighted average of the risks associated with its components.(p. 192) The return on the share is a linear function of the risk. (p. 196)

4. "...An argument can be made for assigning some interest cost to monetary assets, although such a practice may well have no material effect on income." [1, p. 86]

5. See footnote 3, above.

6. The outlay at t_o is $101. The return at t_1 is $109. (1+r) = $109/$101 = 1.0792. The calculations for later years are comparable.

7. I have discussed this more fully [7, pp. 502-504]. Ijiri [23, pp. 334-35] uses very much the same concept of "project."

8. This is not an original idea. I have discussed it at greater length [5, p.133].

9. See, for example, the FASB Statement of Concepts #1, [13, paragraphs 24 - 27.

10. The FASB is changing its attitude on this point. There is no longer any doubt that an asset must provide future benefits [16, paragraphs 25-31, 171-177]. Present value of future returns

is now one of the accepted "attributes" of some assets [15, paragraph 67]. It is difficult to argue that service potential is the critical attribute of an asset without coming to the idea that it is the (present) value of that future service which determines the value of the asset.

11.   This point is emphasized by Davidson et.al. [10, p. 396]. Their example is a truck which can be carried as a single asset, or as a chassis, engine, and tires.

12.   Both Concept Statements #1 [13] and #5 [15] emphasize this in the "Highlights." It is curious, however, that neither Statement gives a reason for this exclusion.

13.   It also leaves open the question of what accountants are trying to measure. A leading text [10, p. 383], insists that "Depreciation is a process of cost allocation, not one of valuation." The accountant is therefore not trying to "value" either the firm or its fixed assets. Nevertheless, credits must equal debits with no entry for net wealth.

14.   This is a statement about equilibrium. There are always take-overs and buy-outs of various kinds because people think that assets are more valuable than equities. New firms are constantly starting because people think that equities are more valuable than assets. The point is that there are market forces which tend to equalize the value of assets and equities. The transactions costs and interactions make it difficult to make similar statements about individual (groups of) assets.

15.   The "classic" reference is Edwards and Bell [12, page 45,

footnote 9. The "crash" of October, 1987, is conclusive evidence, if such were needed, that share prices do not always accurately reflect the future. There is no way that prospects were 20% dimmer on Tuesday than they had been on Friday.

16. I have been arguing this for better than 20 years [4, page 117]. Ijiri has made the same point, and coined the phrase "constructive" cash flows [23, page 343]. The idea has even been accepted by GAAP, when they recommend that the financing of fixed assets by the issue of shares (or bonds) be reflected in the "Statement of Changes in Financial Position" as if the shares (bonds) had been issued for cash, and assets had been bought with cash [10, page 172].

17. Ijiri [23] also advocates integrating financial statements with investment decisions, but goes in a different direction.

18. I struggled with the idea of "accumulating" assets, rather than to charge them with interest costs. This is essentially what GAAP does when it recognizes accrued interest on financial assets as both revenue and an increase in asset value. The counterpart for productive assets would be to recognize the accrual of the anticipated marginal product. While the arithmetic works, the logic of capitalizing costs seems much more in keeping with cost-based accounting than the idea of accruing a marginal product. Logic requires, however, that we either accrue both the interest on financial assets and the marginal product of productive assets, or that we accrue neither. My recommendation for cost-based accounting is to

accrue neither. The only accrual is the interest cost on all
equities.

19. My objection here is primarily semantic. GAAP insists that
forecasting is not the proper role of accounting, yet they
insist on formulating provision for bad debts, and provision for
returns, as if this were forecasting.   Provision for bad debts
should properly viewed as an attempt to measure the current
market value of the financial assets. Provisions for returns
need not be made.   Sales should be recorded, followed by
repurchases.   The difference in the timing will result in
different present (discounted) values.

20. These ideas stem primarily from Friedman [19].

21. Demonstrations abound.   See, for example, Bodenhorn [7,
foonote 8].

22. For a more complete discussion see, for example, Copeland
and Weston [9, pages 384-89].

REFERENCES

1. Anthony, Robert N., _Accounting for the Cost of Interest_, Lexington Books, D. C. Heath and Company, 1975.

2. Barro, Robert J., "Are Government Bonds Net Wealth?," _The Journal of Political Economy_, November/December, 1974.

3. Becker, Gary S., _Economic Approach to Human Behavior_, University of Chicago Press, 1976.

4. Bodenhorn, Diran, "A Cash-Flow Concept of Profit," _The Journal of Finance_, March, 1964.

5. Bodenhorn, Diran, "An Entity Approach to the Measurement of Wealth, Income, and Product," _Abacus_, December, 1972.

6. Bodenhorn, Diran, "An Economic Approach to Balance Sheets and Income Statements," _Abacus_, June, 1978.

7. Bodenhorn, Diran, "Balance Sheet Items as the Present Value of Future Cash Flows," _Journal of Business Finance and Accounting_, Winter, 1984.

8. Chambers, Raymond J., _Accounting, Evaluation and Economic Behavior_, Prentice-Hall, 1966. Reprinted, with an Introductory Essay, by Scholars Book Company, 1974.

9. Copeland, Thomas E., and J. Fred Weston, _Financial Theory and Corporate Policy_, Second Edition, Addison-Wesley Publishing Company, 1983.

10. Davidson, Sidney, Clyde P. Stickney, and Roman L. Weil, _Financial Accounting: An Introduction to Concepts, Methods, and Uses_, Fourth Edition, The Dryden Press, 1985.

11. Department of Commerce, Office of Business Economics, _National Income and Product of the United States, 1929-1950_, 1951 Edition, U. S. Government Printing Office, 1951.

12. Edwards, Edgar O., and Philip W. Bell, _The Theory and Measurement of Business Income_, University of California Press, 1961.

13. Financial Accounting Standards Board, Statement of

Financial Accounting Concepts No. 1, Objectives of Financial Reporting by Business Enterprises, November, 1978.

14. Financial Accounting Standards Board, Financial Accounting Standard #34, "Capitalization of Interest Cost," October, 1979.

15. Financial Accounting Standards Board, Statement of Financial Accounting Concepts No. 5, Recognition and Measurement in Financial Statements of Business Enterprises, December, 1984.

16. Financial Accounting Standards Board, Statement of Financial Accounting Concepts No. 6, Elements of Financial Statements, December, 1985.

17. Fisher, Franklin M., and Karl Shell, The Economic Theory of Price Indices, Academic Press, 1972.

18. Fisher, Irving, The Theory of Interest, Macmillan, 1906.

19. Friedman, Milton, A Theory of the Consumption Function, Princeton University Press, 1957.

20. Hicks, John R., Value and Capital, Oxford University Press, Second Edition, 1946.

21. Hirshleifer, Jack, Investment, Interest, and Capital, Prentice-Hall, 1970.

22. Ijiri, Yuji, Theory of Accounting Measurement, Studies in Accounting Research #10, American Accounting Association, 1975.

23. Ijiri, Yuji, "Cash-Flow Accounting and Its Structure," Journal of Accounting, Auditing & Finance, May, 1978.

24. Ijiri, Yuji, Triple-Entry Bookkeeping and Income Momentum, Studies in Accounting Research #18, American Accounting Association, 1982.

25. Knight, Frank H., The Economic Organization, University of Chicago, 1933.

26. Lerner, Abba P., _The Economics of Control_, Macmillan, 1946.

27. Littleton, Ananias C., _Structure of Accounting Theory_, American Accounting Association, Monograph No. 5, 1953.

28. Marcus, Richard D., "Transferable Tax Liabilities on Real Estate," _Land Economics_, February, 1987.

29. Mattessich, Richard, _Accounting and Analytical Methods_, Richard D. Irwin, 1964.

30. Modigliani, Franco, and Merton H. Miller, "The Cost of Capital, Corporation Finance, and the Theory of Investment," _American Economic Review_, June, 1958.

31. Modigliani, Franco, and Merton H. Miller, "Corporate Income Taxes and the Cost of Capital," _American Economic Review_, June, 1963.

32. Paton, William A., and Ananias C. Littleton, _Corporate Accounting Standards_, American Accounting Association Monograph No. 3, 1940.

33. Rosen, Harvey S., _Public Finance_, Richard D. Irwin, 1985.

34. Ruggles, Richard, _An Introduction to National Income and Income Analysis_, McGraw-Hill Book Company, 1949.

35. Samuelson, Paul A., _Foundations of Economic Analysis_, Harvard University Press, 1948.

36. Solomons, David, _Making Accounting Policy_, Oxford University Press, 1986.

37. Solow, Robert M., _Capital Theory and the Rate of Return_, Rand McNally, 1963.

38. Staubus, George J., _Making Accounting Decisions_, Scholars Book Company, 1977.

39. Sterling, Robert R., _Theory of the Measurement of Enterprise Income_, University Press of Kansas, 1970.

40. Sterling, Robert R., _Toward a Science of Accounting_,

Scholars Book Company, 1979.

41. Stigler, George J., The Theory of Price, Third Edition,
     Macmillan, 1966.

42. Thomas, Arthur L., The Allocation Problem in Financial
     Accounting Theory, Studies in Accounting Research #3, American
     Accounting Association, 1969.

43. Thomas, Arthur L., The Allocation Problem: Part II, Studies
     in Accounting Research #9, American Accounting Association,
     1974.

Accounting Books Published by Garland

■■■■■■■■■■■■■■■■■

NEW BOOKS

■ *Altman, Edward I., *The Prediction of Corporate Bankruptcy: A Discriminant Analysis.*
New York, 1988.

■ Ashton, Robert H., ed. *The Evolution of Accounting Behavior Research: An Overview.*
New York, 1984.

■ Ashton, Robert H., ed. *Some Early Contributions to the Study of Audit Judgement.*
New York, 1984.

■ *Bodenhorn, Diran. *Economic Accounting.*
New York, 1988.

---

* Included in the Garland series Foundations of Accounting
† Included in the Academy of Accounting Historians, Classics Series, Gary John Previt, ed.

■ *Bougen, Philip D. *Accounting and Industrial Relations: Some Historical Evidence on Their Interaction.*
New York, 1988.

■ Brief, Richard P., ed. *Corporate Financial Reporting and Analysis in the Early 1900s.*
New York, 1986.

■ Brief, Richard P., ed. *Depreciation and Capital Maintenance.*
New York, 1984.

■ Brief, Richard P., ed. *Estimating the Economic Rate of Return from Accounting Data.*
New York, 1986.

■ Brief, Richard P., ed. *Four Classics on the Theory of Double-Entry Bookkeeping.*
New York, 1982.

■ Chambers, R. J., and G. W. Dean, eds. *Chambers on Accounting.*
New York, 1986.
Volume I: Accounting, Management and Finance.
Volume II: Accounting Practice and Education.
Volume III: Accounting Theory and Research.
Volume IV: Price Variation Accounting.
Volume V: Continuously Contemporary Accounting.

■ *Clark, John B. (with a new introduction by Donald Dewey). *Capital and Its Earnings.*
New York, 1988.

■ Clarke, F. L. *The Tangled Web of Price Variation Accounting: The Development of Ideas Underlying Professional Prescriptions in Six Countries.*
New York, 1982.

■ Coopers & Lybrand. *The Early History of Coopers & Lybrand.*
New York, 1984.

■ Craswell, Allen. *Audit Qualifications in Australia 1950 to 1979.*
New York, 1986.

■ Dean, G. W., and M. C. Wells, eds. *The Case for Continuously Contemporary Accounting.*
New York, 1984.

■ Dean, G. W. , and M. C. Wells, eds. *Forerunners of Realizable Values Accounting in Financial Reporting.*
New York, 1982.

■ Edey, Harold C. *Accounting Queries.*
New York, 1982.

■ Edwards, J. R., ed. *Legal Regulation of British Company Accounts 1836-1900.*
New York, 1986.

■ Edwards, J. R. ed. *Reporting Fixed Assets in Nineteenth-Century Company Accounts.*
New York, 1986.

■ Edwards, J. R., ed. *Studies of Company Records: 1830-1974.*
New York, 1984.

■ Fabricant, Solomon. *Studies in Social and Private Accounting.*
New York, 1982.

■ Gaffikin, Michael, and Michael Aitkin, eds. *The Development of Accounting Theory: Significant Contributors to Accounting Thought in the 20th Century.*
New York, 1982.

■ Hawawini, Gabriel A., ed. *Bond Duration and Immunization: Early Developments and Recent Contributions.*
New York, 1982.

■ Hawawini, Gabriel A., and Pierre A. Michel, eds. *European Equity Markets: Risk, Return, and Efficiency.*
New York, 1984.

■ Hawawini, Gabriel A., and Pierre Michel. *Mandatory Financial Information and Capital Market Equilibrium in Belgium.*
New York, 1986.

■ Hawkins, David F. *Corporate Financial Disclosure, 1900-1933: A Study of Management Inertia within a Rapidly Changing Environment.*
New York, 1986.

■ *Hopwood, Anthony G. *Accounting from the Outside: The Collected Papers of Anthony G. Hopwood.*
New York, 1988.

■ Johnson, H. Thomas. *A New Approach to Management Accounting History.*
New York, 1986.

■ Kinney, William R., ed. *Fifty Years of Statistical Auditing.*
New York, 1986.

■ Klemstine, Charles E., and Michael W. Maher. *Management Accounting Research: A Review and Annotated Bibliography.*
New York, 1984.

■ *Langenderfer, Harold Q., and Grover L. Porter, eds. *Rational Accounting Concepts: The Writings of Willard Graham.*
New York, 1988.

■ *Lee, T. A., ed. *The Evolution of Audit Thought and Practice.*
New York, 1988.

■ Lee, T. A., ed. *A Scottish Contribution to Accounting History.*
New York, 1986.

■ Lee, T. A. *Towards a Theory and Practice of Cash Flow Accounting.*
New York, 1986.

■ Lee, T. A., ed. *Transactions of the Chartered Accountants Students' Societies of Edinburgh and Glasgow: A Selection of Writings, 1886-1958.*
New York, 1984.

■ *Loft, Anne. *Understanding Accounting in Its Social and Historical Context: The Case of Cost Accounting in Britain, 1914-1925.*
New York, 1988.

■ McKinnon, Jill L.. *The Historical Development and Operational Form of Corporate Reporting Regulation in Japan.*
New York, 1986.

■ *McMickle, Peter L., and Paul H. Jensen, eds. *The Auditor's Guide of 1869: A Review and Computer Enhancement of Recently Discovered Old Microfilm of America's First Book on Auditing by H. J. Mettenheimer.*
New York, 1988.

■ *McMickle, Peter L., and Paul H. Jensen, eds. *The Birth of American Accountancy: A Bibliographic Analysis of Works on Accounting Published in America through 1820.*
New York, 1988.

■ *Mepham, M.-J. *Accounting in Eighteenth-Century Scotland.*
New York, 1988.

■ *Mills, Patti A., trans. *The Legal Literature of Accounting: On Accounts by Diego del Castillo.*
New York, 1988.

■ *Murphy, George J. *The Evolution of Canadian Corporate Reporting Practices: 1900-1970.*
New York, 1988.

■ *Mumford, Michael J., ed. *Edward Stamp—Later Papers.*
New York, 1988.

■ Nobes, Christopher, ed. *The Development of Double Entry: Selected Essays.*
New York, 1984.

■ Nobes, Christopher. *Issues in International Accounting.*
New York, 1986.

■ Parker, Lee D. *Developing Control Concepts in the 20th Century.*
New York, 1986.

■ *Parker, Lee D., ed. *Financial Reporting to Employees: From Past to Present.*
New York, 1988.

■ *Parker, Lee D., and O. Finley Graves, eds. *Methodology and Method in History: A Bibliography.*
New York, 1988.

■ Parker, R. H. *Papers on Accounting History.*
New York, 1984.

■ Previts, Gary John, and Alfred R. Roberts, eds. *Federal Securities Law and Accounting 1933-1970: Selected Addresses.*
New York, 1986.

■ *Reid, Jean Margo, ed. *Law and Accounting: Nineteenth-Century American Legal Cases.*
New York, 1988.

■ *Sheldahl, Terry K., ed. *Accounting Literature in the United States before Mitchell and Jones (1796): Contributions by Four English Writers, through American Editions, and Two Pioneer Local Authors.*
New York, 1988.

■ Sheldahl, Terry K. *Beta Alpha Psi, from Alpha to Omega: Pursuing a Vision of Professional Education for Accountants, 1919-1945.*
New York, 1982.

■ Sheldahl, Terry K. *Beta Alpha Psi, from Omega to Zeta Omega: The Making of a Comprehensive Accounting Fraternity, 1946-1984.*
New York, 1986.

■ *Sheldahl, Terry K., ed. *Education for the Mercantile Countinghouse: Critical and Constructive Essays by Nine British Writers, 1716-1794.*
New York, 1988.

■ Solomons, David. *Collected Papers on Accounting and Accounting Education (in two volumes).*
New York, 1984.

■ Sprague, Charles F. *The General Principles of the Science of Accounts and the Accountancy of Investment.*
New York, 1984.

■ Stamp, Edward. *Edward Stamp—Later Papers. See* Michael J. Mumford.

■ Stamp, Edward. *Selected Papers on Accounting, Auditing, and Professional Problems.*
New York, 1984.

■ *Staubus, George J. *Activity Costing for Decisions: Cost Accounting in the Decision Usefulness Framework.*
New York, 1988.

■ Storrar, Colin, ed. *The Accountant's Magazine—An Anthology.*
New York, 1986.

■ Tantral, Panadda. *Accounting Literature in Non-Accounting Journals: An Annotated Bibliography.*
New York, 1984.

■ *Vangermeersch, Richard G. *Alexander Hamilton Church: A Man of Ideas for All Seasons.*
New York, 1988.

■ Vangermeersch, Richard, ed. *The Contributions of Alexander Hamilton Church to Accounting and Management.*
New York, 1986.

■ Vangermeersch, Richard, ed. *Financial Accounting Milestones in the Annual Reports of the United States Steel Corporation—The First Seven Decades.*
New York, 1986.

■ *Walker, Stephen P. *The Society of Accountants in Edinburgh, 1854-1914: A Study of Recruitment to a New Profession.*
New York, 1988.

■ Whitmore, John. *Factory Accounts.*
New York, 1984.

■ *Whittred, Greg. *The Evolution of Consolidated Financial Reporting in Australia: An Evaluation of an Alternative Hypothesis.*
New York, 1988.

■ Yamey, Basil S. *Further Essays on the History of Accounting.*
New York, 1982.

■ Zeff, Stephen A., ed. *The Accounting Postulates and Principles Controversy of the 1960s.*
New York, 1982.

■ Zeff, Stephen A., ed. *Accounting Principles Through the Years: The Views of Professional and Academic Leaders 1938-1954.*
New York, 1982.

■ Zeff, Stephen A., and Maurice Moonitz, eds. *Sourcebook on Accounting Principles and Auditing Procedures: 1917-1953 (in two volumes).*
New York, 1984.

■ *Zeff, Stephen a., ed. *The U. S. Accounting Profession in the 1890s and Early 1900s.*
New York, 1988.

REPRINTED TITLES

■ *American Institute of Accountants. *Accountants Index, 1920* (in two volumes).
New York, 1921 (Garland reprint, 1988).

■ American Institute of Accountants. *Fiftieth Anniversary Celebration.*
Chicago, 1937 (Garland reprint, 1982).

■ American Institute of Accountants. *Library Catalogue.*
New York, 1919 (Garland reprint, 1982).

■ Arthur Andersen Company. *The First Fifty Years 1913-1963.*
Chicago, 1963 (Garland reprint, 1984).

■ Bevis, Herman W. *Corporate Financial Reporting in a Competitive Economy.*
New York, 1965 (Garland reprint, 1986).

■ Bonini,. Charles P., Robert K. Jaedicke, and Harvey M. Wagner, eds. *Management Controls: New Directions in Basic Research.*
New York, 1964 (Garland reprint, 1986).

■ *The Book-Keeper and the American Counting Room.*
New York, 1880-1884 (Garland reprint, 1988).

■ Bray, F. Sewell. *Four Essays in Accounting Theory.* London, 1953. *Bound with* Institute of Chartered Accountants in England and Wales and the National Institute of Economic and Social Research. *Some Accounting Terms and Concepts.*
    Cambridge, 1951 (Garland reprint, 1982).

■ Brown, R. Gene, and Kenneth S. Johnston. *Paciolo on Accounting.*
    New York, 1963 (Garland reprint, 1984).

■ Carey, John L., and William O. Doherty, eds. *Ethical Standards of the Accounting Profession.*
    New York, 1966 (Garland reprint, 1986).

■ Chambers, R. J. *Accounting in Disarray.*
    Melbourne, 1973 (Garland reprint, 1982).

■ Cooper, Ernest. *Fifty-seven years in an Accountant's Office. See* Sir Russell Kettle.

■ Couchman, Charles B. *The Balance-Sheet.*
    New York, 1924 (Garland reprint, 1982).

■ Couper, Charles Tennant. *Report of the Trial ... Against the Directors and Manager of the City of Glasgow Bank.*
    Edinburgh, 1879 (Garland reprint, 1984).

■ Cutforth, Arthur E. *Audits.*
    London, 1906 (Garland reprint, 1982).

■ Cutforth, Arthur E. *Methods of Amalgamation.*
    London, 1926 (Garland reprint, 1982).

■ Deinzer, Harvey T. *Development of Accounting Thought.*
New York, 1965 (Garland reprint, 1984).

■ De Paula, F.R.M. *The Principles of Auditing.*
London, 1915 (Garland reprint, 1984).

■ Dickerson, R. W. *Accountants and the Law of Negligence.*
Toronto, 1966 (Garland reprint, 1982).

■ Dodson, James. *The Accountant, or, the Method of Bookkeeping Deduced from Clear Principles, and Illustrated by a Variety of Examples.*
London, 1750 (Garland reprint, 1984).

■ Dyer, S. *A Common Sense Method of Double Entry Bookkeeping, on First Principles, as Suggested by De Morgan. Part I, Theoretical.*
London, 1897 (Garland reprint, 1984).

■ *† Edwards, James Don. *History of Public Accounting in the United States.*
East Lansing, 1960 (Garland reprint, 1988).

■ *† Edwards, James Don, and Robert F. Salmonson. *Contributions of Four Accounting Pioneers: Kohler, Littleton, May, Paton.*
East Lancing, 1961 (Garland reprint, 1988).

■ *The Fifth International Congress on Accounting, 1938 [Kongress-Archiv 1938 des V. Internationalen Prüfungs- und Treuhand-Kongresses].*
Berlin, 1938 (Garland reprint, 1986).

■ Finney, A. H. *Consolidated Statements.*
New York, 1922 (Garland reprint, 1982).

■ Fisher, Irving. *The Rate of Interest.*
New York, 1907 (Garland reprint, 1982).

■ Florence, P. Sargant. *Economics of Fatigue and Unrest and the Efficiency of Labour in English and American Industry.*
London, 1923 (Garland reprint, 1984).

■ *Fourth International Congress on Accounting 1933.*
London, 1933 (Garland reprint, 1982).

■ Foye, Arthur B. *Haskins & Sells: Our First Seventy-Five Years.*
New York, 1970 (Garland reprint, 1984).

■ *† Garner, Paul S. *Evolution of Cost Accounting to 1925.*
University, Alabama, 1925 (Garland reprint, 1988).

■ Garnsey, Sir Gilbert. *Holding Companies and Their Published Accounts.* London, 1923. *Bound with* Sir Gilbert Garnsey. *Limitations of a Balance Sheet.*
London, 1928 (Garland reprint, 1982).

■ Garrett, A. A. *The History of the Society of Incorporated Accountants, 1885-1957.*
Oxford, 1961 (Garland reprint, 1984).

■ Gilman, Stephen. *Accounting Concepts of Profit.*
New York, 1939 (Garland reprint, 1982).

■ Gordon, William. *The Universal Accountant, and Complete Merchant ... [Volume II].*
>   Edinburgh, 1765 (Garland reprint, 1986).

■ Green, Wilmer. *History and Survey of Accountancy.*
>   Brooklyn, 1930 (Garland reprint, 1986).

■ Hamilton, Robert. *An Introduction to Merchandise, Parts IV and V (Italian Bookkeeping and Practical Bookkeeping).*
>   Edinburgh, 1788 (Garland reprint, 1982).

■ Hatton, Edward. *The Merchant's Magazine; or, Tradesman's Treasury.* London, 1695 (Garland reprint, 1982).
Hills, George S. *The Law of Accounting and Financial Statements.*
>   Boston, 1957 (Garland reprint, 1982).

■ *A History of Cooper Brothers & Co. 1854 to 1954.*
>   London, 1954 (Garland reprint, 1986).

■ Hofstede, Geert. *The Game of Budget Control.*
>   Assen, 1967 (Garland reprint, 1984).

■ Howitt, Sir Harold. *The History of the Institute of Chartered Accountants in England and Wales 1880-1965, and of Its Founder Accountancy Bodies 1870-1880.*
>   London, 1966 (Garland reprint, 1984).

■ Institute of Chartered Accountants in England and Wales and The National Institute of Social and Economic Research. *Some Accounting Terms and Concepts. See* F. Sewell Bray.

■ Institute of Chartered Accountants of Scotland. *History of the Chartered Accountants of Scotland from the Earliest Times to 1954.*
     Edinburgh, 1954 (Garland reprint, 1984).

■ *International Congress on Accounting 1929.*
     New York, 1930 (Garland reprint, 1982).

■ Jaedicke, Robert K., Yuji Ijiri, and Oswald Nielsen, eds. *Research in Accounting Measurement.*
     American Accounting Association,
     1966 (Garland reprint, 1986).

■ Keats, Charles. *Magnificent Masquerade.*
     New York, 1964 (Garland reprint, 1982).

■ Kettle, Sir Russell. *Deloitte & Co. 1854-1956.* Oxford, 1958. *Bound with* Ernest Cooper. *Fifty-seven Years in an Accountant's Office.*
     London, 1921 (Garland reprint, 1982).

■ Kitchen, J., and R. H. Parker. *Accounting Thought and Education: Six English Pioneers.*
     London, 1980 (Garland reprint, 1984).

■ Lacey, Kenneth. *Profit Measurement and Price Changes.*
     London, 1952 (Garland reprint, 1982).

■ Lee, Chauncey. *The American Accomptant.*
     Lansingburgh, 1797 (Garland reprint, 1982).

■ Lee, T. A., and R. H. Parker. *The Evolution of Corporate Financial Reporting.*
     Middlesex, 1979 (Garland reprint, 1984).

■ *† Littleton, A. C.. *Accounting Evolution to 1900.*
New York, 1933 (Garland reprint, 1988).

■ Malcolm, Alexander. *The Treatise of Book-Keeping, or, Merchants Accounts; In the Italian Method of Debtor and Creditor; Wherein the Fundamental Principles of That Curious and Approved Method Are Clearly and Fully Explained and Demonstrated ... To Which Are Added, Instructions for Gentlemen of Land Estates, and Their Stewards or Factors: With Directions Also for Retailers, and Other More Private Persons.*
London, 1731 (Garland reprint, 1986).

■ Meij, J. L., ed. *Depreciation and Replacement Policy.*
Chicago, 1961 (Garland reprint, 1986).

■ Newlove, George Hills. *Consolidated Balance Sheets.*
New York, 1926 (Garland reprint, 1982).

■ North, Roger. *The Gentleman Accomptant; or, An Essay to Unfold the Mystery of Accompts; By Way of Debtor and Creditor, Commonly Called Merchants Accompts, and Applying the Same to the Concerns of the Nobility and Gentry of England.*
London 1714 (Garland reprint, 1986).

■ *Proceedings of the Seventh International Congress of Accountants.* Amsterdam, 1957 (Garland reprint, 1988).

■ Pryce-Jones, Janet E., and R. H. Parker. *Accounting in Scotland: A Historical Bibliography.*
Edinburgh, 1976 (Garland reprint, 1984).

- *Reynolds, W. B., and F. W. Thornton. *Duties of a Junior Accountant* [three editions].
    New York, 1917, 1933, 1953
    (Garland reprint, 1988).

- Robinson, H. W. *A History of Accountants in Ireland.*
    Dublin, 1964 (Garland edition, 1984).

- Robson, T. B. *Consolidated and Other Group Accounts.*
    London, 1950 (Garland reprint, 1982).

- Rorem, C. Rufus. *Accounting Method.*
    Chicago, 1928 (Garland reprint, 1982).

- Saliers, Earl A., ed. *Accountants' Handbook.*
    New York, 1923 (Garland reprint, 1986).

- Samuel, Horace B. *Shareholder's Money.*
    London, 1933 (Garland reprint, 1982).

- *The Securitites and Exchange Commission in the Matter of McKesson & Robbins, Inc. Report on Investigation.*
    Washington, D. C., 1940 (Garland reprint, 1982).

- *The Securities and Exchange Commission in the Matter of McKesson & Robbins, Inc. Testimony of Expert Witnesses.*
    Washington, D. C., 1939 (Garland reprint, 1982).

- Shaplen, Roger. *Kreuger: Genius and Swindler.*
    New York, 1960 (Garland reprint, 1986).

- Singer, H. W. *Standardized Accountancy in Germany. (With a new appendix.)*
    Cambridge, 1943 (Garland reprint, 1982).

■ *The Sixth International Congress on Accounting.*
    London, 1952 (Garland reprint, 1984).

■ Stewart, Jas. C. (with a new introductory note by T. A. Lee). *Pioneers of a Profession: Chartered Accountants to 1879.*
    Edinburgh, 1977 (Garland reprint, 1986).

■ Thompson, Wardbaugh. *The Accomptant's Oracle: or, a Key to Science, Being a Compleat Practical System of Book-keeping.*
    York, 1777 (Garland reprint, 1984).

■ *Thornton, F. W. *Duties of the Senior Accountant.* New York, 1932. *Bound with.* John C. Martin. *Duties of Junior and Senior Accountants, Supplement of the CPA Handbook.*
    New York, 1953 (Garland reprint, 1988).

■ Vatter, William J. *Managerial Accounting.*
    New York, 1950 (Garland reprint, 1986).

■ Woolf, Arthur H. *A Short History of Accountants and Accountancy.*
    London, 1912 (Garland reprint, 1986).

■ Yamey, B. S., H. C. Edey, and Hugh W. Thomson. *Accounting in England and Scotland: 1543-1800.*
    London, 1963 (Garland reprint, 1982).